Drug Use and Prisons

An International Perspective

Edited by

David Shewan
and
John B. Davies

harwood academic publishers
Australia • Canada • France • Germany
India • Japan • Luxembourg • Malaysia
The Netherlands • Russia • Singapore • Switzerland

Amsteldijk 166
1st Floor
1079 LH Amsterdam
The Netherlands

British Library Cataloguing in Publication Data

A catalogue record for this book is available from the British Library.

ISBN: 90-5823-004-X (softcover)

CONTENTS

LIST OF FIGURES

LIST OF TABLES

PREFACE

Drug users end up in gaol for many reasons, but in the most general terms we might divide the drug-using part of a prison population along three lines. First, there are those who are incarcerated specifically because of their involvement in the 'sharp end' of drug use; that is they use drugs or are involved in the possession of drugs with intent to supply them to others. We may note at the start the lack of an international consensus on this issue. In some countries even the possession of cannabis in any measurable amount may result in harsh penalties, whereas possession of small amounts may not be punished at all in others. Second, there are those who are gaoled for offences other than drug use, but who happen to be involved in drug use at the same time. We may note the association in many Western countries between social deprivation, harmful self-damaging drug use and crime, and the too easy interpretation of the drugs-crime link as self evident on the basis of data that are in fact reflexive, and with the roots of both lying in factors that have little or nothing to do with drugs. Thirdly, there are those who acquired their drug habit whilst in gaol. This indicates that whilst prisons offer the opportunity to influence drug habits in a positive way, as discussed in many of the following chapters, there are instances in which certain settings can conspire with certain individuals to produce exactly the opposite effect.

From a public policy perspective, administrations can have varying views on the issue of drug use in prison. On the one hand, one can take the stance that drug use in prison is simply not to be tolerated and that any attempt to reduce the harm of such use is tantamount to condoning the practise; or one can take the opposite view and do everything possible to reduce drug related harm in prison. Whichever view is taken, there are clear similarities between trying to produce a drug-free prison and a drug-free nation. Both have clear boundaries, and the permeability or rigidity of such boundaries has clear implications for social practices and relationships within those boundaries. We can go a long way towards eliminating drugs in the UK, for example, provided we are all happy to be strip searched every time we leave or enter the country. So it is with prisons. The question 'Which approach is best?' is not solely answerable in simple empirical terms, since science struggles with questions which include or imply the word 'ought'.

Nonetheless, evidence from different places and parts of the world might help in the process of arriving at an informed moral decision.

The contributors to this book are experts from a variety of professional backgrounds, drawn together to provide an international perspective on drug use and prisons. There is, therefore, a diversity of professional opinion and cultural viewpoints contained within the eleven chapters. Common themes are apparent, however. Each contributor stresses the importance of prison as a setting for public health intervention, both in terms of preventing the spread of viral infections and in providing the opportunity for behavioural change. Indeed, it can be argued that the public health requirements for prison systems represent a moral and legal issue. But while it is acknowledged that the quality of health care available in prisons should be comparable to that available in the community, historically prisons have been reluctant to introduce some of the more radical recent developments in drug policy and practice. Whether this has been an overly cautious position is open to debate, but there are strong arguments for the carefully controlled and evaluated introduction of innovative drug services in prisons, and the development of such schemes in European prisons is described in this book. In contrast, in developing countries, where while there is an equal – if not greater – need for the introduction of a range of drug services in prisons, such public health developments are challenged by the range of grave social problems. But even in industrialised countries, there are obstacles to changing drug policy and practice in prisons.

Another common theme throughout the book is that prisons contain a disproportionate number of individuals with serious mental health problems, including addiction. There is both a requirement and an opportunity within prisons to address these problems, although the sheer scale of this problem in prisons puts enormous pressure on treatment services, to an extent that is detrimental to fully effective mental health care and treatment.

The chapters in this book all acknowledge the importance of research as a basis for shaping policy and practice. The role of research in informing policymakers should be pivotal, and it is to be hoped that research findings are fully incorporated into the development of prison drug policy and practice, in such a way that the health, moral and pragmatic dimensions achieve some sort of reasonable balance. A range of organisations will have a role to play in this process, and it is important that policies are developed within prisons which are balanced, and which represent the views and needs of all those involved, including prisoners and prison staff.

Prisons have the potential to act as settings for high risk behaviour. This has implications for the provision of health care, and highlights the need for a pragmatic response that sets realistic but effective targets. The extent and the processes by which high risk behaviour among drug users in prison can lead to the transmission of bloodborne viruses such as HIV and hepatitis C are of primary concern in this context. It has to be noted, however, that while prisons have the capacity to modify drug using behaviour in ways which reduce risk behaviour, there is always the underlying potential for the creation of wide scale health and social problems through imprisoning large numbers of drug users.

The final conclusion of the authors is, therefore, that steps have to be taken to reduce the potential risks associated with the use of illegal drugs in prisons; an aim which requires us to ask some fundamental questions about the appropriateness of prison for certain categories of offender. It may be that we shall eventually conclude that prison is not appropriate for those convicted of offences associated with drug use; and that for those imprisoned for different offences but who also use drugs, harm reduction represents the only solution which has any long-term future. From such a perspective, the idea of a drug-free prison may be as unachievable as a drug-free society. We accept that not everyone would agree.

LIST OF CONTRIBUTORS

A. Graham Bird, Department of Immunology, Churchill Hospital, Oxford, UK

Nick Crofts, The Centre for Harm Reduction, Macfarlane Burnet Centre for Medical Research, Fairfield, Victoria, Australia

John B. Davies, Centre for Applied Social Psychology, University of Strathclyde, Glasgow, UK

Wouter de Jong, Trimbos-institute (Netherlands Institute for Mental Health and Addiction), The Netherlands

Anja Dobler-Mikola, Institute of Addiction Research, Zurich, Switzerland

Kate Dolan, National Drug and Alcohol Research Centre, University of New South Wales, Sydney, Australia

John Dunn, Unidade de Pesquisas em Álcool e outras Drogas (UNIAD), Departamento de Psiquiatria, Escola Paulista de Medicina, Universidade Federal de São Paulo, Brazil

Michael Farrell, National Addiction Centre, Institute of Psychiatry, Maudsley Hospital, London, UK

Andreas Fuhrer, University Psychiatric Services of Berne, Switzerland

Sheila M. Gore, MRC Biostatistics Unit, University of Cambridge, UK

Timothy W. Harding, University of Geneva, Institute of Legal Medicine, Switzerland

Hans-Peter Hirsbrunner, University Psychiatric Services of Berne, Switzerland

Jutta Jacob, Institut fur Politikwissenschaft II, Fachbereich 3, Universitat Oldenburg, Germany

Ralf Jürgens, Project Co-ordinator, Canadian HIV/AIDS Legal Network, Canadian AIDS Society, Montreal, Quebec, Canada

Ronaldo R. Laranjeira, Unidade de Pesquisas em Álcool e outras Drogas (UNIAD), Departamento de Psiquiatria, Escola Paulista de Medicina, Universidade Federal de São Paulo, Brazil

José Ricardo P. Marins, Faculdade de Medicina, PUC, São Paulo and Co-ordinator of the Municipal STD/AIDS Programme, Sorocaba, Brazil

Joachim Nelles, University Psychiatric Services of Berne, Switzerland

Jude U. Ohaeri, Department of Psychiatry, University College Hospital, Ibadan, Oyo State, Nigeria

Roger H. Peters, Department of Mental Health Law and Policy, Louis de la Parte Florida Mental Health Institute, University of South Florida, USA

David Shewan, Department of Psychology, Glasgow Caledonian University, UK

Nicola Singleton, Principal Social Survey Officer, Office for National Statistics, London, UK

Marc L. Steinberg, Department of Mental Health Law and Policy, Louis de la Parte Florida Mental Health Institute, University of South Florida, USA

Heino Stöver, Institut fur Politikwissenschaft II, Fachbereich 3, Universitat Oldenburg, Germany

John Strang, National Addiction Centre, Institute of Psychiatry, Maudsley Hospital, London, UK

Maarten van Doorninck, Trimbos-institute (Netherlands Institute for Mental Health and Addiction), The Netherlands

Chapter 1

HIV/AIDS AND DRUG USE IN PRISONS: MORAL AND LEGAL RESPONSIBILITIES OF PRISONS

Ralf Jürgens

A prisoner retains all civil rights which are not taken away expressly or by necessary implication.

Lord Wilberforce in *Raymond v Honey* (1982), cited in Shaw, Prisoners' Rights, in Sieghart, 1988, p. 40

A sentence of imprisonment should not carry with it a sentence of AIDS.

Note, 1988

This chapter briefly reviews what is known about HIV/AIDS and hepatitis C in prisons. It then presents some of the evidence of the prevalence of high-risk behaviours, in particular, injecting drug use, and resulting HIV transmission behind bars. It discusses what is being done in prisons to prevent HIV infection and to reduce harm from drug use, and shows that where harm reduction measures — such as allowing access to condoms, bleach, sterile injection equipment and methadone maintenance treatment — have been introduced, such measures have been successful, have not created any problems, and are being supported by prisoners, staff, prison administrations and the public. The chapter then briefly discusses why other measures, such as the war on drugs being waged in prisons in many countries, are counterproductive and harmful. Some of the reasons why many prison systems still oppose introduction of harm reduction measures are also addressed. The chapter concludes by arguing that harm-reduction measures in prisons are necessary to prevent the further spread of HIV in prisons, and that prison systems have a moral and legal obligation to implement them.

HIV/AIDS IN PRISONS: AN OVERVIEW

HIV and Hepatitis C Seroprevalence

Worldwide, rates of HIV infection in inmate populations are much higher than in the general population. They are, in general, closely related to two factors: (1) the proportion of prisoners who injected drugs prior to imprisonment; and (2) the rate of HIV infection among injection drug users in the community. The jurisdictions with the highest HIV prevalence in prisons are areas where HIV infection in the general community is 'pervasive among IV drug users, who are dramatically over-represented in correctional institutions' (Hammett, 1988, p. 26). Commenting on the situation in the United States, the US National Commission on AIDS (1991, p. 10) stated that 'by choosing mass imprisonment as the federal and state governments' response to the use of drugs, we have created a *de facto* policy of incarcerating more and more individuals with HIV infection.'

Particularly high rates have been reported from countries in southern Europe; for example, 26 per cent in Spain and 17 per cent in Italy. High figures have also been reported from France (13 per cent; testing of 500 consecutive entries), Switzerland (11 per cent; cross-sectional study in five prisons in the Canton of Berne) and the Netherlands (11 per cent; screening of a sample of prisoners in Amsterdam). In contrast, some European countries, including Belgium, Finland, Iceland and some Länder in Germany, report low levels of HIV prevalence. Relatively low rates of HIV prevalence have also been reported from Australia. In the United States and in Canada, the geographic distribution of cases of HIV infection and AIDS is remarkably uneven. In the United States, many systems continue to have rates under one per cent, while in a few rates approach or exceed 20 per cent. In Canada, rates range between one and 7.7 per cent (seroprevalence data are from Correctional Service Canada (CSC), 1994a, pp. 15–19; CSC, 1994b, pp. 47–79; Jürgens, 1996, appendix 2, with references).

Hepatitis C seroprevalence rates in prisons are even higher: studies revealed rates of between 28 and 40 per cent in three Canadian prisons (Ford *et al.*, 1995; Pearson *et al.*, 1995; Prefontaine and Chaudhary, 1990; Prefontaine *et al.*, 1994); 39 per cent in prisons in Victoria, Australia, and 50 per cent in New South Wales, Australia (Crofts *et al.*, 1995; Brown, cited in Zinn, 1995); 38 per cent among male inmates in prisons in Maryland, US (Vlahov *et al.*, 1993); and 74.8 per cent among IDUs in a prison for women in Vechta, Lower Saxony (Germany), compared to 2.9 per cent among non-IDUs (Keppler, Nolte, and Stover, 1996).

While most hepatitis C positive inmates come to prison already infected, the potential for intramural spread is high: hepatitis C is much more easily transmitted than HIV, and transmission has been documented in prisons in Canada (Jürgens, 1996, at 46), Germany (Keppler, Nolte, and Stover, 1996), and the US (Vlahov *et al.*, 1993).

EVIDENCE OF HIGH-RISK BEHAVIOURS

Drug Use

An increasing number of scientific studies is providing evidence of the existence and extent of injection and other drug use in prisons. The following is an overview of some of these studies.

In Canada, a study on HIV transmission among injection drug users in Toronto found that '[o]ver eighty per cent [of the participating injection drug users] had been in jail overnight or longer since beginning to inject drugs, with twenty-five per cent of those sharing injecting equipment while in custody' (Millson, 1991). In a recent survey, almost 40 per cent of 4,285 federal inmates self-reported having used drugs since arriving in their current institution (CSC, 1996a, pp. 144–148), and eleven per cent reported having injected an illegal/non-prescription drug; of these, only 57 per cent thought that the equipment they used was clean (CSC, 1996a, p. 138 and 1996b, pp. 348–349).

In Australia, '[a]ll commentators agree that it [injection drug use] occurs and that needle sharing is almost always associated with IV drug use in prisons because of the lack of availability of syringes' (Heilpern and Egger, 1989, p. 38 with many references). In an early survey of 'HIV Risk-Taking Behaviour of Sydney Male Drug Injectors While in Prison,' approximately 75 per cent of respondents reported having injected drugs at least once while in prison. Of these, two thirds provided data on the frequency of sharing of injection equipment in prison, with 75 per cent reporting sharing (Wodak, 1991, pp. 240–41). Other more recent studies have confirmed that HIV risk behaviours are frequent in Australian prisons (Dolan, 1994b; Dolan, *et al.*, 1996d).

In the United Kingdom, a number of surveys found that the use and availability of injectable drugs greatly exceeds official estimates and that needles and syringes are commonly shared out of necessity (Thomas, 1990, pp. 7–10; Pickering and Stimson, 1993; see also Bird *et al.*, 1995, and Gore, 1995). One study found that injecting drug use decreased in prisons among inmates who had been injecting drug users on the outside. However, inmates were more likely to inject in an unsafe manner when they did inject. The study concluded that imprisonment increased the risk of contracting HIV infection (Turnbull, Dolan and Stimson, 1992). This is consistent with the results of two other studies of drug using behaviour in Scottish prisons. In the first study, 32 per cent of a purposive sample of 234 prisoners had injected in the community prior to imprisonment. Of this same sample, 11 per cent were injecting during their current sentence. However, whilst the sharing rate in the community had been 24 per cent, it was 76 per cent in prison. (Shewan, Gemmell and Davies, 1994). In the second study, 76 of 227 prisoners (33 per cent) had injected drugs at some time in their lives, and 33 (15 per cent) admitted to injecting in prison. While injectors tended to use drugs on a daily basis outside prison, they would normally inject only weekly or monthly while in prison. However, all those who had injected in prison had shared equipment at least sometimes. Twenty prisoners had always shared it, compared to only two prisoners who had always shared outside (Taylor *et al.*, 1995).

In Germany, nearly 20 per cent of injection drug users who participated in a large epidemiological study were HIV-positive, and about 60 per cent of them had served a prison sentence. While only 10 per cent of participants with no prison experience tested HIV-positive, 26 per cent of those with prison experience tested HIV-positive, and 67 per cent of participants indicated that they continued to inject while in prison (CSC, 1994c, p. 60).

Sexual Activity

Although in prisons sexual activity is generally considered to be a less significant risk factor than sharing of injection equipment, it also puts prisoners at risk of contracting HIV infection. Homosexual activity occurs inside prisons, as it does outside, as a consequence of preferred sexual orientation. In addition, prison life produces conditions that encourage the establishment of homosexual relationships within the institution (Thomas, 1990, p. 5). The prevalence of sexual activity in prison is difficult to estimate, but is based on such factors as whether the accommodation is single-cell or dormitory, the duration of the sentence, the security classification and the extent to which conjugal visits are permitted (Heilpern and Egger, 1989, p. 40 with reference). Studies of sexual contact in prison have shown 'inmate involvement to vary greatly' (Saum, 1995). In a recent study in state prisons and city jails in New York (Mahon, 1996), prisoners and former prisoners reported frequent instances of unprotected sex behind bars. One woman summarized the prevalence and range of sexual activity described by participants in the study when she stated:

> Male CO's are having sex with females. Female COs are having sex with female inmates, and the male inmates are having sex with male inmates.

Male inmates are having sex with female inmates. There's all kinds, it's a smorgasbord up there.

In Canada, six per cent of federal inmates self-reported having had sex with another inmate; of these, only 33 per cent reported using condoms (CSC, 1996c).

Tattooing and Piercing

It has been said that '[o]utside tattooing is not thought to present much of a risk of HIV transmission because the needles are sterilised, but in prison tattooing is a social activity and involves sharing needles which may make it risky' (Curran, McHugh and Nooney, 1989, at 35). Similarly, Heilpern and Egger (1989) stated:

> It is difficult to estimate how much tattooing occurs in prisons although the visible evidence is often quite striking. Because the activity is illegal it is almost certainly conducted with non-sterile equipment.

In Canada, 45 per cent of federal inmates reported having had a tattoo done in prison, and 17 per cent reported having been pierced (CSC, 1996a).

EVIDENCE OF HIV TRANSMISSION

Until recently, few data were available on how many prisoners become infected while in prison, and the data that were available – mostly from studies undertaken in the United States (for a review of five studies, see Parts, 1991) – suggested that 'transmission does occur in correctional facilities, but at quite low rates' (Hammett *et al.*, 1993, p. 43). This was sometimes used to argue that HIV transmission in prisons is rare, and that consequently there is no need for increased prevention efforts.

However, most of the studies that have reported relatively low levels of HIV transmission in prison were conducted early in the HIV epidemic and sampled long-term prisoners who would have been at less risk of infection than short-term prisoners (Dolan, 1997/98). The extent of HIV infection occurring in prisons may have been underestimated. In more recent years, evidence of HIV transmission in prisons in the United States (Mutter *et al.*, 1994), Australia (Dolan *et al.*, 1994a; Dolan *et al.*, 1996a), and other countries (Wright *et al.*, 1994) has been published. In 1994, a study undertaken in Glenochil prison for adult male offenders in Scotland provided definitive evidence that outbreaks of HIV infection can and will occur in prisons unless HIV prevention is taken seriously. Following the diagnosis of two apparently recent seroconversions to HIV infection among prisoners, prisoners were offered confidential counselling and testing for HIV. Of 227 inmates counselled, 76 had a history of injecting; 33 of these admitted injecting in Glenochil, while 43 admitted having injected at some point in their lives, but not in Glenochil. Of the latter, 34 were tested, but none tested positive. In contrast, of the 33 inmates who declared that they had injected in Glenochil prison, 27 were tested and 12 were found to be HIV-positive; the remaining 15 tested negative but were still in the window period. A further two Glenochil injectors had been diagnosed HIV-positive two months previously, giving a total of 14 HIV-positive drug injectors. Of the 14 HIV-positive inmates, definitive evidence of HIV transmission in prison existed for eight inmates. Another six infections also possibly occurred in prison, but acquisition of infection outside prison could not be ruled out. The true number of infections was probably even higher: it has been calculated that the total number of prisoners infected in prison during that period could lie between 22 and 43 inmates (Taylor *et al.*, 1994; see also Christie, 1995; Taylor *et al.*, 1995). Following the outbreak, 12 HIV-positive inmates and 10 other drug injectors were interviewed about their risk behaviours in prison. From the interviews emerged a vivid description of random sharing with a limited number of needles and syringes, which were mostly blunt, broken, or fashioned out of a variety of materials (Taylor and Goldberg, 1996).

 HIV PREVENTION

Initially, responding to the issues raised by HIV/AIDS and drug use in prisons was very slow. Only small steps were made to develop policies and to provide educational programmes for staff and prisoners. In many systems, prisoners with HIV infection or AIDS were segregated from the rest of the prison population and were subject to a variety of discriminatory measures. Neither condoms nor bleach were made available to prisoners, and educational programmes often appeared inadequate or insufficient.

However, in recent years a growing number of prison systems have started undertaking efforts to address HIV/AIDS and drug use in prisons. Often this was done only after they were confronted with sharp increases in the numbers of prisoners with HIV/AIDS in their custody. Some systems have made condoms, bleach, and even sterile injection equipment and methadone maintenance treatment available, abandoned segregation policies, and introduced better educational programmes delivered or supplemented by community-based outside organizations and/or peers.

The following section describes some of the harm reduction measures introduced behind bars.

Condoms

According to the World Health Organization's network on HIV/AIDS in prison, 23 of 52 prison systems surveyed late in 1991 allowed condom distribution (Harding and Schaller, 1992, p. 767). Significantly, no system that has adopted a policy of making condoms available in prisons has reversed the policy, and the number of systems that make condoms available continues to grow every year.

In some systems, however, making condoms available in prisons is still opposed on the grounds that sexual activity is illegal in public and that prisons are public spaces. Other systems make condoms available only through prison medical services, upon the express request of a prisoner, although national and international recommendations agree that condoms should be made easily and discreetly available (see, e.g., CSC 1994a, at 58).

In an important recent development, in New South Wales in Australia, 50 prisoners launched a legal action against the state for non-provision of condoms (*Prisoners A to XX inclusive* v *State of NSW*; see Jürgens, 1996, at 48). Their lawyer noted that '[i]t is no proper part of the punishment of prisoners that their access to preventative means to protect their health is impeded.' Since then, at least in part because of the legal action, the NSW government decided to make condoms available, initially in three prisons on a trial basis, but later also in other prisons and on a permanent basis.

Bleach

As reported by Harding and Schaller (1992b, Table 10.1), 16 of 52 systems surveyed late in 1991 made bleach available to prisoners, often accompanied by instruction on how to clean needles. However, results of an Australian study – the first in the world to allow the independent monitoring of a bleach distribution programme for prisoners – provide evidence of the limitations of making bleach available in prisons for syringe decontamination (Dolan *et al.*, 1994b). The study found that three years after the distribution of bleach began, 62 per cent of inmates still found it difficult to gain access to it, and pointed out other shortcomings of a syringe disinfecting programme, such as uncertainty about whether other blood-borne viruses can be effectively and rapidly decontaminated from injecting equipment with the use of bleach. It concluded that other prevention measures need to be explored and that one such measure that requires consideration is piloting a syringe exchange programme in prisons. One year later, a follow-up study found that there had been improvement in access to bleach from the first study. Nevertheless, it found shortcomings in the bleach programme and again recommended that consideration be given to a pilot study of syringe exchange in prisons (Dolan *et al.*, 1996b at 23).

Sterile Injection Equipment

Particularly because of the questionable efficacy of bleach in destroying HIV and other viruses (US Department of Health and Human Services, 1993), providing sterile needles to inmates has been widely recommended. In Canada, the Expert Committee on AIDS and Prisons (ECAP) observed that the scarcity of drug-injection equipment in correctional facilities almost guarantees that inmates who persist in drug-injecting behaviour will share their equipment:

> Some injection drug users have stated that the only time they ever shared needles was during imprisonment and that they would not otherwise have done so. Access to clean drug-injection equipment would ensure that inmates would not have to share their equipment. (CSC, 1994a, p. 77):

The Committee concluded that making injection equipment available in prisons would be 'inevitable' (CSC, 1994a).

Recently, an increasing number of prisons worldwide has established — or is planning to do so in the near future — needle and syringe exchange or distribution programmes.

In Switzerland, distribution of sterile injection equipment has been a reality in some prisons since 1993. Sterile injection equipment first became available to inmates in 1993, at Oberschöngrün prison for men, a minimum-security institution housing approximately 75 prisoners. Dr Probst, a part-time medical officer working at Oberschöngrün was faced with the ethical dilemma of as many as 15 of 70 inmates regularly injecting drugs, with no adequate preventive measures:

> Unlike most of his fellow prison doctors, all of whom feel obliged to compromise their ethical and public health principles daily, Probst began

distributing sterile injection material without informing the prison director. When this courageous but apparently foolhardy gesture was discovered, the director, instead of firing Probst on the spot, listened to his arguments about prevention of HIV and hepatitis, as well as injection-site abscesses, and sought approval from the Cantonal authorities to sanction the distribution of needles and syringes. Thus, the world's first distribution of injection material inside prison began as an act of medical disobedience. (Nelles and Harding, 1995).

Three years later, distribution is ongoing, has never resulted in any negative consequences, and is supported by prisoners, staff, and the prison administration. According to the warden, Mr Fäh, initial scepticism by front-line staff has been replaced by their full support:

> Staff have realized that distribution of sterile injection equipment is in their own interest. They feel safer now than before the distribution started. Three years ago, they were always afraid of sticking themselves with a hidden needle during cell searches. Now, inmates are allowed to keep needles, but only in a glass in their medical cabinet over their sink. No staff has suffered needle-stick injuries since 1993. (Jürgens, 1996, p. 59)

About 700 sterile injection units are handed out yearly by Dr Probst, at a cost of only 400 Swiss francs (approximately US$350), 'much less than would be the costs of caring for the cases of hepatitis and abscesses we avoid by handing out sterile equipment' (ibid). From the physician, who comes to the institution once every week, inmates can obtain more than one injection unit at a time, and distribution is not undertaken on a strict one-for-one basis. As emphasized by Mr Fäh:

> It is more important to make sure that prisoners who are injection drug users can always use sterile equipment than to insist on a one-for-one exchange scheme. We have a fairly good return rate, and are not concerned about not all equipment being returned to Dr Probst. What we do care about is safety of staff – and staff has not been exposed to any hidden needles.

In June 1994, another Swiss prison — Hindelbank institution for women in the Canton of Berne — started a one-year pilot AIDS prevention programme including needle distribution. Hindelbank houses up to 110 inmates, of whom the majority have been sentenced for narcotics offenses.

One year after it started, Hindelbank's needle-distribution programme was scientifically evaluated by external experts, demonstrating clear positive results: the health status of prisoners improved; no new cases of infection with HIV or hepatitis occurred; an important decrease in needle sharing was observed; there was no increase in drug consumption; and needles were not used as weapons (Nelles and Fuhrer, 1995). During one year, 5335 needles were distributed, an average of 14 per day. Their utilization seemed to depend primarily upon two factors: the availability of drugs, and prisoners' capacity to purchase them. Importantly, the evaluation showed that only about 20 per cent of staff did not agree with the installation of the needle distribution machines. The report concluded by saying that (ibid, at 19):

> The feasibility of distributing needles and syringes, the positive consequences it had on the sharing of needles, and the considerable acceptance of the project by inmates and staff ... lead to the conclusion that the distribution of sterile needles and syringes could also be justified in other prisons.

Following the evaluation, a decision was taken to continue the programme at Hindelbank. One year later, a follow-up evaluation confirmed that there was neither evidence of needle misuse nor an increase in drug consumption. The sterile needle distribution programme continued to run without complications (Nachevaluation, 1997). Other prisons have since started, or are planning to start, their own programmes (for more details, see Jürgens, 1996, at 60–66; Jürgens, 1997). In Switzerland, distribution of sterile injection equipment to injection drug users started in at least one prison for men in Geneva on 1 March 1996, in the prison of Realta in the Canton of Grisons on 3 February 1997, and in three more prisons in the Canton of Berne in early 1998 (Editor, 1998). In Germany, it started at Vechta (Lower Saxony), a women's prison with 170 inmates; at a men's prison with 230 inmates in Lingen (Lower Saxony) (for a preliminary review, see Jacob and Stöver, 1997); at a men's prison with a capacity of 300 in Hamburg in May 1996; and in Berlin, the Senator of Justice has expressed her intention to start it in a prison for women. In Spain, it is being piloted at the Trinidad Youth Prison in Barcelona and Basaure Prison near Bilbao. In Austria, according to an announcement made by Dr Jörg Pont at the 3rd European Conference on AIDS and Drug Use in Prisons in February 1997, it will be piloted in at least one prison (Jürgens, 1997). Finally, in Australia, a study concluded that needle and syringe exchange is feasible (Rutter *et al.*, 1996).

The experience of the prisons where sterile injection equipment has been made available has shown that it can be made available in a manner that is non-threatening to staff and indeed seems to have increased staff's safety; it has further shown that staff can be brought to understand that making sterile injection equipment available to inmates does not mean condoning drug use and 'giving up' on drug use in prisons, but is a pragmatic health measure. Because staff don't feel threatened by the distribution of sterile injection equipment, and because they understand the rationale behind it, they are supportive of it.

There is not one, but several models of distribution of sterile injection equipment. Thus far, every institution has chosen its own model: installation of dispensing machines, one-for-one exchange, or distribution through the physician or health-care services. This shows that what can and should be done in a particular institution depends on many factors, including, but not limited to, the size of the institution, the extent of injecting drug use, the security level, whether it is a prison for men or for women, the commitment of health-care staff, and the 'stability' of the relations between staff and inmates. A measure such as making sterile injection equipment available could not, and does not necessarily have to be, introduced in all institutions at the same time and in the same fashion, but can be undertaken immediately, easily, and at low cost, with good results, in some institutions. In other institutions, other measures may be more feasible and are being introduced, such as methadone maintenance programmes or the establishment of drug-free wings.

Methadone

Many national and international organizations have recommended the introduction or expansion of methadone maintenance treatment (MMT) in prisons (e.g. WHO, 1993; Advisory Committee on the Misuse of Drugs, 1993; Scottish Affairs Committee, 1994) and worldwide, a small but increasing number of prison systems is offering MMT to inmates (for a comprehensive review, see Dolan and Wodak, 1996). Treatment with methadone is seen as an AIDS-prevention strategy that allows people dependent on drugs an additional option to get away from needle use and sharing. As stated by Gore, the main aim of methadone maintenance:

> ... is to help people get off injecting, not off drugs. Methadone dose reduction — with the ultimate goal of helping the client to get off drugs – is a longer term objective. (cited in Jürgens, 1996, p. 70).

Indeed, it has been suggested that methadone is the best available option to prevent needle sharing in prisons (McLeod, 1991, at 245, 248), and that increasing the number of places available for MMT in prisons should be considered as a matter of urgency particularly for HIV-positive drug-dependent prisoners (Heilpern and Egger, 1989, at 94).

Community MMT programmes have rapidly expanded in a number of countries in recent years. There are ample data supporting their effectiveness in reducing high-risk injecting behaviour and in reducing the risk of contracting HIV. There is also compelling evidence that MMT is the most effective treatment available for heroin-dependent IDUs in the community in terms of reducing mortality, heroin consumption and criminality. Further, in most countries where it has been introduced, MMT attracts and retains more heroin injectors than any other form of treatment (Dolan and Wodak, 1996, with numerous references). Finally, there is evidence that people who are on MMT and who are forced to withdraw from methadone because they are incarcerated often 'return to narcotic use, often within the prison system, and often via injection' (CSC, 1994a, at 73; Shewan, Gemmell and Davies, 1994). It has therefore been widely recommended that prisoners who were on MMT outside prison be allowed to continue it in prison.

Further, with the advent of HIV/AIDS, the arguments for offering MMT even to those who were not following such a treatment outside, are compelling: prisoners who are injection drug users are likely to continue injecting in prison, and are more likely to share injection equipment, creating a high risk of HIV transmission among prisoners and to the public. As in the community, MMT, if made available to prisoners, has the potential of reducing injecting and syringe sharing in prisons (Dolan *et al.*, 1996c).

Nevertheless, many prison systems are still reluctant to make MMT available, arguing that imprisonment should be a time when injection drug users are forced to abstain from drug use for their own and the community's benefit:

> Methadone is considered by many correctional staff as just another mood altering drug, the provision of which further delays the necessary personal growth required to move beyond a drug centred existence. (Dolan and Wodak, 1996).

In the absence of education about its rationale, some prison staff regard MMT as 'pandering' to addicted prisoners by giving them free access to an opiate drug; they believe that its main rationale is the reduction of recidivism rather than the prevention of HIV transmission in prison. Some also object to MMT on moral grounds, arguing that it merely replaces one drug of dependence with another. If there were reliably effective alternative methods of achieving enduring abstinence, this would be a meagre achievement. However, there are no such alternatives:

> [T]he majority of heroin-dependent patients relapse to heroin use after detoxification; and few are attracted into, and retained in drug-free treatment long enough to achieve abstinence. Any treatment [such as MMT] which retains half of those who enrol in treatment, substantially reduces their illicit opioid use and involvement in criminal activity, and improves their health and well-being is accomplishing more than 'merely' substituting one drug of dependence for another (ibid, with reference).

This has been recognized in a recent Canadian case (*R* v *Povilaitis*), in which a man with a long-standing, 'serious heroin problem', who had committed a number of acquisitory crimes and had been in treatment, without success, several times already, was convicted to two years minus one day imprisonment — and thus to imprisonment in a provincial prison in Québec — because that prison had agreed to provide him with methadone treatment. The defense in the case had submitted that it was necessary to deal with the root causes of the man's crimes, namely his heroin addiction, and that treatment with methadone was essential to overcome that addiction. This was the first case in which an accused in a criminal case was sentenced to a term of imprisonment with the specific aim that he be allowed to undergo methadone treatment.

In another Canadian case, an HIV-positive woman undertook legal action against a provincial prison system for failing to provide her with methadone. The woman, who at the time of her sentence was on a methadone maintenance programme, had been refused continuation of the treatment in prison. She petitioned the court for relief in the nature of habeas corpus (see McLeod, 1996), arguing that, under the circumstances she found herself in, her detention was illegal. In response to the petition, and despite the position it had originally taken, the prison system arranged for a staff doctor to examine the woman, and he prescribed methadone for her. After this, she withdrew her petition. The provincial prison policy has since been changed to allow for methadone treatment of prisoners.

Heroin Maintenance Treatment

As part of the Swiss national experiment with prescribing of heroin and other drugs to users, in Oberschöngrün institution a heroin prescription programme started in September 1995. Up to a maximum of eight inmates participated in the project. To be eligible for participation, inmates had to be 20 years of age or older; have been dependent on heroin for a minimum of two years; have been in treatment, without success, in the past; have 'deficits in the social sphere', and have sufficient time left in the institution.

Participants lived in a separate unit of the institution, worked seven days a week, participated in group discussions and individual psychosocial counselling, and injected themselves with heroin three times a day under medical supervision. The main aims of the project were to: establish the feasibility of heroin maintenance in prisons; assist the institution in solving its drug-related problems; and study its advantages and disadvantages, for clients and institution, as compared to methadone maintenance.

First results derived from qualitative analyses show that prescribing heroin under medical control in prisons is feasible:

> All the medical and social problems could be resolved in a satisfactory way. ... the participants experienced an improvement in their quality of life. After a few start-up problems, adapting to the requirements of the prison sentence was considered to be satisfactory by the prison staff. For the prison itself, this pilot project was a major challenge that, thanks to the extra efforts of motivated and available staff, could be carried out successfully. (Kaufmann, Drelfuss and Dobler-Mikola, 1997/98).

THE WAR ON DRUGS IN PRISONS

Despite the examples of successful harm reduction programmes in prisons described above, many prison systems are still reluctant to embrace a harm reduction approach, and abstinence often remains the primary goal of their drug policy. The war on drugs, but not on AIDS, continues behind bars. The following section briefly discusses why such an approach could be counterproductive and contribute to the spread of HIV behind bars.

Measures have traditionally aimed at eliminating drug use in prisons, rather than reducing the harms from it. Stress has been placed on interdiction and apprehension, education and the treatment of addicted offenders. Some of the measures undertaken or planned, such as implementation of effective drug education, are uncontroversial and widely supported, but others have been criticized. In particular, it has been argued that drug-testing programmes such as those undertaken in a number of prison systems are costly and hardly a good use of scarce resources: such programmes cost more than appropriate public health responses to drug use, namely evaluated drug reduction and rehabilitation programmes in all prisons, would cost (Bird, Gore, and co-signatories, 1995). Further, they are intrusive, requiring prisoners to urinate on command and in full sight of staff. And finally, they are likely to have a negative impact on efforts to reduce the harms from drug use. In theory, drug testing should reduce the amount of drug use in prisons because people should be dissuaded from using drugs through fear of disciplinary action. However, the long-term effects on levels of drug use remain to be seen. According to inmates in Canadian federal prisons, the urinalysis programme may, if at all, have led to a slight decrease in drug use: according to a majority, the programme had 'no impact' on drug use among inmates (CSC, 1996a, at 360). Importantly, even if urinalysis programmes did result in a decrease in drug use, this should not be overvalued. Reduction of drug use is an important goal, but reduction of the spread of HIV and other infections is more important: 'the spread of HIV is a greater danger to' individual and public health than injection drug use itself' (NAC-AIDS Working Group on HIV Infection and Injection Drug Use, 1994). In particular, there is a fear that, because of urine testing, inmates' drug use, rather than diminishing, may shift from drugs (such as marijuana) that are detectable in urine for up to one month, to drugs (such as cocaine, heroin, PCP and LSD) that have much shorter windows of detection. As a result, injection drug use may increase, and with it the risk of HIV transmission and other harms from drug use (Riley 1995; Kommission, 1995). Canadian prisoners confirm that this is happening (Jürgens, 1996, at 24, with reference):

> We agree that urinalysis testing is encouraging some inmates to change their drug of choice from marijuana and hashish to harder drugs like cocaine and heroin because they are flushed out of your system faster, thus making random detection much harder. There is also a good portion of inmates that really do not care and will take their chances with random testing. In my opinion, this strategy is not reducing the amount of drugs in prison, instead it is increasing the amount of 'hard' drugs available.

ADDRESSING PRISON SYSTEM'S CONCERNS

Prison systems and governments have argued that harm reduction measures cannot be introduced in prisons for safety reasons, and that making them available would mean condoning sexual activity and drug use in prisons. This section will address these concerns and point out that introduction of harm reduction measures in prisons is in the interest of all concerned — prisoners, staff, the prison administration, and the public; and that it does not mean condoning sexual activity and drug use.

THE PERCEIVED CONFLICT OF VALUES BETWEEN THE PENAL SYSTEM AND MEDICAL CARE

Correction is a public safety (law enforcement) rather than a public health activity (Brewer, 1991), and prison life is not organized on the basis of care, but of coercion. Outside the prison setting, it has long been recognized that coercive interventions are counter-productive in controlling HIV transmission and its consequences; that HIV/AIDS interventions need to be based on respect for persons and their rights and dignity; and that personal responsibility has to be encouraged. Prevention of disease and the provision of medical care in prisons, however, require reconciling or balancing a medical model of prevention, diagnosis, care and treatment with the correctional requirements of custody and control (Dubler, 1990, p. 365). The punitiveness inherent in the prison system, and security concerns, have often been seen as obstacles to effective prevention of HIV/AIDS in prisons.

However, the promotion of health in prisons does not necessarily entail lessening the safety and security of prisons. The interest of prisoners in being given access to the means necessary to protect them from contracting HIV infection are compatible with the interest of staff in their security in the workplace and of prison authorities in the maintenance of safety and order in the institutions. Indeed, promotion of health in the prison population and the education of both prisoners and staff may be the best ways to create safety and security (PASAN, 1992, p. 3). Any measure undertaken now to prevent the spread of HIV infection will benefit prisoners, staff, and the public. First, it will protect the health of prisoners, who should not, by reason of their imprisonment, be exposed to the risk of a deadly condition. Second, it will protect staff in correctional institutions. Lowering the prevalence of infections in prisons means that the risk of exposure to these infections will also be lowered. Importantly, the experience of those countries that have made condoms, bleach, and sterile injection equipment available to inmates has shown that this can be done with the cooperation and support of staff, taking staff's security concerns into account. Finally, measures to prevent the spread of HIV infection in prisons also protect the public. Indeed, they are mandated by a sound public health policy. Most inmates are in prison only for relatively short periods of time and are then released into their communities. In order to protect the general population, HIV/AIDS prevention measures need to be available in prisons, as they are outside.

CONDONING DRUG USE OR CONDONING HIV TRANSMISSION?

Many prisoners are in prison because of drug offenses or because of drug-related offenses. Preventing their drug use is seen as an important part of their rehabilitation. In the eyes of many, acknowledging that drug use is a reality in prisons, would be to acknowledge that prison authorities have failed:

> And doesn't this mean that the government is basically admitting defeat — saying it can't control illegal drug use in prisons... ?'*Edmonton Sun*, 1994

Another argument that is often used is that making condoms, bleach, or sterile needles available to inmates would mean condoning behaviour that is illegal in prisons. Far from condoning sexual activity and drug use in prisons, however, making available to inmates the means that are necessary to protect them from HIV transmission acknowledges that protection of prisoners' health, rather than elimination of drug use, needs to be the primary objective of drug policy in prisons. As the Scottish report *Drug Use and Prisons* pointed out, 'the idea of a drug free prison does not seem to be any more realistic than the idea of a drug free society', and 'stability may actually be better achieved by moving beyond this concept' (Shewan, Gemmell, and Davies, 1994, at 24).

Furthermore, introducing harm-reduction measures is not incompatible with a goal to reduce drug use in prisons: making sterile needles available to drug users has not led to an increase in drug use, but to a decrease in the number of injection drug users contracting HIV and other infections (see, e.g., Centers for Disease Control and Prevention, 1993, at iii–vii; Wodak, 1996). Similarly, making methadone available to some users does not mean giving up on the ultimate goal of getting people off drugs; rather, it is a realistic acknowledgment that for some users this requires time, and that they need an option that will allow them to break the drug-and-crime cycle, reduce their contact with the black market, link with needed services, and reduce the risk of their becoming infected with HIV.

On the other hand, refusing to make condoms and bleach or sterile needles available to inmates, knowing that activities likely to transmit HIV are prevalent in prisons, could be seen as condoning the spread of

HIV among prisoners and to the community at large. As stated by Martin Lachat, Interim Director of Hindelbank institution:

> The transmission of HIV or any other serious disease cannot be tolerated. Given that all we can do is restrict, not suppress, the entry of drugs, we feel it is our responsibility to at least provide sterile syringes to inmates. The ambiguity of our mandate leads to a contradiction that we have to live with (Lachat, 1994).

This has been recognized by police forces in many countries, which, although continuing their fight against drugs, allow and even promote needle exchanges and other harm-reduction approaches. As the Head of the Merseyside Police Drug Squad has stated (cited in Riley, 1994, p. 156):

> As police officers, part of our oath is to protect life. In the drugs field that policy must include saving life as well as enforcing the law. Clearly, we must reach injectors and get them the help they require, but in the meantime we must try and keep them healthy, for we are their police as well... People can be cured of drug addiction, but at the moment they cannot be cured of AIDS.

A MORAL AND LEGAL OBLIGATION TO ACT?

Because of the reluctance of many prison systems to provide prisoners with the means that would allow them to protect themselves against contracting HIV, a question has been raised about whether governments and prison systems have a moral and legal obligation to provide such means, even if prisoners 'voluntarily' engage in illegal or forbidden behaviours (drug use and sexual activity). Can they be held liable for not providing condoms, bleach, and sterile needles and for the resulting transmission of HIV in prisons?

Two early US articles argue that HIV/AIDS prevention programs have a constitutionally mandated place within prison systems, born out of prisoners' right to personal security. According to the first (Note, 1988), prison officials who ignore the risk and fail to respond to it with appropriate protective policies violate the constitutional proscription against cruel and unusual punishment. The second also addresses the question of prison authorities' liability for HIV transmission in prisons (Note, 1989). However, both suggest that coercive measures be taken to prevent the spread of HIV, and do not mention the possibility of making condoms, bleach, and sterile needles accessible to prisoners: the latter argues that '[s]egregating inmates with AIDS in medical infirmaries and housing seropositive and ARC inmates together provides protection to all inmates'; the former recommends that prison officials take 'affirmative action consisting of mass screening, privilege-conscious segregation, and informative training.'

However, such coercive measures have been rejected by the vast majority of the other authors and reports, which argue that they are not only overly intrusive, but also costly and ineffective in curbing the spread of HIV. For example, Parts (1991, at 217; see also Dubler, 1990, at 389; Comment, 1989, at 354; Coughlin, 1988, at 63, 66; Note, 1987, at 288–89) rejects testing and segregation and, instead, argues that prison officials need to:

> take affirmative steps to prevent the transmission of AIDS, including establishment of AIDS prevention programs entailing provision of condoms to sexually active inmates and clean needles or bleach for cleaning needles to inmates who use intravenous drugs.

According to Parts, 'in light of the threat presented by AIDS, specific effective preventive health measures are more than just a good idea; they are constitutionally required.' The World Health Organization also emphasizes that '[a]ll prisoners have the right to receive health care, *including preventive measures*, equivalent to that available in the community without discrimination' [emphasis added], and that the general principles adopted by national AIDS programs 'should apply equally to prisons as to the general community' (WHO, 1993). Acknowledging this so-called equivalency principle, the Swiss Federal Office of Justice concludes that provision of sterile syringes in prisons is judicially admissible and compatible with a responsible health policy: 'If prison establishments wish to fulfil their duty to provide medical assistance, the provision of syringes and disinfectants is recommended' (Federal Office of Justice, 1992). Another legal opinion prepared in Switzerland in 1994 agrees and suggests that the state has 'a duty to make sure that persons dependent on drugs are provided with sterile injection equipment while in detention' (Wehrlin, 1994). Similarly, the commission mandated, by the Senator for Justice of Hamburg, Germany, with the development of a drug policy for prisons, concluded that 'the state has a legal obligation to care for prisoners in its custody,' and that this includes not only 'activities directed at caring for the sick, but measures directed at preventing threats to the health and well-being of prisoners' (Kommission, 1995, at 61).

INTERNATIONAL LAW

By its very nature, imprisonment involves the loss of the right to liberty. However, a prisoner 'retains all civil rights which are not taken away expressly or by necessary implication' (Lord Wilberforce in *Raymond v Honey* (1982), cited in Shaw, Prisoners' Rights, in Sieghart, 1988, at 40). In particular, prisoners, as every other person, have 'a right to the highest attainable level of physical and mental health' (El-Badry, 1989, at 11, with reference to the Constitution of the World Health Organization and Art 25, Universal Declaration of Human Rights; Art 12, International Covenant on Social, Economic and Cultural Rights; Art 11, American Declaration of the Rights and Duties of Man; Art 11, European Social Charter; Art 16, African Charter on Human and Peoples' Rights, etc.): the states' duty toward health, which includes giving people the means to protect themselves from exposure to HIV, does not end at the gates of prisons.

International recommendations on HIV/AIDS and drug use in prisons all stress the importance of prevention of transmission of HIV in prisons, and suggest that condoms and sterile needles or bleach should be available to prisoners (see, e.g. WHO, 1987; WHO, 1993; Council of Europe, 1988, paras. 14A(i) to 14A(viii); United Nations, 1990, p. 167; UNAIDS, 1997). In particular, according to the 1993 WHO Guidelines on HIV/AIDS in Prisons, preventive measures for HIV/AIDS in prisons should be complementary to and compatible with those in the community; and prison administrations have a responsibility to define and put in place policies and practices that will create a safer environment and diminish the risk of transmission of HIV to prisoners and staff alike (WHO, 1993, at 1–2).

LEGAL ACTION UNDERTAKEN BY PRISONERS

It is being increasingly argued that law (constitutional law, the law of negligence, and criminal law) could be used to force prison systems to introduce long overdue harm-reduction measures, or to hold them liable for not providing them and for the resulting transmission of HIV in prisons (for an overview, see Jürgens, 1996, at 81–94 and appendices 1 and 2).

Prisoners have shown a willingness to take action against government inaction by initiating legal action in order to obtain access to condoms (see supra at 7) and to methadone treatment (see supra at 13). This has provided the catalyst necessary for the institution of long-recommended changes. Courts have not even had to pronounce themselves on the substantive issues raised in the cases: governments and correctional authorities, at least in part because of the cases, have acted before the courts forced them to do so, and have made condoms and methadone treatment available.

Further, in at least two cases, Australian prisoners initiated legal action to secure damages for having contracted HIV in prison. The first prisoner seroconverted while in a maximum-security institution in Queensland and launched an action for damages for negligence against the Queensland Corrective Services Commission (Kennedy, 1995). The second prisoner testified from his hospital bed that he had contracted HIV while under the control and custody of the New South Wales prison authorities, and instituted a negligence claim against the authorities for failing to provide him with access to condoms and sterile syringes while he was incarcerated. Because he died shortly after the commencement of the pre-trial hearing and left no estate or dependants, the case ended with his passing (Malkin, 1997).

Such legal cases are important, but it would be 'a shame if incarcerated persons were obliged to have recourse to the courts in order to claim and have recognized certain rights, in particular with regard to access to preventive means for protecting oneself against HIV transmission' (Morissette, cited in Jürgens, 1996, at 94). There can be no question that the issue of providing protective means to prisoners would be more appropriately dealt with by swift action by correctional systems than by court action.

Prisoners, however, have indicated that, if necessary, they would continue to resort to legal action. Representatives of the Inmate Committee of one Canadian federal institution expressed agreement with the idea to 'pressure the authorities into supplying prisoners with a 'full range' of protective devices ... through legal means', saying that they 'view the present policy concerning hypodermic syringes as a blatant disregard for human life,' and that 'responsibility should fall squarely on their [the authorities'] shoulders' (cited in Jürgens, 1996, at 121). Inmates from another institution said that:

> if I were to contract a fatal disease in prison due to negligence on the part of C.S.C. [the Correctional Service of Canada] to provide me with the necessary prevention material and education, (that we are... entitled to on the street), I would personally hold C.S.C. fully responsible and liable. (ibid).

CONCLUSIONS

Prisoners are the essential captive audience. With such an audience, effective HIV prevention and care programmes can be implemented. But there needs to be the political will, the knowledge, and the resources to devote to these issues. UNAIDS calls on governments to address the needs of prisoners in a non-discriminatory and comprehensive manner (United Nations Commission on Human Rights, 1996).

Prison systems have a moral, but also a legal responsibility to prevent the spread of infectious diseases among inmates and to staff and the public. Currently, many systems are failing to meet this responsibility, because they are not doing all they could: measures that have been successfully undertaken outside prison with government funding and support, such as making sterile injection equipment and methadone maintenance available to injection drug users, are not being undertaken in most prisons, although some prison systems have shown that they can be introduced successfully, and receive support from prisoners, staff, prison administrations, politicians and the public.

It is to be hoped that governments and prison systems will act without prisoners having to undertake legal action to hold them responsible for the harm resulting from their refusal to provide adequate preventative means. Prisoners, even though they live behind the walls of a prison, are still part of our communities and deserve the same level of care and protection that people outside prison get. They are sentenced to prison, not sentenced to be infected:

> [B]y entering prisons, prisoners are condemned to imprisonment for their crimes; they should not be condemned to HIV and AIDS. There is no doubt that governments have a moral and legal responsibility to prevent the spread of HIV among prisoners and prison staff and to care for those infected. They also have a responsibility to prevent the spread of HIV among communities. Prisoners are the community. They come from the community, they return to it. Protection of prisoners is protection of our communities. (United Nations Commission on Human Rights, 1996).

If governments and prison systems do not take proper steps, they risk being condemned as irresponsible and morally negligent in the safekeeping of prisoners. As Justice Kirby stated, we owe it to the prisoners, and we owe it to the community, to protect prisoners from infection in prison:

> This requires radical steps before it is too late... The infection of a person who is in the custody of society, because that person does not have access

to ready means of self-protection and because society has preferred to turn the other way, is ... unpalatable. ... As a community we must take all proper steps to protect prison officers and prisoners alike. By protecting them we protect society. (Kirby, 1991, p. 19).

References

Advisory Committee on the Misuse of Drugs (1993) *AIDS and Drug Misuse Update*. London: HMSO.

Bird, A.G., *et al.* (1995) Anonymous HIV Surveillance with Risk Factor Elicitation at Scotland's Largest Prison, Barlinnie. *AIDS*, 9, 801–808.

Bird, A.G., Gore, S. and co-signatories (1995) Letter to M Forsyth, Secretary of State for Scotland, dated 14 September.

Brewer, T.F. (1991) HIV in Prisons: The Pragmatic Approach. *AIDS*, 5, 897.

Centers for Disease Control and Prevention (1993) The Public Health Impact of Needle Exchange Programs in the United States and Abroad. Summary, Conclusions and Recommendations. The Centers.

Christie, B. (1995) Scotland: Learning from Experience. *British Medical Journal*, 310, (6975), 279.

Comment (1989) AIDS behind Bars: Prison Responses and Judicial Deference. *Temple Law Review*, 62, 327–354.

Correctional Service Canada (1994a) *HIV/AIDS in Prisons: Final Report of the Expert Committee on AIDS and Prisons*. Ottawa: Minister of Supply and Services Canada.

Correctional Service Canada (1994b) *HIV/AIDS in Prisons: Background Materials*. Ottawa: Minister of Supply and Services Canada.

Correctional Service Canada (1996a) *1995 National Inmate Survey: Final Report*. Ottawa: The Service, Correctional Research and Development.

Correctional Service Canada (1996b) *1995 National Inmate Survey: Main Appendix*. Ottawa: The Service, Correctional Research and Development.

Coughlin (1988) AIDS in Prisons: One Correctional Administrator's Recommended Policies and Procedures. *Judicature*, 72, 63.

Council of Europe (1988) Recommendation 1080 on a Co-ordinated European Health Policy to Prevent the Spread of AIDS in Prisons of 30 June 1988.

Crofts, N. *et al.* (1995) Spread of Bloodborne Viruses among Australian Prison Entrants. *British Medical Journal*, 310(6975), 285.

Curran, L., McHugh, M., Nooney, K. (1989) HIV Counselling in Prisons. *Counselling Psychology Quarterly*, 2(1), 33–51.

Dolan, K., Hall, W., Wodak, A., Gaughwin, M. (1994a) Evidence of HIV Transmission in an Australian Prison. *The Medical Journal of Australia*, 160, 734.

Dolan, K., *et al.* (1994b) *Bleach Availability and Risk Behaviours in New South Wales*. Technical Report No 22. Sydney: National Drug and Alcohol Research Centre.

Dolan, K., *et al.* (1996a) A Network of HIV Infection among Australian Inmates. Abstract No 6594, XIth International Conference on AIDS, Vancouver, 7–11 July 1996.

Dolan, K., *et al.* (1996b) *Bleach Easier to Obtain But Inmates Still at Risk of Infection in New South Wales Prisons*. Technical Report. Sydney, National Drug and Alcohol Research Centre.

Dolan, K. *et al.* (1996c) Methadone Maintenance Reduces Injecting in Prison. *British Medical Journal*, 312, 1162.

Dolan, K. and Wodak, A. (1996) An International Review of Methadone Provision in Prisons. *Addiction Research*, 4(1), 85–97.

Dolan, K., *et al.* (1996) HIV Risk Behaviour of IDUs before, during and after Imprisonment in New South Wales. *Addiction Research*, 4(2), 151–160.

Dolan, K. (1997/98) Evidence about HIV Transmission in Prisons. *Canadian HIV/AIDS Policy and Law Newsletter*, 3(4)/4(1), 32–35.

Dubler, N.N. *et al.* (1990) Management of HIV Infection in New York State Prisons. *Columbia Human Rights Law Review*, 21, 363.

Editor. (1998) Needles in Bernese Penitentiaries. *Spectra*, 11, 4.

Edmonton Sun (1994) *Terribly Modern.* 29 March, p. 10.

El-Badry, A. (1989) *Health and Human Rights.* Report Prepared for the United Nations Expert Group Meeting on Population and Human Rights, Geneva, 3–6 April 1989. UN Doc IESA/P/AC.28/9 of 21 March 1989.

Federal Office of Justice (1992) *Provision of sterile syringes and of disinfectant*: Pilot project in correctional institutions; judicial admissibility. Berne, 9 July.

Ford, P.M. *et al.* (1995) Seroprevalence of Hepatitis C in a Canadian Federal Penitentiary for Women. *Canada Communicable Disease Report* 21(14): 132–134.

Gore, S.M. (1995) Drug Injection and HIV Prevalence in Inmates of Glenochil Prison. *British Medical Journal*, 310, 293–296.

Hammett, T.M. (1988) *AIDS in Correctional Facilities: Issues and Options. Third Edition.* Washington, DC: US Department of Justice.

Harding, T.W. and Schaller, G. (1992) HIV/AIDS Policy for Prisons or for Prisoners? In J.M Mann,., D.J.M. Tarantola, and T.W. Netter, (Editors), *AIDS in the World*. Cambridge, MA: Harvard University Press.

Harding, T.W. and Schaller, G. (1992b) *HIV/AIDS and Prisons: Updating and Policy Review. A Survey Covering 55 Prison Systems in 31 Countries.* Geneva: WHO Global Programme on AIDS.

Heilpern, H. and Egger, S. (1989) *AIDS in Australian Prisons — Issues and Policy Options.* Canberra: Department of Community Services and Health.

Jacob, J. and Stöver, H. (1997) Germany — Needle Exchange in Prisons in Lower Saxony: A Preliminary Review. *Canadian HIV/AIDS Policy and Law Newsletter*, 3(2/3), 30–31.

Jürgens, R. (1996) *HIV/AIDS in Prisons: Final Report.* Montréal: Canadian HIV/AIDS Legal Network and Canadian AIDS Society.

Jürgens, R. (1997) More Needle Exchange Programs in Prisons. *Canadian HIV/AIDS Policy and Law Newsletter*, 3(2/3), 30.

Kaufmann, B., Drelfuss, R., Dobler-Mikola, A. (1997/98) Prescribing Narcotics to Drug-Dependent People in Prison: Some Preliminary Results. *Canadian HIV/AIDS Policy and Law Newsletter*, 3(4)/4(1), 38–40.

Kennedy, M. (1995) Prison Discrimination Case Continues. [Australian] *HIV/AIDS Legal Link*, 6(2),12.

Keppler, K., Nolte, F., Stover, H. (1996) Transmission of Infectious Diseases in Prison — Results of a Study in the Prison for Women in Vechta, Lower Saxony, Germany. Reported in *Canadian HIV/AIDS Policy and Law Newsletter*; 2(2), 18–19.

Kirby, M. (1991) WHO Global Commission, AIDS Recommendations and Prisons in Australia. In J. Norberry, M. Gaughwin, and S.A. Gerull (eds). *No 4 HIV/AIDS and Prisons Conference Proceedings.*

Kommission zur Entwicklung eines umsetzungsorientierten Drogenkonzeptes für den Hamburger Strafvollzug (1995) Abschlussbericht. Hamburg, Germany: The Commission.

Lachat, M. (1994) Account of a pilot project for HIV prevention in the Hindelbank Penitentiaries for Women — Press conference, 16 May 1994. Berne: Information and Public Relations Bureau of the Canton.

Mahon, N. (1996) New York Inmates' HIV Risk Behaviors: The Implications for Prevention Policy and Programs. *American Journal of Public Health*, 86(9), 1211–1215.

Malkin, I. (1997) Australia — Not Giving Up the Fight: Prisoners' Litigation Continues. *Canadian HIV/AIDS Policy and Law Newsletter*, 3(2/3): 32–33.

McLeod, F. (1991) *Methadone, Prisons and AIDS.* In J. Norberry *et al.* (Eds.), HIV/AIDS and Prisons. Canberra: Australian Institute of Criminology.

McLeod, C. (1996) Is There a Right to Methadone Maintenance Treatment in Prison? *Canadian HIV/AIDS Policy and Law Newsletter*, 2(4), 22–23.

Millson, P. (1991) *Evaluation of a Programme to Prevent HIV Transmission in Injection Drug Users in Toronto*. Toronto: Toronto Board of Health.

Mutter, R.C., Grimes, R.M., Labarthe, D. (1994) Evidence of Intraprison Spread of HIV Infection. *Archives of Internal Medicine*, 154, 793–795.

NAC-AIDS Working Group on HIV Infection and Injection Drug Use. (1994). Principles and Recommendations on HIV Infection and Injection Drug Use. In: *Second National Workshop on HIV, Alcohol, and Other Drug Use: Proceedings, Edmonton, Alberta, February 6-9, 1994*. Ottawa: Canadian Centre on Substance Abuse.

Nachevaluation der Drogen- und HIV-Prävention in den Anstalten in Hindelbank (1997) Schlußbericht zu Handen des Bundesamtes für Gesundheit. Berne: BAG.

Nelles, J., Fuhrer, A. (1995) *Drug and HIV Prevention at the Hindelbank Penitentiary. Abridged Report of the Evaluation Results*. Berne: Swiss Federal Office of Public Health.

Nelles, J. and Harding, T. (1995) Preventing HIV Transmission in Prison: A Tale of Medical Disobedience and Swiss Pragmatism. *The Lancet*, 346, 1507.

Note. (1987) AIDS in Prisons: Are We Doing the Right Thing? *New England Journal on Criminal and Civil Confinement*, 13, 269.

Note. (1988) Sentenced to Prison, Sentenced to AIDS: The Eighth Amendment Right to be Protected from Prison's Second Death Row. *Dickinson Law Review*, 92, 863–892.

Note. (1989) AIDS in Correctional Facilities: A New Form of the Death Penalty? *Journal of Urban and Contemporary Law*, 36, 167–185.

Parts, M. (1991) The Eighth Amendment and the Requirement of Active Measures to Prevent the Spread of AIDS in Prisons. *Columbia Human Rights Law Review*, 22, 217–249.

Pearson, M. *et al.* (1995) Screening for Hepatitis C in a Canadian Federal Penitentiary for Men. *Canada Communicable Disease Report*, 21(14), 134–136.

Pickering, H. and Stimson, G.V. (1993) Syringe Sharing in Prison. *The Lancet*, 342, 621–22.

Prefontaine, R.G. and Chaudhary, R.K. (1990) Seroepidemiologic Study of Hepatitis B and C Viruses in Federal Correctional Institutions in British Columbia. *Canadian Disease Weekly Report*, 16, 265–266.

Prefontaine, R.G. *et al.* (1994) Analysis of Risk Factors Associated with Hepatitis B and C Infections in Correctional Institutions in British Columbia. *Canadian Journal of Infectious Diseases*, 5, 153–156.

Prisoners with AIDS/HIV Support Action Network (PASAN) (1992) *HIV/AIDS in Prison Systems: A Comprehensive Strategy*. Toronto: The Network.

Riley, D. (1994) Drug Use in Prisons. In *Correctional Service Canada* (1994b), pp. 152–161.

Riley, D. (1995) Drug Testing in Prisons. *The International Journal of Drug Policy*, 6(2), 106–111.

Rutter, S. *et al.* (1995) *Is Syringe Exchange Feasible in a Prison Setting? An Exploration of the Issues*. Technical Report No 25. Sydney: National Drug and Alcohol Research Centre.

Saum, C.A., *et al.* (1995) Sex in Prison: Exploring the Myths and Realities. *Prison Journal* December 1995.

Scottish Affairs Committee. (1994) *Drug Abuse in Scotland: Report*. London: HMSO.

Shewan, D., Gemmell, M. and Davies, J.B. (1994) Prison as a Modifier of Drug Using Behaviour. *Addiction Research*, 2(2), 203–216.

Shewan, D., Gemmell, M., and Davies, J.B. (1994) *Drug Use and Scottish Prisons: Summary Report*. Scottish Prison Service Occasional Paper, no 5.

Sieghart, P. (1988) Editor. *Human Rights in the United Kingdom*. London: Pinter Publishers.

Taylor, A. *et al.* (1994) Outbreak of HIV Infection in a Scottish Prison. Paper presented at the Tenth International Conference on AIDS, Yokohama, August 1994.

Taylor, A. *et al.* (1995). Outbreak of HIV Infection in a Scottish Prison. *British Medical Journal*, 310(6975): 289–292.

Taylor, A. and Goldberg, D. (1996) Outbreak of HIV in a Scottish Prison: Why Did It Happen? *Canadian HIV/AIDS Policy and Law Newsletter*, 2(3), 13–14.

Thomas, P.A. (1990) HIV/AIDS in Prisons. *The Howard Journal of Criminal Justice*, 29, 1–13.

Turnbull, P.J., Dolan, K.A., Stimson, G.V. (1992) Prison Decreases the Prevalence of Behaviours but Increases the Risks (Poster Abstract No. PoC 4321). VIIIth International Conference on AIDS, Amsterdam, 19–24 July 1992.

UNAIDS. (1997) *Prisons and AIDS — UNAIDS Point of View*. Geneva: Joint United Nations Programme on HIV/AIDS.

United Nations (1990) Infection with human immunodeficiency virus (HIV) and acquired immunodeficiency syndrome (AIDS) in prisons: Resolution 18 of the Eighth United Nations Congress on the Prevention of Crime and the Treatment of Offenders, Havana, Cuba, 27 August–7 September 1990. In *Report of the Eighth United Nations Congress on the Prevention of Crime and the Treatment of Offenders*. U.N. Doc. A/CONF.144/28 of 5 October 1990.

United Nations Commission on Human Rights (1996) Fifty-second session, item 8 of the agenda. HIV/AIDS in Prisons — Statement by the Joint United Nations Programme on HIV/AIDS (UNAIDS). Geneva, Switzerland, April 1996.

US National Commission on AIDS (1991) *Report: HIV Disease in Correctional Facilities*. Washington, DC: The Commission.

US Department of Health and Human Services, Public Health Service, Centers for Disease Control and Prevention. *HIV/AIDS Prevention Bulletin*, 19 April 1993.

Vlahov, D. *et al.* (1993) Prevalence and Incidence of Hepatitis C Virus Infection among Male Prison Inmates in Maryland. *European Journal of Epidemiology*, 9(5), 566–569.

Wehrlin, M. (1994) Gutachten. Verweigerung der Abgabe von Sterilem Injectionsmaterial in Bernischen Strafvollzugsanstalten und Allfällige Rechtliche Sanktionen gegen die HIV-Präventionspolitik des Kantons Bern. Berne: Advokaturbüro Wehrlin, Fuhrer, Hirt.

W.H.O. (1987) *Statement from the Consultation on Prevention and Control of AIDS in Prisons*. Geneva: WHO Global Programme on AIDS.

W.H.O. (1993) *Guidelines on HIV Infection and AIDS in Prisons*. Geneva: WHO Global Programme on AIDS.

Wodak, A. (1991) Behind Bars: HIV Risk-Taking Behaviour of Sydney Male Drug Injectors While in Prison. In J. Norberry *et al.* (Eds), *HIV/AIDS and Prisons*. Canberra: Australian Institute of Criminology, 181–191.

Wodak, A. Prevention Works! Effectiveness of Prevention of HIV Spread among Injecting Drug Users. *International AIDS Society Newsletter*, 5, 12–13.

Wright, N.H., *et al.* (1994) Was the 1988 HIV Epidemic among Bangkok's Injecting Drug Users a Common Source Outbreak? *AIDS*, 8, 529–532.

Zinn, C. (1995) Australia: Climbing the Political Agenda. *British Medical Journal*, 310(6975), 279

Cases

Prisoners A to XX inclusive v *State of NSW* (Supreme Court of NSW, Dunford J, 5 October 1994).

R v *Povilaitis*, unreported judgment of 27 June 1996 (Superior Court, Criminal Division, Province of Québec, no 450-01-004040-965, Gérald Desmarais J).

ACKNOWLEDGEMENTS

Writing of this Chapter was made possible, in part, by funding received from Health Canada and The Centre on Crime, Communities and Culture of the Open Society Institute.

Chapter 2

REDUCTION OF DRUG AND HIV RELATED HARM IN PRISON: BREAKING TABOOS AND APPLYING PUBLIC HEALTH PRINCIPLES

Joachim Nelles, Hans-Peter Hirsbrunner, Andreas Fuhrer, Anja Dobler-Mikola, and Timothy W. Harding

THE NECESSITY OF HARM REDUCTION IN PRISONS

At first sight, the prison environment appears as a mirror of society. A prisoner's life, as does everybody's, consists of work and recreation. In prisons, there is an economy, where people deal in privileges and goods like cigarettes or drugs. Everyday life is controlled by written and un-written rules. There is a culture of hierarchies, of daily routines and stable coalitions between prisoners and their fellow inmates as well as between prisoners and staff (Quensel, 1997). But from a closer view, prison reality turns out to reflect the outside world in a highly distorted way: 95 per cent of the prison population are male (Council of Europe, 1993), mostly of young age (for Switzerland: Estermann, 1997). The prevalence of infectious diseases, such as tuberculosis, HIV and viral hepatitis is considerably higher than in the community (Harding, 1990; Thomas and Moerings, 1994; Dolan *et al.*, 1995; Crofts *et al.*, 1995; Gostin, 1995). Compared with the general population, a markedly higher proportion of people imprisoned suffer from psychiatric diseases such as schizophrenia, bipolar psychosis, major depression or organic psychosis — often without receiving appropriate treatment. The number of mentally ill inmates in US prisons for example is estimated to reach 170,000 (Gunn *et al.*, 1991; Torrey, 1995). The proportion of drug addicted persons in prisons varies from 30 per cent to 80 per cent (Nelles *et al.*, 1995). The risk of suicide in prison as well as mortality following release from prison is high (Harding-Pink, 1990).

More than 5 million people are imprisoned world-wide (Africa, Far East and South America not included). In industrialised countries, per-manently about 0.1 per cent of the population are incarcerated; in the US this figure exceeds 0.5 per cent and a further increase is predicted. The turnover of the inmate population is high, essentially due to a growing number of short-term sentences. As a result, prisons play an increasingly significant role in the random mixing of marginalised groups; in the long term, prison-specific health problems concern the whole of society. To sum up, prisons may be described as places which concentrate health problems, and create public health risks.

Exchange of contaminated syringes among drug consumers and unprotected sexual contacts are the most important pathways of the spread of HIV and hepatitis. Health prevention in the classic sense has limited chances to be effective in prison, since both the heterogeneity and the high fluctuation of the inmate population undermine well targeted, long-term strategies. Furthermore, prevention aiming at hindering people from starting drug consumption, at changing their sexual behaviour, or at reducing the number of drug addicts encounters the problem that those people most in need of prevention are the most difficult to reach (Uchtenhagen, 1997). This applies especially for prisoners. As an alternative, the concept of harm reduction aims at minimising the health risks associated with incarceration instead of totally obviating them. Harm reduction measures, such as provision of sterile syringes, have been proven to reduce the risk of HIV infection among drug users in the community (for Switzerland: Dubois-Arber, 1994). Preliminary data from the Swiss national study on the prescription of opiates (heroin included) suggest comparable results (Rihs-Middle, 1996). Considering these findings, harm reduction might play an important role in improving the health situation in prisons.

But the principle of equivalence, postulating equal health provision offers inside and outside prisons, is far from being carried out. Guidelines and recommendations by both the WHO (1993) and the Council of Europe (1993) regarding adequate prevention measures in prison, have carried little weight so far (Nelles and Harding, 1995). Drug prohibition and pragmatic aid for drug addicts are often said to contradict each other. This assumed dilemma is more obvious in prison than in the society, where harm reduction has, at least in Switzerland, attained broad acceptance (Gutzwiller, 1997). This applies especially to syringe provision, methadone maintenance and prescription of heroin or injectable substitutes — elements of harm reduction that until today remain almost completely withheld from prisoners on a world-wide scale.

CONSEQUENCES

Prisons are rarely included in health policy formulation for the community. Prison authorities have to seek solutions to problems almost on their own. But prisons are hopelessly overcharged with this task.

None of the far-reaching harm reduction instruments has been implemented generally in prison (Siegel-Itzkovich, 1995; Nelles *et al.*, 1995). The prisoners, whose crime is most often related to social deficiencies, mental illness or drug dependency, have to deal not only with their individual problems but also with the health risks described above. And none of the various recommendations in scientific publications has improved this situation (Crofts *et al.*, 1995; Gill *et al.*, 1995; Gore *et al.*, 1995; Taylor *et al.*, 1995).

The resistance of prison staff, prison authorities and politicians against far-reaching harm reduction measures is often justified with fears like that provision of syringes might enhance drug intake because of its stimulating effect, that syringes might be used as weapons against fellow inmates or staff, and that undisposed contaminated syringes might cause injuries and infections, e.g. with HIV. The refusal of prison authorities to consider such measures meant that no systematic experience from prison projects was available to test such fears and concerns with objective observations.

PRAGMATIC PROJECTS IN SWISS PRISONS

Despite political opposition, whenever harm reduction programmes were intended to be introduced in prisons, pragmatic arrangements were taken into Swiss prisons by medical services, prison staff or administrations from 1985. Condom availability to prisoners was introduced in Geneva's remand prison in 1985. By 1989, with the support of the federal health authorities, most Swiss Cantons had accepted the principle of condom availability and several promoted open distribution in medical services or living quarters. In 1989, prisons in Zurich and Geneva introduced disinfectant with instructions on cleaning injection equipment. From 1990, methadone maintenance became possible for prisoners on methadone treatment prior to entry to prison in a growing number of remand prisons. In the Zurich penitentiary of Regensdorf, a special unit for prisoners on long term methadone treatment was opened in 1989. In several Cantons, the possibility of starting methadone maintenance *de novo* while in prison has been introduced. Despite widespread political opposition, the federal structure of Switzerland, with decentralised decision making and strong support from the federal health authority, has encouraged innovation and a pragmatic approach to harm reduction during the first decade of the AIDS epidemic. However, syringe distribution in prison remained taboo for a long time. It was finally initiated in 1993 as an act of medical disobedience, when the physician of Oberschöngrün Prison in the Canton of Solothurn decided to provide inmates with syringes without being authorised (Nelles and Harding, 1995).

As a result of a combined initiative of members of prison staff, prison administration and the Federal Office of Public Health, the first pilot project on HIV prevention, including distribution of sterile syringes, was started in 1994 in Hindelbank prison for women in the Canton of Berne. This initiative had originated in 1991, when the medical service of Hindelbank prison presented alarming figures about drug abuse, HIV prevalence and syringe sharing among drug dependent inmates. The process to launch this pilot study was carried on by the Swiss Federal Office of Public Health, which made it possible to overcome the doubts and reservations of political authorities in the Canton of Berne (Nelles *et al.*, 1994).

Recently even prescription of injectable heroin to a limited number of severely drug addicted inmates has become possible in the framework of a scientific study that started in July 1995 in the prison of Oberschöngrün (Kaufmann and Dobler-Mikola, 1997).

DISTRIBUTION OF SYRINGES IN OBERSCHÖNGRÜN PRISON

The prison of Oberschöngrün is a small penitentiary for about 75 male inmates, predominantly of Swiss origin. Duration of sentence varies from 3 months to 20 years. Offences are related to all types of crime. Some 15 drug addicts are permanently incarcerated in this prison. The physician of Oberschöngrün Prison hands out about 700 syringes a year. The syringes are given to the prisoners on their request (usually in exchange for used syringes returned for disposal). At the beginning the physician provided syringes on his own responsibility; only later he was authorised to do so by the political authorities. Syringe distribution is still ongoing in Oberschöngrün Prison. The effect of the syringe distribution has not been evaluated scientifically, but there are some informally reported facts: no incidents related to the distribution and use of syringes occurred, nor was there an increase in the number of overdoses or drug related deaths. No new abscesses caused by injecting in prison and no increase in drug intake was reported. Used syringes did not cause injuries to inmates or staff. Syringes have not been misused in any harmful way.

DRUG- AND AIDS- PREVENTION IN HINDELBANK PRISON

Study Design

Hindelbank serves about 100 female offenders of different nationalities. Sentences are related to all types of offences. Duration of imprisonment varies within a range of few months up to lifetime sentence.

The Hindelbank pilot project was carried out over a period of twelve months (June 1994–May 1995). Prevention efforts and evaluation were performed by two different independent external groups (B. Bürki and colleagues for drug prevention measures under guidance of the Cantonal Police Administration, and J. Nelles and colleagues from the Psychiatric University Services of Bern, Department East, for project evaluation; Nelles et al., 1994).

The prevention programme consisted of lectures given to all prisoners, small group discussions, personal socio-medical counselling, provision of information leaflets and distribution of condoms and sterile syringes. The latter have been issued by means of one-to-one automatic dispensers, installed in each of the six divisions of the prison (all prisoners received a dummy syringe, so that they could activate the dispenser for the first time). Group sessions and personal counselling took place in rooms reserved for the project. The prevention programme was aimed at all prisoners and, as far as convenient, at the staff, too. The information meetings focused upon topics such as hepatitis and HIV infection, the corresponding protection measures, and assistance in drug-related emergencies. The group meetings included discussions and role playing. The whole programme was held in German, English, French, and Spanish.

The objective of the subsequent evaluation was to analyse the efficacy of the prevention programme, to detect any undesirable developments and to elaborate, on the basis of the obtained results, general recommendations on how to proceed after termination of the pilot project, as well as on the introduction of syringe distribution in other prisons. The evaluation was based mainly on standardised interviews, carried out before launch of the prevention programme as well as three, six and twelve months thereafter. The interviews included questions on the socio-cultural context of the individual, on the consumption of drugs (past and present), on risk behaviour concerning sexuality and drug consumption, on the level of knowledge about HIV/AIDS and hepatitis, as well as on the acceptance and use of the preventive offers. Additional data such as the number of syringes used, the number, nature and course of disciplinary sanctions (e.g. locking of the cells, restriction in holiday regime), particular incidents, and data from the prisoners' medical examinations were also gathered.

Participation

The rate of participation in the interviews by the inmates was high. From a total of 189 women, 155 were invited for interview, and 137 participated. On the other hand, acceptance of the detailed interview by the staff was lower: 48 out of 111 persons working at Hindelbank Prison participated in the initial interviews. Consequently modified questionnaires (handed out to all staff members) did not change the situation significantly. Nevertheless, a total of 86 members of the personnel participated in at least one interview or returned a questionnaire. The data presented below as a rule concern interviewed inmates only. Comparisons of socio-demographic data of participating inmates and those who refused revealed no systematic differences.

The inmate population of Hindelbank Prison was very international; less than half of the inmates were of Swiss origin (Figure 2.1). The data on age, education level, and further socio-demographic aspects were comparable to other prisons for women. 60 per cent of the inmates have been sentenced because of offences against the Swiss law on narcotics, 26 per cent of them in combination with other offences.

Acceptance of the Programme

The offer of preventive measures — such as information, counselling, and discussions — was considered very positively by almost all prisoners and personnel. Only the distribution of syringes turned out to be controversial among staff, but not among prisoners (which reflects the current political debate on this issue). About one in five staff members stated their disagreement with the installation of syringe distribution machines. This proportion remained stable during the pilot project. Those staff members who did not participate in the interviews turned out to be the most critical about prevention efforts. This observation was confirmed by the results of the written questionnaires indicating that the position a person took with respect to the syringe distribution correlated with his or her general attitude towards drug politics (e.g. personal liberal opinion about general drug policy correlates with acceptance of syringe distribution dispensers in prison).

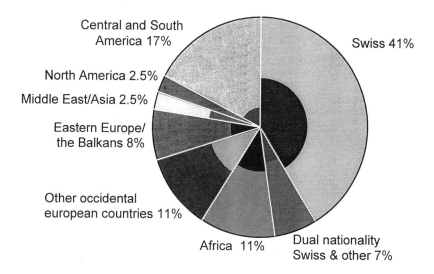

Central and South America 17%

Swiss 41%

North America 2.5%

Middle East/Asia 2.5%

Eastern Europe/ the Balkans 8%

Other occidental european countries 11%

Africa 11%

Dual nationality Swiss & other 7%

FIGURE 2.1 NATIONALITY OF THE INMATES (STUDY POPULATION, N=161). HATCHED AREAS CORRESPOND TO THE PROPORTION OF INMATES OF THE RESPECTIVE NATIONALITY WHO REFUSED INTERVIEW PARTICIPATION.

Drug Consumption before and During Imprisonment

The spectrum of drugs consumed before and while being in prison is presented in detail in Figure 2.2. A decrease in reported use of both heroin and cocaine was observed, while consumption of cannabis showed an increase. A comparable increase was also observed in intake of sleeping, tranquillising and anti depressant drugs. The interviews three, six and twelve months after the beginning of the project indicate that the spectrum of drug intake remained stable during the pilot phase. Analgesics, sedatives, antidepressants, neuroleptics, and other medications were prescribed by the prison medical service.

Prisoners taking illicit drugs were predominantly of Swiss nationality: 83 per cent of Swiss inmates (n = 46), but only 22 per cent of foreign origin (n = 16) reported having taken drugs regularly before being in prison; 72 per cent (n = 44) and 13 per cent (n = 9) respectively a month preceding incarceration; 67 per cent (n = 36), and 13 per cent (n = 9) respectively, reported taking illicit drugs while currently in prison. The covariance of drug intake and nationality unfortunately restricts identification of co-variables for drug intake such as age, education level, and marital status. The observed extent of drug intake did not increase during the pilot phase. No new drug consumers

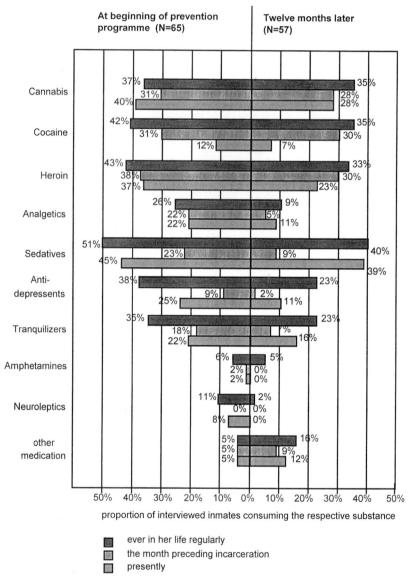

FIGURE 2.2 SPECTRUM OF DRUG INTAKE AT BEGINNING OF THE PREVENTION PROGRAMME AND AFTER ONE YEAR.

were found either. Those few inmates who re-started drug intake in prison, had already taken illicit drugs regularly for some time before being incarcerated. Summarising the results, it can be concluded that the syringe distribution did not provoke an increase in drug intake as feared by some prior to the pilot project.

Risk Behaviour Related to Drug Intake

High risk behaviour related to drug intake consists in exchange of contaminated syringes among IV drug users. From a total of 137 inmates interviewed, 11 reported having shared syringes with other inmates in Hindelbank prison. Eight inmates reported having shared syringes in prison with various persons before the project started. At the end of the project, only one woman still continued to share, with her friend. Exchange of used syringes almost disappeared over the course of the project.

Five of the women who reported sharing of syringes had been tested voluntarily for HIV and hepatitis infections. None of these was HIV positive, but two showed positive results for hepatitis A, B and C; one was hepatitis A and B positive, one was hepatitis A and C positive, and one was hepatitis B and C positive. Of the six women not tested, one reported she was HIV positive. These data indicate that risk of transmission of bloodborne viruses in Hindelbank prison, predominantly concerning hepatitis C, is high.

Utilisation of Distributed Syringes

The number of distributed syringes and the course of disciplinary sanctions are presented in Figure 3.3. The curve of syringe distribution starts on a high level and reaches another peak in October and November 1994. In the following months it decreases and remains finally on a low level when compared with the beginning (linear fit: syringe distribution over time, $r^2 = 0.87$, p<0.001). The course of sanctions related to drug intake correlates with the distribution curve, whereas the course of other sanctions does not ($r = 0.80$, p < 0.001, and other sanctions (r = 0.35, p > 0.1). This allows the conclusion that increased syringe distribution is due to increased drug intake, which was subsequently confirmed by the staff. In October and November 1994, Hindelbank Prison was apparently flooded with illegal drugs. The low syringe distribution from January to June 1995 is associated with low drug use at that time and a smaller proportion of drug dependent women in prison. These observations indicate that supply of syringes is closely related to availability and use of illegal drugs. This finding is confirmed by another observation: distribution of syringes was increased in the week after inmates received their monthly wages (0.14 ± 0.02 [SEM] syringes/inmate/day versus 0.24 ± 0.03 [SEM] syringes/inmate/day, Wilcoxon, p = 0.01). Obviously having money in prison is associated with increase in drug acquisition, increase of drug

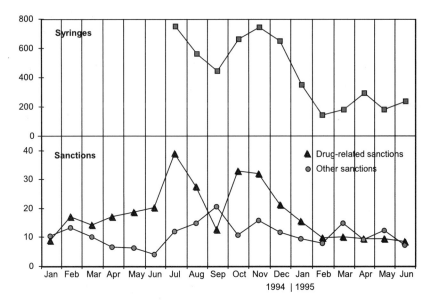

FIGURE 2.3   NUMBER OF DISTRIBUTED SYRINGES AND COURSE OF DIFFERENT TYPES OF SANCTIONS

intake and supply of syringes, followed by a rise in surveillance and sanctions.

Some of the fears most often expressed concerning the issue of syringes in prison could not be confirmed by the study: syringes have never been misused by inmates (e.g. as a weapon). Disposal of syringes was uncomplicated (because of one-to-one exchange machines) and no injuries were caused by unproperly disposed of syringes. The number of overdoses (1 in 12 months) and the number of drug related deaths (1 in 12 months) did not increase.

Knowledge of HIV/AIDS and Hepatitis Infection

The inmates showed themselves to be well informed on HIV infection and AIDS already at the beginning of the project, and during the time, only slight differentiation of the pre-existing knowledge occurred. Despite this solid knowledge base, however, 35 per cent of the prisoners committed 'fatal' judgement errors: behaviours which undeniably include the risk of infection, e.g. sexual relations between women, were falsely estimated to be out of risk. Surprisingly, drug addicted prisoners most often committed such errors, even though they showed themselves to be better informed in almost all of the other awareness areas than did the other prisoners (46 per cent fatal errors by drug addicts versus 24 per cent by non drug users).

Inmates' knowledge about HIV infection and AIDS was high even at the beginning of the project. Strikingly, the prisoners showed themselves to possess very little knowledge concerning hepatitis. This is in contrast to the fact that, as is shown below, this infection is widespread at Hindelbank. 60 per cent of the inmates interviewed could not answer the question: 'What is a viral hepatitis (infectious jaundice)?'. Only half of the prisoners knew how the hepatitis virus is transmitted. Most of the prisoners were not able to respond to more specific questions concerning hepatitis infection. The results obtained from the staff were comparable.

Prevalence of HIV and Hepatitis Infection

Upon their arrival at the prison, 94 women underwent a voluntary blood analysis within the framework of the pilot project. The results revealed, in addition to a proportion of 6 per cent (n = 6) HIV positive tests, a strikingly high infection rate concerning viral hepatitis. Of the women examined, about one out of two (n = 45) was hepatitis B positive and more than one in three (n = 35) was hepatitis C positive (Table 2.1). In follow-up tests (n = 51, just before release) no seroconversion, neither concerning HIV nor viral hepatitis, was observed.

Interpretation of the Findings

The proportion of drug consumption, the prevalence of drug-related risk behaviour and the rate of HIV and hepatitis infections in the prison of Hindelbank compare with the situation known from international studies (overview in Nelles *et al.*, 1995).

The results of the pilot project carried out at Hindelbank prison do not furnish any arguments against the continuation of the distribution of sterile syringes. The initial fears that were expressed — that the

Table 2.1 Results of serological testing (n = 94).

Serological Testing	Positive	Active	Unclear/ no result
HIV	6		0
HAV	69		3
HBV	45	5	3
HCV	35		3
HBV **and** HCV	28		
Lues	9	0	4

consumption of drugs would increase, syringes would be used negligently or as weapons, or would cause injuries — did not occur at all. In contrast, no abscesses related to drug injection in prison were observed during the pilot project, the exchange of syringes among prisoners almost ceased, and no new cases of HIV or hepatitis infection surfaced. Abolishing the distribution of sterile syringes would undermine the success achieved so far. The findings compare with the experience of syringe distribution in Oberschöngrün prison, indicating that distribution of syringes is feasible in prisons for women and men. However, a considerable limitation of validity of the conclusions has to be mentioned: both prisons are of relatively small size.

Though knowledge of risks is not predictive for less harmful behaviour, it may serve as the rationale for change of behaviour. The basic level of knowledge about HIV infections and AIDS was sufficient already before launching the project, but the proportion of 'fatal errors' (misinterpreting existing infection pathways) was astonishingly high, especially in the group of drug addicts. Awareness of hepatitis infections was alarmingly low in both groups, the inmates and the personnel. There is an urgent need to provide more, and continuous information in prisons regarding these harmful infections, especially concerning viral hepatitis.

The positive effects of syringe distribution on harm reduction in Hindelbank and in Oberschöngrün, and the fact that the consumption of drugs, behaviour detrimental to good health and a high prevalence of HIV and hepatitis infections all are undeniable realities of prison life lead to the conclusion that syringe distribution should be considered in addition to routine prevention activities in other prisons.

As a consequence of the project results, providing inmates of Hindelbank prison with sterile syringes has been prolonged by the Cantonal police director for at least one year, but with a lower level of accompanying preventive measures (part-time employed nurse in charge of prevention measures).

CONTROLLED OPIATE MAINTENANCE IN OBERSCHÖNGRÜN PRISON

The pilot project in Oberschöngrün is part of the Swiss multicenter opiate trial (Rihs-Middle, 1996). It follows the same basic objectives as such trials outside prison: to reach addicts unable to profit from other forms of treatment, to improve health and social status, and to reduce risk taking behaviour. However, in the special environment of the penal system there are special questions concerning the participants: 'Is there an improvement in the general adjustment of the participants because of the heroin substitution in the penal institution?'. And also concerning the organisation and realisation: 'Which are the negative and positive effects related to the heroin substitution in penal institutions?'

Study Design

The participants in the prison have to fulfil the same entry criteria as in the trials outside prison walls. They have been proven to be heroin dependent for at least two years and to have failed in earlier therapeutic programmes. They should not be younger than twenty years and deficiencies concerning social integration, psychological well-being and health should be presented. In the prison, the target population includes only heroin addicted inmates with at least nine months of sentence remaining. The trial is also open for inmates from other penal institutions, however their sentences have to be compatible with a semi-confined imprisonment regime.

In the prison of Oberschöngrün, the trial setting is separated from the main part of the prison and located about three kilometres outside the main buildings. The participants of the project live and work in small groups. The heroin (individual medical prescription) is provided three times a day by trained female staff (nurses), provision is supervised by a prison warder, and prisoners inject their heroin themselves. Additionally, the participants receive psycho-social counselling and care based on general guidelines for the Swiss heroin trials.

The first participants entered the trial in September 1995. After some initial difficulties, the daily routine normalised rapidly. These difficulties were based on new elements in the penal setting: inmates as well as warders had to get familiar with the unusual situation that intake of in general still illegal drugs takes place in prison under the supervision of prison staff.

Preliminary Results and Conclusions

Quantitative and qualitative data from the initial period with the four first participants have been collected only so far. Summarising first impressions, it can be said that new forms of interactions within the penal system arose, due to heroin maintenance, and that these interactions are very different from traditional interaction patterns between the two main groups of actors, staff and inmates. Enhanced compliance and personal contacts, caused by active care-taking, are one of the main results of the first period. Despite these positive findings, the contradiction concerning intake of illegal drugs under supervision of prison staff was recognised by inmates and staff. It seems to be necessary to develop individual coping mechanisms for these contradictions. Preliminary findings however suggest that the passing of time may play an important role in getting used to this unfamiliar situation.

From the preliminary results it can be concluded that prescription of heroin within the penal system is feasible. But heroin maintenance in prison causes changes in understanding of the traditional prison function: in order to implement heroin maintenance in the daily routine in a useful way, the penal system needs to shift its main function from merely incarcerating people to care taking processes for inmates.

DISCUSSION

What can be learned from the pragmatic approaches in Swiss prisons? First, in two prisons, the desired effect of providing inmates with sterile syringes was fully achieved, since no increase of drug intake was observed, syringes have not been used as weapons, disposal of syringes was uncomplicated, and high risk behaviour — exchange of pre-used syringes — disappeared almost completely. These results belie fears that have often been used to hinder introduction of syringe distribution in prison. Second, acceptance of the programmes in the prisons of Oberschöngrün and Hindelbank was high, both among inmates and staff. Even prescription of heroin to inmates revealed good acceptance among staff and inmates, as can be concluded from preliminary data of the feasibility study in Oberschöngrün prison. Third, in the prison of Hindelbank, the inmates' knowledge about drugs, HIV infection, AIDS and risk behaviour is in general sufficient. However, a third of the inmates, among them a high proportion of drug addicts revealed individual 'fatal errors' (infection pathways were assessed to be harmless). Knowledge on viral hepatitis was alarmingly low for both inmates and staff, and in contrast to the fact that prevalence of viral hepatitis B and C among inmates was high. These findings indicate the necessity of permanent education and counselling efforts in prison. From the point of view of health policy, it would be a serious mistake to restrict education in prison to HIV and AIDS campaigns of public health organisations conducted in the general public. Fourth, in implementing the two pilot projects the Swiss Federal Office of Public Health played a remarkable role. Without its support for the political process of acceptance as well as its financial aid, neither of the projects could have been realised. This office's clear concept based on the principle of equivalence and embedded in the drug policy of the Swiss government (BAG 1993) was of major importance. But in the end, only the combined initiative of courageous members of prison staff, prison administration and health organisation made the programmes possible.

Do prisons need special health strategies adapted to the closed and highly controlled environment? The following conclusions can be drawn: prisons should be seen as an integral part of the community with a constant flow in both directions. Typical problems of prisons such as high prevalence of viral hepatitis, HIV infection and tuberculosis therefore should not be seen as specific issues for 'prison medicine.' If harm reduction measures already proven to be successful in the community are comparably efficient when introduced in prisons, there is no need to develop special harm reduction strategies for prisons. The results of the pilot projects in two Swiss prisons may be interpreted as a first indication in this direction. However, we do not yet know to what extent these positive results obtained from small prisons in an industrialised country are applicable to other prisons (e.g. remand prisons, large prisons, and prisons in developing countries). We therefore need still further experience. In Germany and Switzerland, new scientifically evaluated projects are already running and their results will be available soon. These projects include provision of syringes (Hamburg/D: Pape *et al.*, 1996; Vechta and Groß-Hespe/Lower Saxony/D: Meyenberg *et al.*, 1996; Realta, Canton of Grisons/CH) and prescription of injectable methadone (Bale/Switzerland: Nelles *et al.*, 1997).

The introduction of complete harm reduction programmes in prison is still far beyond broad political acceptance, even in Switzerland. But selective pragmatic attempts, as described in this paper, may be the step-by-step way out of the unsatisfactory health situation in most prisons.

References

BAG (Bundesamt für Gesundheitswesen) und Eidgenössische Kommission für Aidsfragen (Hrsg.), (1993) HIV-Prävention in der Schweiz. Ziele, Strategien, Massnahmen, Bern, Bundesamt für Gesundheitswesen.

Council of Europe (1993) Recommendation no. R(93)6 of the Ministers of Member States, Strasbourg, Council of Europe.

Crofts, N., Stewart T., Hearne P., Ping X.Y., Breschkin A.M. Locarnini, S.A., (1995) Spread of blood-borne viruses among Australian prison entrants. *British Medical Journal*, 310, 285–288.

Dolan, K., Wodak, A., Penny, R. (1995) AIDS behind bars: preventing HIV spread among incarcerated drug injectors, *AIDS*, 9, 825–832.

Dubois-Arber, F., Barbey, P. (1994) Evaluation der AIDS-Präventionsstrategie in der Schweiz: Vierter zusammenfassender Bericht, 1991–1992, im Auftrag des Bundesamtes für Gesundheitswesen, Institut univérsitaire de médecine sociale et préventive, Lausanne.

Estermann, J. (1997) Die Verfolgung des Drogenkonsums und Drogenkonsumenten in Schweizer Gefängnissen. Ein Überblick; in: *Harm Reduction in Prison. Strategies against AIDS, Drugs, and Risk Behaviour*, J. Nelles, and A. Fuhrer, eds. (Bern, Lang-Verlag), pp. 61–82.

Gill, O.N., Noone A., Heptanstall, J. (1995) Imprisonment, injecting drug use, and bloodborne viruses. *British Medical Journal*, 310, 275–276.

Gore, S.M., Bird, A.G., Burns, S.M., Goldberg, D.J., Ross, A.J., Macgregor, J. (1995) Drug injection and HIV prevalence in inmates of Glenochil prison. *British Medical Journal*, 310, 293–296.

Gostin, L.O. (1995) The resurgent tuberculosis epidemic in the era of AIDS. *Maryland Law Review*, 64, 1–131.

Gunn, J., Maden, A., and Swinon, M. (1991) Treatment needs of prisoners with psychiatric disorders. *British Medical Journal*, 303, 338–341.

Gutzwiller, F. (1997) Schadensreduktion als Teil einer kohärenten Drogenbekämpfungsstrategie, Ein Überblick; in: *Harm Reduction in Prison. Strategies against AIDS, Drugs, and Risk Behaviour*, J. Nelles, and A. Fuhrer, eds. (Bern, Lang-Verlag), 35–44.

Harding, T.W., Manghi, R., Sanchez, G. (1990) *Le SIDA au milieu carceral, Les stratégies de prévention das les prisons suisses*. Rapport mandaté par l'OFSP, Institut univérsitaire de médecine légale, Gèneve.

Kaufmann, B. und Dobler-Mikola A. (1997) Die kontrollierte Opiatabgabe in der Strafanstalt Oberschöngrün — Forschungsplan und erste Zwischenergebnisse; Ein Überblick; in: *Harm Reduction in Prison. Strategies against AIDS, Drugs, and Risk Behaviour*, J. Nelles, and A. Fuhrer, eds. (Bern, Lang-Verlag), pp. 135–160.

Meyenberg, R., Stöver, H., Jacob, J., Pospeschill, M. (1996) Infektionsprophylaxe im Niedersächsischen Justizvollzug. bis, Oldenburg.

Nelles, J., Bernasconi S., Bürki, B., Hirsbrunner, H.P., Maurer, C., Waldvogel, D. (1994) Drogen- und AIDS-Prävention im Gefängnis: Pilotprojekt mit freier Spritzenabgabe in den Anstalten Hindelbank bei Bern/Schweiz. in: Heino Stöver (Hrsg.), Infektionsprophylaxe im Strafvollzug. Eine Übersicht über Theorie und Praxis, AIDS Forum D.A.H., Band XIV, Berlin, Deutsche AIDS- Hilfe e.V., 101–109. (*English translation available*)

Nelles, J., Harding, T.W. (1995) Preventing HIV transmission in prison: a tale of medical disobedience and Swiss pragmatism. *Lancet*, 346, (8989), 1507–1508.

Nelles, J., Waldvogel, D., Maurer, C., Aebischer, C., Fuhrer, A., Hirsbrunner, H.P. (1995) *Drogen- und HIV-Prävention in den Anstalten von Hindelbank*. Evaluationsbericht, Bern, Bundesamt für Gesundheitswesen.(*Abridged report in English and French available*).

Nelles, J., und Fuhrer, A. (1997) *Kurzevaluation des Pilotprojekts 'Drogen- und Aidsprävention in den Basler Gefängnissen'*, Evaluation report by order of the Swiss Federal Office of Public Health, Bern [internal publication].

Pape, U., Böttger, A., und Pfeiffer, Ch. (1996) Wissenschaftliche Begleitung und Beurteilung des geplanten Spritzentauschprogramms im Rahmen eines Modellversuchs der Justizbehörde der Freien Hansestadt Hamburg. Konzeption eines empirischen Forschungsprojekts, KFN Hannover, Forschungsbericht Nr. 54.

Quensel, S. (1997) Drogen im Gefängnis — muss das sein?. Ein Überblick; in: *Harm Reduction in Prison. Strategies against AIDS, Drugs, and Risk Behaviour*, J. Nelles, and A. Fuhrer, eds. (Bern, Lang-Verlag), 45–60.

Rihs-Middle, M. (1996) Ärztliche Verschreibung von Betäubungsmitteln. Wissenschaftliche Grundlagen und praktische Erfahrungen, Huber Verlag, Bern/Göttingen/Toronto/Seattle.

Siegel-Itzkovich J. (1995) Prison policies put inmates at risk. *British Medical Journal*, 310, 278–283.

Taylor, A., Goldberg, D., Cameron, S., Emslie, J. (1995) Outbreak of HIV infection in a Scottish prison, *British Medical Journal*, 310, 289–292.

Thomas, P.A. and Moerings, M. (Eds.) (1994) *AIDS in prison*. Dartmouth, Aldershot/ Brockfield USA/Singapore/ Sidney.

Torrey, E.F., 1995: Jails and prisons — America's new mental hospitals. *American Journal of Public Health*, 85, 1611–1613.

Uchtenhagen, A. (1997) Drug Prevention Outside and Inside of Prison Walls. Ein Überblick; in: *Harm Reduction in Prison. Strategies against AIDS, Drugs, and Risk Behaviour*, J. Nelles, and A. Fuhrer, eds. (Bern, Lang-Verlag), 201–212.

WHO (World Health Organization) (1993) *Global Programme on AIDS, WHO guidelines on HIV infection and AIDS in prison*, Geneva, World Health Organization.

[This study was supported by the Swiss Federal Office of Public Health.]

Chapter 3

HIV, DRUG USE, CRIME AND THE PENAL SYSTEM: COMPETING PRIORITIES IN A DEVELOPING COUNTRY — THE CASE OF BRAZIL

John Dunn, Ronaldo R. Laranjeira, and José Ricardo P. Marins

Geographically speaking, Brazil is the fifth largest country in the world, and has an estimated population of over 146 million. Although a developing country, it is rich in natural resources and has a strong agricultural industry. Three quarters of the population live in cities, the largest of which is São Paulo with a population of around 15 million.

The Portuguese colonised the country in the fifteenth century and Brazil finally achieved independence in 1822. From 1964 to 1985 the country was run as a military dictatorship and after a transitional government became a democratic republic in 1989. The first elected president to take office was impeached following allegations of corruption but a degree of both political and economic stability have been established under the following two presidents. Despite political and economic reforms, massive social inequalities persist and over one third of the population live below the poverty line. Striking inequalities can often be seen side by side, with luxury apartments and mansions rubbing shoulders with *favelas* or shanty towns, where the houses are made of wood and cardboard, there is no sanitation, and children run semi-naked in the litter strewn streets.

CRIME

Statistics suggest that there is a high level of crime in Brazil, but published figures do not fully represent the true picture. It is believed that many crimes, particularly theft and robbery, go unreported because the victims have little confidence in the police. A recent survey undertaken by the Latin American Institute of the United Nations for the Prevention of Crime and the Treatment of Delinquency (ILANUD) suggested that only one third of crimes such as theft, assault and robbery were reported to the police.

Figures released by the Secretary for Public Security for São Paulo estimated that in São Paulo alone there are 325 thefts, 275 robberies, 288 car thefts and 21 homicides per day. Most homicides are a result of gunshot wounds, gun possession being widespread, although a recent law has been introduced to reduce the facility with which guns can be purchased.

LAW ENFORCEMENT AND THE PENAL SYSTEM

There are two main divisions of the police: the civil and military. The former are mainly responsible for investigating criminal and civil offences and the latter for policing the streets and repressive actions. Policing is undertaken on a sectorized basis, linked to population size and local crime levels. The police are poorly paid and allegations of corruption are common. Police officers themselves complain about lack of resources, saying that criminals are often better equipped than they are, with more powerful firearms and faster cars. Each police station has a cell where offenders can be locked up whilst awaiting charging or transfer to prison. Because of overcrowding in the prison system, police stations often end up having to accommodate offenders for considerable periods of time with the result that they too become subject to overcrowding.

Prisons in Brazil are the responsibility of the individual State Governments. Federal input to the prison system is limited to issuing guidelines, overall monitoring, and financing. Consequently, there can be considerable variation between States in the custodial models used, for example in terms of prison sizes and the ratio of open to closed regimes. In open regimes prisoners undertake work in the community during the day and only return to prison in the evening.

It is common for 10 to 12 prisoners to share a cell designed for just two people. Due to this high level of overcrowding, the limited facilities available in prisons and the appalling conditions found in many of them, there has been increasing political pressure to reform the penal system and develop alternatives to custodial sentences, for example, community service, particularly for less serious offences. Several problems have been identified in the penal system apart from overcrowding. These include: an insufficient number of prisons, a need for smaller prison units, insufficient prison wardens (on average around five prisoners to one warden), lack of training and an inefficient administrative structure. In recent years there have been numerous rebellions in prisons throughout Brazil, often with prison staff and relatives being held hostage and large-scale breakouts.

As a consequence of overcrowding, many offenders are completing their sentences in police cells. Apart from the obvious lack of space and amenities, such as toilets and bathrooms, police cells have no facilities for rehabilitation, education or even basic exercise. Since levels of security are lower, breakouts and rioting are not uncommon.

The need for a reform of the penal system is well recognised but whether there is the political will to undertake one is debatable. Improving the infrastructure of the prison system is not a vote winner and is just one of many competing priorities in a country beset by serious social problems and inequalities.

PRISON POPULATION

A survey of the prison population in 1995 showed that there were 148,760 people incarcerated in Brazilian prisons, but there was considerable variation in the prison population between states (http://www.mj.gov.br). The highest figure was for São Paulo with 174.4 prisoners per 100,000 population compared to 17.8 per 100,000 in the north-eastern State of Alagoas. Over 95 per cent of prisoners were men. The majority were being held in closed regimes with just over 11 per cent in open or semi-open prisons. The most common reasons for having being imprisoned were as follows: robbery (32 per cent), theft (16 per cent), homicide (15 per cent) and drug trafficking (11 per cent).

CRIMINAL BEHAVIOUR AMONG DRUG USERS

We have recently completed a survey of 294 cocaine users who were in contact with a wide range of treatment services in São Paulo, including outpatient clinics, detoxification centres, rehabilitation units, counselling agencies and non-governmental organisations (Dunn and Laranjeira, *in press*). The study aimed to provide details of patient characteristics, drug history, HIV risk behaviour and other associated behaviours, including criminal history. Patients were asked how they financed their drug use and a variety of activities were reported including: selling one's own belongings, especially training shoes, sound systems and compact discs (65 per cent), selling objects belonging to other family members (39 per cent), theft of objects belonging to non-family members (38 per cent) and armed robbery (21 per cent). Trafficking of drugs was not uncommon with 18 per cent having sold cannabis, 16 per cent cocaine powder and 12 per cent crack. Thirteen per cent of the sample said that they had prostituted themselves in order to obtain money to buy drugs (12 per cent of men and 24 per cent of women).

DRUG USERS' EXPERIENCE OF PRISON

Fifty-six per cent of the above sample of 294 cocaine users from treatment agencies in São Paulo had been arrested at some stage in their life, with 42 per cent having spent time locked up in police cells and 16 per cent in prison. Thirty-two per cent of cocaine users who had been incarcerated, either in police cells or prisons, reported having used drugs whilst there. Only 3 per cent had injected drugs whilst in prison and just 2 per cent said that they had shared injecting equipment.

Two per cent of cocaine users had had sex with another prisoner whilst incarcerated but only 1.4 per cent said that they had had penetrative sex without a condom. This compares with 10 per cent of prisoners who reported having had sex with another inmate in a study of 917 prisoners from a large prison in Sorocaba, São Paulo (Marins, 1996).

HIV AND AIDS IN BRAZIL

The Global AIDS Programme of the WHO puts Brazil in the top four countries in the world in terms of cumulative numbers of AIDS cases. Since 1980 when the first case of AIDS was reported, over 110,872 cases have been notified to the Ministry of Health (http://www.aids.gov.br). However, the Ministry itself works on an estimated level of under reporting of 30 per cent. For the combined years 1996/97, the primary exposure categories for reported AIDS cases (n = 20,123) were as follows: homosexual 16 per cent, bisexual 8 per cent, heterosexual 31 per cent, intravenous drug use 19 per cent, haemophilia 0.3 per cent, blood transfusion 3 per cent, perinatal transmission 3 per cent and unknown 20 per cent. Heterosexual transmission has shown a steady increase over the last decade, as illustrated by the falling male to female ratio. In 1987 there were 9 male patients with AIDS for every female, by 1990 the figure had fallen to 6 to 1 and in 1996/97 to 2.5 to 1. Data from females with AIDS shows that the main risk factor for infection was having had a sexual relationship with a drug user.

There have been no HIV prevalence studies undertaken of the general population in Brazil, but a study of blood donors in the city of Santos showed the prevalence of HIV to be 0 per cent, whilst that for hepatitis C was 2 per cent and hepatitis B 23 per cent (Carvalho *et al.*, 1996).

The WHO multi-city study of HIV prevalence among intravenous drug users, included two Brazilian cities, the port town of Santos and Rio de Janeiro (WHO Collaborative Study Group, 1993). In this study roughly half the sample came from drug treatment agencies and the other half were recruited directly from the community. The prevalence of HIV among drug users in Santos was 60 per cent and in Rio de Janeiro 40 per cent. In a more recent study, Carvalho *et al.*, (1996) used a snowball sample to investigate the prevalence of various infectious agents among intravenous drug users in Santos. They found the following figures: HIV 62 per cent, hepatitis B 75 per cent, hepatitis C 75 per cent and syphilis 34 per cent. A multi-city study of the prevalence of HIV among intravenous drug users in five Brazilian cities, with a sample size of 701, has recently been completed with blood samples having been collected between August 1995 and December 1996 (Mesquita, 1997). The prevalence of HIV varied considerably between cities, ranging from 28 per cent in Rio de Janeiro to 71 per cent in Itajaí in the State of Santa Catarina.

These seroprevalence studies suggest that intravenous drug users are involved in high levels of HIV risk behaviour. This question was investigated in the above-mentioned study of 294 cocaine/crack users from 15 different treatment services in São Paulo (Dunn and Laranjeira, unpublished). In this study we investigated injecting history, in particular the sharing of injecting equipment. Thirty-two per cent (95) of the sample had injected a drug at least once in their life and 25 per cent (74) had been regular injectors. Cocaine was the drug most commonly injected. Sixty-eight per cent of injectors described having borrowed a previously used syringe, 64 per cent had lent their used syringe to someone else and 72 per cent said that they usually shared injecting equipment. Apart from syringes, other injecting 'works' were frequently shared, including spoons (78 per cent) and rinse water (88 per cent). Eighty-two per cent of injectors said that they usually washed their syringe prior to use, but the majority used ineffective disinfecting agents, like cold tap water (71 per cent).

HIV/AIDS AND HEPATITIS AMONG PRISONERS

A governmental research organisation recently reviewed the literature on the prevalence of HIV and other sexually transmitted diseases among prisoners in Brazil (NUPAIDS, 1996). They gathered together all published studies, including theses and conference abstracts that had been published between 1986 and 1996. Most of these studies were performed in single prisons, although one study used a state-wide sample of prisoners from Rio de Janeiro (Matida *et al.*, 1992). Many of the studies do not clearly specify how the samples were obtained but most used either volunteers or high-risk groups, such as known intravenous drug users. Few studies used random samples or systematic samples of all prisoners. Lorenço *et al.*, (1992) studied the prevalence of HIV in São Paulo's largest prison using a systematic sample of all new prisoners detained between 1990 and 1991. Among the 1692 prisoners tested,

16.5 per cent were already infected on entry into prison. In this study, prisoners were prospectively followed up and re-tested at the end of the study period. He found a new infection rate among initially HIV negative prisoners of 0.6 per cent per annum. The usual risk factors were associated with HIV seropositivity in all studies that investigated this question, namely intravenous drug use, homosexual or bisexual activity and a previous history of sexually transmitted diseases.

The prevalence of syphilis among prisoners has been reported as between 7 and 25 per cent, depending on the type of sample used. Only two studies have measured the prevalence of hepatitis C, neither of which used random or systematic samples (Rozman et al., 1996; Soares et al., 1995). Soares et al. (1995) found a prevalence of 6 per cent among 63 volunteers from a prison with a total population of 70 in the State of Minas Gerais, whilst Rozman et al. (1996) found a prevalence of 34 per cent among 631 prisoners from a total prison population of 4677. Likewise, the prevalence of hepatitis B varied widely depending on the type of sample used and whether HBsAg or anti-HBs were being measured. Souza et al., (1989) measured both in a systematic sample of prisoners in the city of Bauru, São Paulo and found a prevalence of HbsAg of 4 per cent and anti-HBs of 15 per cent among 52 prisoners.

Recently, Ferreira et al. (1996) used a prospective cohort design to measure the prevalence of tuberculosis and HIV among 350 female inmates of a prison in São Paulo and also looked at the incidence of new tuberculosis cases during a 12-month follow-up period. The prevalence of HIV was 25 per cent and tuberculosis 5.7 per cent. The incidence of new tuberculosis cases was 9.9 per 100 person-years for HIV-positive inmates and 0.7 per cent per 100 person-years for HIV-negative inmates, a relative risk of over 14.

DRUG USE IN BRAZIL

There have been no epidemiological studies of the prevalence of illicit drug misuse in the general population, although two are currently being developed. The most methodologically rigorous studies of drug use have been undertaken in specific populations, in particular among primary and secondary school pupils (Galduróz et al., 1994; Carlini-Cotrim and Carlini, 1993) and among homeless street children (Armando et al., 1990). In the study of primary and secondary school children aged between 10 and 18 years, the most commonly used illicit drugs were solvents (15.4 per cent), anxiolytics (5.5 per cent) and cannabis (5.0 per cent). Among treatment populations cocaine, either in the form of cocaine powder or crack, is the most commonly reported drug of misuse (Bastos *et al.*, 1988; Castel and Malbergier, 1989). There is evidence that the number of patients using crack has been increasing since the start of the 1990s (Dunn *et al.*, 1996). Heroin and other opiates are virtually unknown in most of Brazil, but there have been sporadic reports of heroin use in São Paulo in recent years (Laranjeira *et al.*, 1997).

In the study of primary and secondary school children, the prevalence of cocaine use was found to be increasing. The first time the survey was undertaken in 1987 with a sample of over 16,000 pupils from ten Brazilian cities, the lifetime prevalence of cocaine use was 0.9 per cent among boys and 0.3 per cent among girls (Carlini-Cotrim and Carlini, 1993). The study was repeated again in 1989 and 1993 and the corresponding figures for boys and girls were 1.4 per cent and 0.3 per cent in 1989 and 2.0 per cent and 0.6 per cent in 1993 (Galduróz *et al.*, 1994). Among homeless street children cocaine use was much higher. Two studies have been undertaken of drug use among street children using samples from five Brazilian cities (Armando *et al.*, 1990). The first study was carried out in 1989 using a sample of 284 children and showed a lifetime prevalence of cocaine use of 12 per cent. It was repeated in 1983 with a sample of 564 children and the lifetime prevalence of cocaine use had risen to 21 per cent.

DRUG USE AMONG PRISONERS

There is remarkably little data available on illicit drug use among prisoners in Brazil, only three studies have investigated this question in any detail (Marins, 1995; Kallás, 1996; Lorenço, 1992). Lorenço (1992), using a systematic sample of 557 new admission to the largest prison in São Paulo and reported that 56 per cent of prisoners had used illicit drugs prior to incarceration but only 18 per cent had injected drugs in the past. Once incarcerated, 51 per cent continued to use some from of illicit substance, but only 1.5 per cent continued injecting drugs. Kallás (1996) reported that 18 per cent of prisoners had used intravenous drugs prior to imprisonment but only 1.5 per cent continued using them in prison. Marins (1995) found a lifetime prevalence of illicit drug use of 78 per cent among 917 inmates from a prison in Sorocaba, São Paulo, 28 per cent of whom had injected drugs. Only 2 per cent (n = 19) continued injecting after incarceration, but the majority of these shared their injecting equipment with other prisoners. The prevalence of HIV among those prisoners who had ever injected drugs was 35 per cent compared to 4.5 per cent of those who had never used any illicit substance, a relative risk of 7.8.

HIV PREVENTION CAMPAIGNS

HIV educational and prevention campaigns have been running for many years in Brazil. They are mainly financed and co-ordinated by the Ministry of Health through a committee known as the Coordenação Nacional de DST/AIDS. There are usually two main campaigns per year, one that starts on the 1st December (the International Fight Against AIDS Day) and the second in the run up to the annual Carnival in February/March. All major media are used including television, radio, cinema, newspapers, magazines, billboards and pamphlets. The prevention themes are also discussed in the popular soap operas, programmes that have the highest national audience ratings.

Carnival, a national public holiday, is a festivity traditionally associated with heavy alcohol consumption, drug use and freer sexual activity (Dunn, 1994). The campaign prior to Carnival tends to be more humorous than the December one. For example, the 1997 campaign used turkeys dressed up in carnival costumes (in Portuguese the word for turkey is *peru*, which is also the slang word for penis), with the suggestion that one's peru should always be dressed up in its costume (condom) during Carnival.

Non-governmental organisations are also actively involved in educational and prevention campaigns, often doing outreach work with so-called 'high risk' groups, such as prostitutes and intravenous drug users. The most famous non-governmental organisation to act in this area is GAPA (Grupo de Apoio à Prevenção à AIDS), which works primarily with drug users but also distributes condoms free of charge to the general population during Carnival.

Although educational campaigns have been running for many years, the Government has had much more difficulty implementing direct action such as the introduction of needle exchanges for intravenous drug users. Despite the prevalence of HIV among intravenous drug users, various attempts to introduce needle exchanges in cities with the highest prevalence have been thwarted by legal interventions, usually instigated by the local Justice Departments. In the port city of Santos, where studies suggest that 60 per cent of intravenous drug users are HIV positive, various unsuccessful attempts have been made to introduce a needle exchange (Dunn and Laranjeira, 1995). Only as late as 1997 did the State Legislator of São Paulo authorise needle exchanges and there are two currently functioning in the City of São Paulo.

HIV PREVENTION CAMPAIGNS AMONG PRISONERS

In 1995 the Ministry of Health, through its AIDS co-ordinating committee (Coordenação Nacional de DST/AIDS), began to directly finance and support HIV prevention and educational campaigns in prisons. Contracts for the development of such campaigns were signed with 10 State governments in 1996 and further contracts were planned for 1998.

The main aim has been to increase the general level of HIV awareness and knowledge among both prison staff (including wardens, administrators, nurses, doctors, teachers) and the prisoners themselves. Some of these interventions have been quite innovative, for example, in the State of São Paulo comic strips have been distributed to prisoners featuring a character known as *Vira Lata* (Street Dog), to educate prisoners about AIDS. *Vira Lata*, an ex-con, is seen in a series of explicit sexual adventures but is always seen using a condom. A comic book character was chosen to get the HIV message across because it is primarily visual and does not necessitate much in the way of literacy skills on behalf of the prisoner.

Although needles and syringes are not distributed to intravenous drug users in Brazilian prisons, in the State of Rio Grande do Sul a programme has been developed whereby prisoners have access to disinfecting agents, such as bleach, so that clandestine injecting equipment can at least be sterilised.

A feature, perhaps unique to Brazilian prisons, is the *visita íntima* (intimacy visits). These were introduced as a specific measure to try to reduce the incidence of new HIV infections occurring in prisons caused by prisoners having sex with other inmates. The intimacy visits are aimed at male prisoners who have a stable relationship with a female outside the prison. A room is set aside where the prisoner and his partner are able to have sexual relations on a regular basis. Condoms are usually available in these rooms. Intimacy visits are not permitted for female prisoners on the perhaps sexist grounds that they would increase the risk of female prisoners becoming pregnant and having babies in prison, where conditions are inadequate for their care and protection.

CONCLUSIONS

As this brief review shows, Brazil is a country with a serious crime problem, a growing cocaine/crack problem and one of the highest prevalences of AIDS in the world. The prevalence of HIV among intravenous drug users is between 28 per cent and 71 per cent and HIV positive drug users have acted as a channel through which HIV has spread into the general population, as evidenced by the current heterosexual epidemic. Many drug users become involved in criminal activity such as theft, robbery and drug trafficking and at some stage are likely to come into contact with the judicial system and spend time either in police cells or prison. Prisons are unsanitary, dilapidated and seriously overcrowded. This combination of factors would suggest that prisons are high-risk environments in which the spread of HIV and other infectious diseases, such as hepatitis and tuberculosis, are facilitated. Clearly action is needed on several fronts if the current situation is not to worsen. Education and prevention campaigns for the general population must continue but priority should be given to more active approaches, such as outreach work with high-risk groups. The systematic introduction of a countrywide network of needle exchanges and expansion of the HIV prevention programmes in prisons are two measures that could have a significant impact. In addition urgent consideration should be given to the introduction of some form of prison diversion scheme, to redirect drug-using offenders away from the custodial system into treatment agencies and/or community service.

As has already been mentioned, although HIV, drug use and crime are serious problems in Brazil, they are just three of the many equally if not more grave social problems that the country faces. The Government is under pressure from all sides to spend more money on social programmes. Reform priorities include, the redistribution of agricultural land, improving the quality of and access to public health services, better primary and secondary education to combat the relatively high levels of illiteracy and school evasion and investment to improve the basic infrastructure (sanitation, water supply, electricity and roads) of the many large shanty towns. To maintain economic stability and prevent a return to runaway inflation (40 per cent per month in 1993), public spending is under tight Governmental control and many worthy schemes have had to be put on hold. Despite this, several innovative schemes have already been introduced to try to combat the rising prevalences of HIV, drug misuse and crime, but clearly much more needs to be done.

References

Armando, R *et al.* (1990) Uso de psicotrópicos por meninos de rua: comparação entre os dados coletados em 1987 e 1989. In: *Abuso de drogas entre meninos emeninas de rua do Brasil.* São Paulo: CEBRID. pp. 1–28.

Bastos, F.I.M., *et al.* (1988) Perfil de usuários de drogas I — estudo de características de pacientes do NEPAD/UFRJ — 1986/87. *Revista ABP-APAL,* **10**, 47–52.

Carlini-Cotrim, B. and Carlini, E.A. Illicit use of psychotropic substances among Brazilian students: 1987 and 1989 surveys. In: *Brazil — United States Binational Research,* M.G. Monteiro, and J.A. Inciardi, eds. (São Paulo: CEBRID), pp. 151–163.

Castel, S. and Malbergier, A. (1989) Farmacodependência – estudo comparativo de uma população atendida em serviço especializado: 1984–1988. *Revista ABP-APAL,* **11**, 126–132.

Carvalho, H.B. *et al.* (1996) HIV and infections of similar transmission pattern in a drug injectors community of Santos, Brazil. *Journal of the Acquired Immune Deficiency Syndrome and Human Retrovirology,* **12**, 84–92.

Dunn, J. (1994) Carnival and condoms. *Psychiatric Bulletin,* **18**, 575–76.

Dunn, J *et al.* (1996) Crack cocaine: an increase in use among patients attending clinics in São Paulo: 1990–1993. *Substance Use and Misuse,* **31**, 519–27.

Dunn, J and Laranjeira, R. (1995) News from Latin America. *Addiction,* **90**, 295–299.

Dunn, J and Laranjeira, R. Transitions in the route of cocaine administration: characteristics, direction and associated variables (ADDICTION, *in press*).

Ferreira, M.M. *et al.* (1996) Tuberculosis and HIV infection among inmates in São Paulo, Brazil: a prospective cohort study. *Journal of the Acquired Immune Deficiency Syndrome and Human Retrovirology,* **13**, 177–83.

Galduróz, J.C. *et al.* (1994) *III levantamento sobre o uso de drogas entre estudantes de 1° e 2° graus em 10 capitais Brasileiras, 1993.* CEBRID, São Paulo.

Kallás, E.G. (1996) *Prevalência e identificação dos fatores de risco para infecção pelo vírus da imunodeficiência humana na Casa de Detenção de São Paulo.* Masters Thesis. Department of Infectious Diseases and Parasitoses, Escola Paulista de Medicina, São Paulo.

Laranjeira, R. *et al.* (1997) Heroína: a próxima epidemia de drogas no Brasil? *Journal brasileiro de Psiquiatria,* **46**, 5–7.

Lorenço, R. (1992) *Epidemiologia da infecção pelo VIH-1 nas instituições carcerária masculinas do complexo penitenciário do Carandiru — São Paulo.* Masters Thesis. São Paulo: Department of Infectious Diseases and Parasitoses, Escola Paulista de Medicina,.

Marins, J.R.P. (1996) *Soroprevalência da infecção pelo HIV em população carcerária.* Masters Thesis. Faculdade de Ciências Médicas, UNICAMP, SãoPaulo.

Matida, A.H. *et al.* (1992) Prevalência de soropositividade para o vírus HTLV-III/LAV em populações carcerárias masculinas do estado do Rio de Janeiro — resultados preliminares. In: *Inventário de recursos de pesquisa em SIDA — América Latina e o Caribe 1983–91.* Brazil, OPS, p. 117.

Mesquita, F. (1997) Projeto Brasil — aumento do consumo de heroína no Brasil. (1996) *Encarte do Boletim Epidemioógico — AIDS, Ano IX,* No. 6, 3–4.

NUPAIDS *Pesquisa para diagnóstico rápido (PDR) a partir de fontes secundárias sobre a situação do HIV/AIDS e outras DSTs do sistema prisional.* Núcleo de Pesuqisa Epiedmilógicas em AIDS, Universidade de São Paulo.

Rozman, M.A. (1995) *AIDS e tuberculose na Casa de Detenção de São Paulo.* Masters Thesis. Faculdade de Medicina, Universidade de São Paulo, 1995.

Soares, B.C.C. *et al.* (1995) Soropreval6encia de HIV-1, HTLV-I/II, hepatites B e C, sífilis e chagas em população de Manhuçu, M.G. *Congresso Brasileiro de Epidemiologia,* **1035**, p. 270.

Souza, P. *et al.* (1990) SIDA/AIDS prevention for risk behaviour individuals: a health promotion programme under way in Brazil. *International Conference on AIDS,* San Fransisco, USA. Poster S.C. 682.

WHO Collaborative Study Group (1993) An international comparative study of HIV prevalence and risk behaviour among drug injectors in 13 cities. *Bulletin of Narcotics,* **45**, 19–46.

Chapter 4

DRUG USE, DRUG CONTROL AND DRUG SERVICES IN
GERMAN PRISONS: CONTRADICTIONS,
INSUFFICIENCIES AND INNOVATIVE APPROACHES

Jutta Jacob and Heino Stöver

Currently about 60,000 people are held in German prisons. This reflects an overall ratio of 72 inmates per 100,000 inhabitants. The German prison system is covered by the Prison Act of 1977 which provides that federal legislation must be implemented by the various states. This is the reason for differences in the handling of drug consumers and HIV- or hepatitis-infected prison inmates in the various states.

Because consumers of illegal drugs were presented as criminals, many of them were taken into custody at least one time or repeatedly during their 'career' for dealing with or taking drugs. At some stages during their 'career' the prison becomes the centre of life for the drug users. It is assumed that the total number of drug addicts held in custody amounts to approx. 10,000–20,000. In other words, despite vigorous controls every third to sixth inmate in a German prison is or has until recently consumed illegal drugs (with varying consumption patterns and frequencies), particularly injection drugs.

Injection drug use is everyday routine among inmates in German prisons, despite wide-ranging preventive measures in the fields of security, addiction and drug abuse. Some empirical studies (e.g. Koch and Ehrenberg, 1992; Kleiber and Pant, 1996) have revealed that the conditions of drug consumption in prisons advance the spreading of viral infections like HIV or some forms of hepatitis. High rates of infected inmates not only entail long illnesses and states of emergency at the individual level, but in the long run they also cause increased follow-up costs due to the rising demand on social and medical service providers.

Considering the specific dynamics of illness spreading among prison inmates and its possible or likely implications on public health, penal institutions increasingly become a matter of interest for public health care institutions which have to meet the obligation to safeguard public health. Thus the social and political significance of risks of infection in penal institutions becomes apparent. Accepting these interrelations as facts makes it necessary to focus on new lines in the evaluation of possible infectious diseases arising from injection drug use in prison. The new strategies to be undertaken should provide the basis for an effective infection prophylaxis and a general promotion of health care measures in penal institutions.

PREVALENCE OF INJECTING DRUG USE AND INFECTION DISEASES (HIV AND HEPATITIS) IN PENAL INSTITUTIONS

During the past 20 years the extent of injection drug use and the spreading of infectious diseases among prisoners has risen considerably. This is true for all European countries. Drug abuse, psychological disorders and infectious diseases are the major problems, besides overcrowding, in European penal institutions (Tomasevski, 1992).

The majority of those infected with HIV/AIDS or other infectious diseases (hepatitis) are (former) drug consumers. In prisons, HIV and particularly hepatitis B and C are mostly transmitted through sharing unsterile needles. Whereas Kleiber and Pant (1996) found that the number of those who share their needles with other drug consumers has dropped significantly outside prisons between 1988 and 1992/3, it is striking that this trend has not been observed in prisons. The readiness to take the risks involved in needle sharing has not diminished during the past years. 'The readiness to pass on contaminated needles to others after use despite the knowledge about being sero-positive is above average if the recipient is unknown or if needles are scarce as in prisons.'(Kleiber and Pant, p. 169).

PREVALENCE OF DRUG USE IN PENAL INSTITUTIONS

At some stages a prison becomes the centre of life for many drug users. In total the number of drug addicts held in custody in Germany is assumed to amount to approximately 10,000–20,000. Despite vigorous controls every third to sixth inmate in a German prison is or has been until recently a consumer of illegal drugs (with varying consumption patterns and frequencies), particularly of injection drugs. The proportions of drug addicts in the various penal institutions differ widely. Whereas in women's prisons the share of addicts frequently exceeds 50 per cent, the proportion is significantly lower in men's prisons. Mr. Krumsiek, the former Minister of Justice of the state holding the largest population, Northrhine-Westphalia, has pointed out that the number of drug addicts held in custody has doubled between 1982 and 1992. Several studies in which drug addicts outside prisons were interviewed revealed that two thirds of the drug consumers surveyed had already been in prison, on average for more than 12 months (Koch and Ehrenberg, 1992; Kleiber and Pant, 1996). Moreover empirical findings have shown that drug consumers have spent more time in prison than in therapy facilities (AMSEL study of 1991: 342ff).

In an epidemiological study Koch and Ehrenberg (1992) found that those drugs that were available and used outside prisons were also available and used inside prisons. The frequencies of consumption indicated by inmates ranged from 'several times per day' to 'more rarely than once a month'. There seemed to be hardly any problems in the prisons as to the supply of heroin or cocaine (p. 53). However, the supply situation varied from prison to prison and even between several sections of the same prison. But despite these fluctuations it is relatively easy to get hold of drugs; therefore those inmates who did not consume illegal drugs when they were taken in custody can hardly avoid doing so in prison. This 'detention-induced addiction' is a frequently observed phenomenon. Cannabis seems to be easily available in most prisons and is widely in use. Tightened controls sometimes cause bottlenecks in supply which give rise to an increased use of mixed drugs.

Prevalence of Viral Infectious Diseases in Penal Institutions

Reports of HIV prevalence and sero-conversions in penal institutions are inconsistent. Whereas the legal authorities at state level proceed on the assumption that in most prisons the number of HIV-positive inmates is low and decreasing, and the number of unrecorded cases is also low and only comprises a few known cases of sero-conversion, outside investigations revealed statistically significant correlations between HIV transmission and imprisonment (injection drug use is continued in prison).

As for hepatitis, it must be assumed that hepatitis infections are widely spread among injection drug users, not only outside but also inside prisons. Longitudinal studies have already revealed several sero-conversions with prison inmates. It must be pointed out here that due to the particular study area; drug use and infectious diseases, and due to the special nature of the subject under study; viral infectious diseases in penal institutions (voluntary testing, varying incubation and antibody detection times), precise statements on the transmission and the course of infections in penal institutions are difficult to make. Moreover, the issue has only rarely been approached through research.

Due to the drawbacks mentioned above, it is hardly possible to analyse the spreading of infections in penal institutions by means of the mostly applied method — conducting cross-sectional surveys at the beginning of detention. If longitudinally collected serological data are complemented by information from social science it is more likely that reliable results will be obtained.

HIV TESTING PRACTICES

In most regional states of Germany the inmates are advised to take a voluntary HIV test at the beginning of their prison sentence. The legal authorities of the various states gather the test results and publish them in the Statistical Quarterly Surveys on HIV and AIDS Infections. However, it must be noted here that the results of the surveys are misleading because generally a considerable number of inmates refuse to take a test. To test inmates for HIV without their consent would counteract the liberal goals to be achieved by the German health care policy which is designed to achieve bring about changes in behaviour through education and providing information. Compulsory tests would be aimed at controlling and recording epidemics and at criminal prosecution. The practice currently applied in penal institutions, giving inmates the opportunity to take voluntary HIV tests, corresponds to practice applied outside prisons. Some inmates do not use the opportunity to take voluntary tests for fear that they will entail disadvantages during detention. On the other hand there are some states (Bavaria, Baden-Wurttemberg, Hesse, Saarland) where the refusal to take a test will definitely result in disadvantages during detention. Those prisoners refusing to take a test are treated as if they were HIV positive. The testing practices within prisons in the various states differ widely. In some states test rates of more than 90 per cent have been achieved (e.g. Hamburg), while in other states (e.g. Bremen) no reliable data material is available because the tests are taken anonymously and outside prisons.

In general, HIV tests are not repeated at the end of detention, so sero-conversions which may have occurred during detention are not recorded. Baden-Württemberg is the only exception. Here a two year test series was conducted, including repeated tests. The number of those refusing to take part was low. If the states pursued the policy of conducting consistent follow-up examinations this would mean that an additional test would have to be taken after detention and after the time during which HIV-antibodies may be detected. Owing to the lack of longitudinally collected data on sero prevalence in penal institutions, the number of sero conversions during detention is unknown in most states. Only in Berlin and Hesse two cases in each state have become known during the past years (BMG, 1995:9).

Besides, it must be pointed out that systematic testing is restricted to HIV infections, a procedure which reflects the fact that HIV is considered the greatest challenge in health care. However, particularly with injection drug users in prison, the number of hepatitis infections is assumed to be considerably higher. The significance of this epidemiological fact has not been given adequate attention in public discussions and in expert discussions on AIDS. Only in recent years have all groups involved developed an awareness of the problem.

In summary it can be stated that the currently available data on the sero-status of prisoners do not yield transparent information with respect to the spread and dynamics of HIV and hepatitis infections. Only by considering additional data material[1] and by taking the varying objectives pursued and methodologies applied into account will it be possible to make epidemiologically relevant statements on infectious diseases which are currently widely spread (hepatitis and HIV) and if necessary, to identify factors that affect the transmission or development of infectious diseases among the risk group of injection drug users in penal institutions.

Under no circumstances must this be mistaken for a plea in favour of an increased data collection or in favour of compulsory testing for research purposes. It is not the quantity but the quality of the serological data (longitudinal) that is important.

Helpful information needed for implementing adequate preventive measures may be obtained by identifying specifically risky modes of conduct in detention, the individual's readiness to use violence, his/her awareness of risks involved or his/her handling of risks. All this must be viewed against the background of the inmates' biographical records.

HIV/AIDS

The official registers listing the recorded cases of AIDS and new infections (AIDS register and HIV-registrations according to the laboratory report ordinance), are available at the Robert Koch Institute in Berlin. The recently issued 'Report on the epidemiological situation in the Federal Republic of Germany until 31.12.95' points out that HIV as well as AIDS cases among injection drug users have stabilised during the past few years.

Looking at several more recent studies of sero-prevalence it appears that the spread of infections is on the decrease. HIV prevalence with drug-related deaths amounted to 9.2 per cent (46 in 498) (Heckmann *et al.*, 1993:86f), whereas of the examined 183 drug addicts treated as emergencies in Hamburg hospitals 8.7 per cent were HIV-AK-positive (Heckmann *et al.*, 1993:139). Stark *et al.*, (1995) examined 405 drug consumers in Berlin and found an HIV prevalence of 18 per cent.

The most important German epidemiological study of the correlations between drug use and HIV/AIDS, conducted by Kleiber and Pant at three different times, reveals a decrease in the spreading of HIV among the interviewees. The percentage dropped from 19.4 per cent in 1988/89 to 16.4 per cent in 1990/91 and dropped further to 12.7 per cent in 1992/93. However, on closer inspection it becomes clear that this trend is affected by shifts in the population under study: more and more older HIV-antibody positive drug addicts stop using drugs and begin methadone treatments (at least in Berlin). 'Our investigations revealed that at the core of the drug scene the number of new HIV infections has not dropped.' (Kleiber and Pant, 1996:137). This finding is substantiated by the invariable readiness of the interviewees to take risks. Admittedly the number of those using unsterile syringes has dropped between 1988 and 1993 from 65 per cent to 48 per cent and further to 40 per cent, but 25 per cent of the needle sharers still do not disinfect injection equipment of other users effectively. 'The greater the social distance between those exchanging needles was, the greater was their readiness to take risks (and thus to take the risk of getting infected with HIV). In detention this readiness to take risks was particularly marked.' (Kleiber and Pant, 1996:257). Müller *et al.*, (1995) confirmed that needle sharing was very frequent among drug addicts held in custody. Whereas drastic changes in behaviour have been observed with a great number of injection drug users, considerably many of them take great risks, particularly in places where clean injection equipment is difficult to come by (Hamouda *et al.*, 1996:12).

Several studies conducted outside penal institutions reveal that a strong correlation exists between previous detention and the spreading of the above infectious diseases (Kleiber, 1991:35; Müller *et al.*, 1995). In their study Stark and Müller (1994) point out that 'with those persons who frequently used the syringes of other inmates during detention, the risk of getting infected with HIV is more than 10 times greater than with those who have never been in prison. 50 per cent of addicts who had used the syringes of other inmates more than 50 times were HIV infected and 97 per cent of them were infected with the hepatitis C virus. By contrast, with those who had never been in custody the infection rates only reached levels of 5 per cent and 71 per cent respectively' (Stark and Müller, 1994, p. 2).

Kleiber (1991) also established a connection between detention and the spreading of HIV infections. In his epidemiological study of HIV prevalence among drug users (n = 1253) he found a correlation rate of 19.9 per cent. Further analysis revealed that 10 per cent of drug users without experience of detention (n = 499) were HIV-antibody positive. With those who had been in prison the rate was 26 per cent. Of the interviewees who also stated that they had consumed injection drugs during detention, 33.7 per cent were HIV positive. The more often addicts have been in prison the more likely is it that they get infected with HIV. This became most strikingly apparent with the women surveyed: 'More than 40 per cent (29 in 70) of the junkies who had been in prison more than 3 times were HIV-infected. This finding most clearly reveals the correlation between HIV infection and another variable.' (Kleiber, 1995, p. 16). Koch and Ehrenberg (1992) confirmed these results. Their survey of 660 people revealed that with injection drug users who had been in prison HIV prevalence was twice as high (23.7 per cent) as with those consumers of these drugs who had never been in custody (12.5 per cent). HIV prevalence of women who had been in prison was three times higher than with those who had never been in custody.

According to state authorities (BMG, 1995:6) 0.12–2.8 per cent of male and 0.48–8 per cent of female drug users in German prisons are HIV infected.[2] These figures do not include the number of unrecorded cases mentioned above. Other studies on HIV-prevalence in detention yielded similar results: (cf. Albota, 1993; Albota et al., 1995; Nelles et al., 1995; Keppler, Nolte, and Stöver, 1996). The above-mentioned two-year test series on injection drug use in detention (n = 6255) conducted in the state of Baden Württemberg revealed an HIV prevalence of 5.3 per cent. One third of the tests were repeated examinations of inmates whose test results had been negative previously. No sero-conversion had been detected (Ministry of Justice of Baden Württemberg 1994)[3] Statistical surveys of AIDS infections and AIDS diseases provided by the judicial authorities of the various states only give an incomplete picture of HIV/AIDS infections and diseases respectively. By 31 March 1995, 46 per cent (27,509) of the total of 58,875 inmates had been tested for HIV-antibodies. 1 per cent of the inmates were HIV-antibody positive (a repeated test at the end of 1995 revealed that 1.13 per cent of the people examined were HIV-antibody positive).

Hepatitis

Outside prisons the number of hepatitis infections among injection drug users has risen considerably, despite the provision of infection-preventive aids. In part this is due to the fact that hepatitis viruses are much more resistant to environmental influence and thus are much more easily communicable than for instance the HI-virus. However, the high prevalence may also be attributed to the lack of hygiene among certain consumers of drugs when injecting drugs intravenously: either they share needles or injection equipment and drugs respectively. Finally the epidemiological conditions must also be taken into account. The number of hepatitis-infected drug users is very high. The risk of getting infected by handling injection equipment carelessly or by not exercising proper care is extremely high.

Prevalence studies of the populations investigated in Germany revealed a hepatitis B prevalence of 36.6–58 per cent (Heckmann, 1993; Stark *et al.*, 1995); and a hepatitis C prevalence of 43–83 per cent (Heckmann *et al.*, 1993; Stark *et al.*, 1995). In their epidemiological study conducted outside prison, Rieger-Ndakorerwa *et al.* (1994) found a relative and absolute increase in hepatitis B infections with the risk groups of injecting drug users and (former) prison inmates. The proportion of those infected with hepatitis B by far exceeds the one assumed for the general population. Of the 4659 HCV-infected persons surveyed by Laufs *et al.*, (1994) in the area of Hamburg 23.4 per cent were injection drug users and 12.5 per cent of them had been in detention. These figures do not include the vast number of unrecorded cases of hepatitis infections: Rieger-Ndakorerwa (1994) estimates that this group makes up 80–90 per cent of all infections. During the epidemiological interviews conducted by Kleiber and Pant (1996) more than half of the interviewees mentioned that they had been ill with hepatitis; of those who were HIV seropositive the rate even reached 78.5 per cent.

The correlation between injection drug use and HIV or hepatitis infections becomes even more apparent in the test results obtained by Hämmig (1996). In this study, 114 participants in the PROVE project conducted in Bern (provision of narcotics to heroin addicts) were tested in order to study the correlation between hepatitis diseases, HIV/AIDS diseases and injecting drug use. The examination revealed that an HIV disease only occured in conjunction with either hepatitis C, or hepatitis B and C. In most cases (60 per cent) a hepatitis B infection occurred in conjunction with hepatitis C. Therefore, the efforts undertaken to prevent infections should not be restricted to reduce the spreading of HIV but should also be designed to reduce the risk of getting infected with hepatitis, particularly with injecting drug users in detention.

In a survey conducted in Wolfenbüttel, Gaube *et al.* (1993) found that the rate of hepatitis A, B and C infections was 100–200 times higher among prison inmates than among the general population. However, these figures reflect the epidemiological situation of the convicts at the beginning of their prison sentence. The finding that hepatitis infections occur much more frequently in detention is supported by a study conducted by Keppler, Nolte, and Stöver (1996) in the women's prison in Vechta, Lower Saxony. This study found that 78 per cent of the drug-consuming women were infected with hepatitis B and 74.8 per cent of them were infected with hepatitis C. Furthermore, the authors found that the number of sero-conversions during detention was considerable: 20 out of the 41 women with sero conversions (48.8 per cent) had been infected with hepatitis during detention.

THE RESPONSE OF PENAL INSTITUTIONS TO THE DRUG PROBLEM

The current situation in which judicial authorities find themselves is paradoxical: they have to find a solution to a problem which is not supposed to exist. The situation in prisons can be compared to the one outside prisons ten years ago. However, in that time the attitude of society towards illegal drugs has changed. Terms like acceptance, tolerance, indifference, capitulation may be used for describing this attitude change. After 10 years directors of penal institutions have realised that they cannot avoid adapting to the new situation: in some prisons (mainly in North Germany) urine tests do not include testing for cannabis consumption anymore. As regards the attitude to be taken towards consumers of opiates, a widely held view is that 'actually' they do not belong in prison. Just like their counterparts outside prison they should be given the opportunity of undergoing an adequate treatment.

The increasing use of drugs changes life in prison: the penal system as a whole changes, the behaviour of drug users in detention changes and drug service providers are faced with new demands. Prisons reflect social and individual problems. Thus the rising spread of illegal drug consumption outside prisons and the implications arising from it may also be observed in prisons: drug-related deaths, drug-induced cases of emergency, increase in the number of drug users, dealer hierarchies, debts, mixed drugs or drugs of poor quality, the purity of which is incalculable and risks of infection (HIV and hepatitis) resulting from the fact that no sterile syringes are available in detention and therefore contaminated injection equipment is shared.

The increase in drug consumption entails major implications for the penal system: drugs become the focus of prison subcultures, and many routine activities of inmates focus on the acquisition, smuggling, consumption, sale and financing of drugs. If the acquisition and the use of drugs dominate the life of prison inmates, prison directors and staff have to make increased efforts to safeguard a regular course of prison sentences. This is the primary goal to be achieved. Solving the problem of drug addiction in detention is secondary.

Prison managements are faced with increased public pressure to keep prisons drug-free. This affects all forms of detention for men and women: punitive detention, pre-trial detention, detention of juveniles. Only a small number of prison managers talk about the issue in public and offer aid. Frequently, however, this approach is mistaken for failing to maintain security in prisons: the prison system which is supposed to be impenetrable for drug trafficking, has turned out to be penetrable. The number of prison managers who deny or ignore drug use in prison for political reasons is still high. Before this background it becomes obvious why the dealing with addicts in detention is difficult: on the one hand the goal to achieve the convicts rehabilitation[4] must be pursued, on the other hand prison managements are faced with constantly rising drug consumption among inmates and with political and economic restrictions which make it even more difficult to solve the drug problem.

Reduction of Drug Supply and Demand

To combat these developments there are courses of action that may be pursued. An attempt can be made to reduce drug availability in prisons, for example by restricting the inmates' rights to receive packages, by restricting the number of visitors, more rigid checking of letters written or received, and restriction of previously granted relaxations in detention. These measures sharply contrast with the goal of inmates' rehabilitation, and it seems doubtful that they will actually help to reduce drug supply and consumption. Moreover inmates who do not use drugs would also be hit by these measures. Finally the results of a survey conducted in various states should also be mentioned here. The study revealed that in some cases prison staff provided inmates with drugs.

In this context drug testing is of particular importance. The meaningfulness of urine tests for detecting drug use is controversial. For some these tests are unrenounceable to gain an overview of the extent of drug consumption in prison and for deterrence purposes. Others hold the view that urine tests may even induce inmates to consume more injectable drugs: because cannabis is detectable in urine for a considerably lengthy period of time and heroin can only be detected in urine during a short period of time after consumption, some inmates start to use heroin instead of cannabis. This finding may have been the reason why some prison managements have stopped testing inmates for cannabis use by means of urine tests. Another reason may have been that due to the widely spread consumption of cannabis, many inmates cannot be granted relaxations in detention. These relaxations can only be granted to those inmates who are assumed to be able to lead a life without offending the law after they have completed their prison sentence. Consumers of illegal drugs (including cannabis) do not fall into this group.

Cannabis consumption is a controversial matter. Outside prisons approximately 4 million people in Germany consume cannabis, although this is still illegal. Cannabis use is considered a minor offence because it is a 'victimless crime'. By contrast, in detention cannabis consumption has become *the* standard applied in evaluating if rehabilitation has been successful or if a prisoner is entitled to relaxations in detention.

Physicians frequently criticise the use of mandatory urine tests (i.e. those that are conducted against the patient's expressed will) which burden the confidential relationship between patient and physician. This fact is particularly important because prison inmates cannot choose a doctor, so the relationship between patient and doctor is burdened anyway. Furthermore, physicians criticise that the number of false positive or false negative test results or mix-ups in the laboratory is very high. Apart from this the procedure applied to obtain urine from inmates is susceptible to failure because urine specimens can be manipulated or falsified even if supervisors exercise proper care. Finally it must be mentioned that the tests themselves yield inaccurate results (85–90 per cent reliability). Admittedly analyses of hair or 'drug wipes' yield more reliable results, but they are very costly and not easily available.

Reduction of demand primarily means prevention, however not primary prevention because most members of the target group, prison inmates, are already addicted to drugs. The goal to be achieved is rehabilitation, which should lead to a drug-free life. For this reason most aid projects offered are designed to induce addicts to live abstinently. It is doubtful if the objective to make inmates start a drug-free life during detention and to keep it up, is realistic, all the more so because drugs are relatively freely available in detention and the inmates' past which was dominated by drugs cannot simply be wiped out. In many cases the implications of a criminal lifestyle become apparent in detention: blackmailing and debts.

In view of the constant rise in drug consumption in prisons it is imperative to provide adequate aids which meet the needs of those affected. The measures taken must be balanced with the requirements for security and good order. The goals pursued should also be pragmatic, not only with respect to the prison system but also with respect to the inmates: harm reduction should be the guiding philosophy behind the measures. The spatial and methodical range of action for implementing remedial measures in prisons is very limited because drug consumption is not tolerated and security and order in prison are more important than the inmates' drug problems.

Which objectives to be achieved by the help provided to drug users in detention can be formulated despite the above-mentioned hindrances? As has been mentioned before the standards applied in prisons for the help provided to drug users must be adjusted to the standards applied outside prisons. It seems unrealistic that drug using inmates are expected to change their behaviour drastically in detention, i.e. to live abstinently. Providing help to drug-users in detention is designed to give them an idea of a realistic and alternative lifestyle: 'Providing help to drug-users aims to raise and strengthen the inmates' self-motivation and their feeling of responsibility. Changes only occur gradually. These attempts must be supported by providing a variety of aids which help drug-users to become aware of alternatives.' (Borkenstein, 1994, p. 80f).

PROVISION OF HEALTH CARE AND SOCIAL SUPPORT TO DRUG ADDICTS IN DETENTION

Stabilisation of Drug Addicts' Physical and social Conditions

Promotion of health care involves ensuring that the prevailing conditions in prison are studied more closely to find out which factors put inmates under stress or induce them to take greater risks. These factors then need to be eliminated. The areas to be investigated are:

— housing (cell, block, office, place of work);
— autonomy (competence, residence);
— healthy and varied nutrition;
— offers for spare-time activities at weekends and after 16:00 h;
— physical exercise, sports;
— visiting and leave regulations;
— availability of therapeutic treatments;
— medical treatment in general.

Promotion of health care should be designed to improving living conditions in detention in general because many inmates are desperate and without hope, and do not believe that they can improve their situation permanently. This may be one reason for the increased readiness of inmates to take greater risks and to dismiss the implications.

However, it will not suffice to only look into the options the individual prisoner has of changing his/her behaviour. Instead 'structural prevention' is required, in that the actual living conditions of prisoners and the necessity for behavioural changes must be investigated. By only looking into the individual's options for changes in behaviour the blame is put on the prisoners who act 'riskily' and 'desperately'.

This paper focuses on drug addicted prisoners (in women's and men's prisons). The following organisational-conceptual improvements and adjustments to outside standards need to be implemented.

DIFFERENTIATION INSIDE PRISONS

Due to the varying requirements of (formerly) drug-addicted prisoners different forms of housing should be available. Those prisoners who intend to live abstinently and prove to do so by testing negative for drugs should be given the opportunity to live in 'areas with a low drug availability', just like those prisoners who intend to undergo a therapy outside prison to become drug-free or who prepare for open detention. Prisoners who show little willingness to change their behaviour should be offered information on safer-use practices as well as stimulation and basic self-help in safer injecting, in order to avoid unnecessary and possibly irreversible damage, and to encourage prisoners to use clean equipment.

Networking between Drug Service Providers Inside and Outside Prisons and Adjustment to the Standards Applied Outside Prisons

Among other things the Prison Act provides is that the help provided to drug users inside prisons is balanced with the support services available outside prisons. The special status of support services inside the walls can only be overcome if all the services available to drug users outside prisons are also made available to those inside prisons. In particular, outside experts should also offer counselling and care inside the walls. This can only be achieved if all parties involved are willing to co-operate, a precondition which is not natural. A policy of demarcation is not only pursued by prison managers but also by service providers outside prisons who disregard inmate drug use, mostly because their experience of the control and security regime of prisons has been negative. Hence it is difficult to balance support services inside prisons with those outside prisons. In the presence of mistrust and a reluctance to pass on information, co-operative links from which both parties could benefit and which are urgently needed cannot be established. However, it must be considered that a co-operation between outside experts and the trained staff in prisons requires compatible working strategies. Despite the different conditions inside and outside prisons concepts that can be implemented in both areas must be developed.

Networking between service providers inside and outside prisons is particularly important to imprisoned (drug-addicted) women. Since their average period of detention ranges from 3 to 9 months (owing to the short time available a detention schedule is not made), the goal that is pursued from the beginning is to prepare them for the time after detention. This can be done most effectively if the service providers inside and outside the walls co-operate. As regards the health status of inmates for instance, a methadone treatment that was started during detention could be continued without interruption after imprisonment. Inmates could be prepared for a therapeutic treatment after detention; gynaecological and dental treatments as well as the treatment of diseases resulting from illegal activities would be possible, just like healthy nutrition and offers for spare time activities. As regards social aspects, co-operating service providers inside and outside prison could help (former) inmates to cope with the loss of family ties (to their children, partners, their original family) and to avoid isolation.

The rising extent of problems among this group (imprisoned, drug-addicted women) stems from their social situation prior to imprisonment: impoverishment which mainly becomes apparent through increased homelessness, and frequently, lacking financial security. Securing existence and providing compensation for the under-supply situation of the affected men and women are the main goals to be achieved by social service providers responsible for preparing inmates for release (cf. von den Driesch and Kawamura, 1995). Another objective that might be achieved by granting increased leaves from prison and relaxations of detention respectively (safety aspects are not a real obstacle to this) may be better chances of former inmates to find a job or occupation. Finally it must be mentioned that premature release (mainly as a result of participation in a methadone therapy) after two thirds or half of the sentence has been completed, is handled in an exemplary manner in some women's prisons.

Drug-addicted women in prisons are exposed to physical and emotional strain. They try to cope with prostitution, abuse and violence by consuming intoxicating drugs. This mode of behavior, i.e. to try to solve a problem inwardly or even to blame oneself for it, is typical of women. Frequently psychological help to cope with the problems that arise in detention can only be provided to a limited extent. There is a particular need, therefore, for female outside workers to offer this help.

Opening up Prisons to Outside Groups and Service Providers

The drug addict must be able to realise that the steps he has to take can be taken and that they open up new prospects. To orient towards the outside world is a strong motivation for prisoners. To date, drug addicts in detention have been a group which, in contrast to other inmates, was only rarely granted relaxations of detention, open detention or premature release (according to §57 Criminal Code and §88 Juvenile Criminal Code). The negative test results of urine controls which frequently also included testing for cannabis residues (which can be detected up to 30 days after consumption) and which were required to be granted these relaxations have been and still are a major hurdle which is difficult to overcome.

The objectives of service provision mentioned above, strengthening the inmates self-esteem and autonomy, would be reduced to absurdity if possibilities for acquiring and testing (their) physical skills were not accessible to prisoners outside the walls. Borkenstein (1994) states that not being granted relaxations in detention makes inmates think about their drug use. This time should instead be used to induce them to change their behaviour.

PRACTICAL SUPPORT

Prevention of Drug use and/or Addiction

The goals pursued in the field of prevention of drug abuse and addiction must be realistic. To try to make inmates do without drugs altogether by outlining the disastrous consequences of drug use to them, would be an unrealistic objective. Neither prisoners who have already used drugs nor those who have never used drugs can be reached in this way. Rather, efforts made inside and outside prisons should focus on the prevention of addiction by taking the conditions in detention and the implication of a continued drug use in prison into account: debts, blackmailing, the use of brutal methods to recover money, murder, extension of the sentence due to drug use, dependence on dealers, health hazards. The main goal to be achieved is to impart knowledge and to enable the individual prisoner to realise when a situation is risky or which living conditions (like imprisonment) involve a lot of risks and to make them act in a (more) carefully considered way.

COUNSELLING

In almost all states of the Federal Republic of Germany, outside drug service providers are involved in the taking care of inmate drug users. Some prisons even have their own advisory bureau on drug issues, and in some prisons the social workers take care of these problems. Including outside workers promotes the necessary orientation towards the outside world. In contrast to inside workers, outside workers are more widely accepted and trusted by prisoners because the outsiders have a duty to maintain confidentiality and have the right to refuse to give evidence. Moreover the outside workers are more experienced and know about the content of and requirements for the various support services offered. Counsellors on drug issues in prison should primarily provide information about the various support services/programmes available inside and outside prisons. As a second step their efforts should focus on motivating prisoners to overcome their drug use. The main goal to be pursued by outside workers is to encourage drug addicts to participate in outside therapy programmes (in compliance with §35 of the Law of Narcotics) and to prepare inmates for these therapies. The applied concept of the therapy-providing institution/facility should be discussed with the inmate, just like the question of who bears the costs and who takes care of the prisoner during the therapy. Many prisoners, however, were greatly scared of and had many reservations about a long-term inpatient treatment. The readiness to participate in these treatments decreases with the number of therapies already undergone (some of which included restrictive methods) and with the extent of the period of incarceration. Outpatient treatments (in compliance with §35 of the Law of Narcotics) are still rare and most of them are not accepted by the prosecution.

Support is also provided to prisoners expressing the wish to change their behaviour and to participate in methadone programmes, who need to settle health-related issues or who wish to switch to open detention. Furthermore, prisoners must be induced to help themselves, and service providers need to develop and apply new working methods like group work or 'streetwork'.

It is a major advantage of outside drug counselling that it establishes a link between life inside and outside prison and thus is very helpful for continuing treatments that were started in prison beyond completion of the sentence. In this way long-term contacts can be forged, ensuring continuity.

TREATMENT

Detoxification

In many clinic settings in Germany withdrawal of opiates or partial withdrawal in case of multiple addiction are increasingly treated by means of medication. 'Cold turkey' (immediate reduction of the dosage to zero) is considered a deterrent because it aims at total renunciation of opiate consumption, and has been replaced with a more pragmatic approach: addicts are treated with medication which permits an intense analysis of the psychosocial causes of addiction. In several clinics the dosage is gradually reduced; the process of detoxification is orientated by the patients' requirements, abilities and resources to overcome or at least cope with their drug problem. The treatments also included ear acupuncture or the application of methods of experiential pedagogics. Furthermore in-patient treatment during withdrawal was replaced with out-patient treatments with or without medication.

Contrary to these new therapeutic standards addicts are exposed to 'cold turkey' upon incarceration, either deliberately, i.e. the prisoners have to cope with the symptoms of withdrawal on their own (not least in order to punish them) or they are not treated in time or not at all. Sometimes the problem is not recognised at all. Frequently prisoners have good reasons for concealing their opiate addiction for fear of restrictive measures or stigmatisation. There are also cases in which staff of the health care units give tranquillisers to inmates which do not have any effect on most of the withdrawal symptoms. While withdrawal from methadone outside prisons is done gradually, the dosages given inside prisons are reduced rapidly. Only in a small number of prisons methadone treatments are implemented properly so that the considerable physical and psychological withdrawal symptoms are really reduced. A specialist withdrawal treatment that is based on medication also permits detection and handling of side effects and potential sources of infection (cf. Commission, 1995).

Training programmes in which the staff of prison health care units participate at regular intervals should provide the necessary knowledge on the latest standards in withdrawal treatments of opiate addiction or in case of multiple addiction, detoxification treatments of alcohol, benzodiazepine and barbiturate addiction. It is advisable to seek the advice of outside doctors who are specialised in medication-based withdrawal treatments.

Counselling and support services for inmates participating in withdrawal treatments in prison cannot be effective without the aid of·outside drug service providers. It has become apparent that the staff in many health care units of prisons works unsystematically, has no clear idea about the course of the treatment and do not document the data properly: This applies to examinations at the beginning and end of infectious diseases as well as to examination of other typical side effects of opiate consumption as for instance tuberculosis.

INNOVATIVE APPROACHES

In view of the increasing number of HIV and hepatitis infections in prisons, injection drug use of men and women in detention is given increasingly more attention. This resulted in changes in the fields of order policy, health-care policy and in detention practices.

Due to the injurious effects of drug consumption in prison which bears great risks of infection, the number of those who demand that a health care policy minimising risks for inmates is given priority over correctional concerns constantly rises. Although preventive measures taken to avoid the spreading of infectious diseases in prisons which are not aimed at a total renunciation of drugs are not compulsory to date, a lot of methadone programmes have already been set up in prisons. There are projects, e.g. in Switzerland, under which addicts are provided with original substances. Similarly, innovative model projects under which clean drug injection equipment is made available in prisons have already been launched as trial projects in Germany. It is hoped that they will not only help to raise general acceptance and efficiency of preventive measures but they are also expected to yield the data required to give a fresh impetus to the 'tough' prison system.

Besides the classical objectives to be achieved by imprisonment, pragmatic, attainable goals should also be pursued which should initially be aimed at keeping damage as little as possible. These strategies are based on the following premises:

— drug addiction is curable;
— harm-reduction strategies are particularly important because certain infections related to illegal drug consumption (e.g. HIV or hepatitis C infections) are incurable and thus pose a threat to existence.

Before the background of these premises, support to drug consumers should be provided according to the following list of priorities:

— securing survival;
— securing survival without contracting irreversible damage;
— stabilising the addict's physical and social condition;
— supporting the addicts in their attempt to lead a drug-free life.

The support programmes launched so far which initially are designed to minimise damage, not only comprise crucial communicative strategies at the personal level (i.e. education and provision of information) but they also include instrumental measures. These will be described in detail in the next sections. The goal pursued, i.e. to incite inmates to change their behavior, can only be achieved if prisoners have sufficient room for movement. Improvement of the situation is impossible if this correlation between desired behavioural change and eased living conditions is not considered (for more details cf. Jacob, Schaper and Stöver, 1996).

PROVISION OF STERILE INJECTING EQUIPMENT

In many big cities there are places where addicts can go and exchange injection implements, or where machines supplying sterile syringes have been set up so that sterile equipment is available at any time and can be obtained anonymously. This help is not provided in prison, despite the WHO guideline on HIV infection and AIDS in Prison, suggesting that 'In all countries where sterile syringes and needles are available to drug users outside prisons it should be considered if inmates who request sterile equipment should also be provided with it'. It is an undisputed fact that the most effective strategy to avoid new or re-infection is the availability of sterile injecting equipment. Since the mid-1980s this strategy has internationally been acknowledged and demanded by experts in the field (cf. Stöver, 1994). In the following sections, the experience and results obtained in pilot projects under which sterile equipment was made available in Germany will be presented and discussed.

Pilot Project: 'Prevention of infectious Diseases in Prison' in Lower Saxony, Germany

The project resulted from extensive subject-specific and political discussions and was launched by the Lower Saxonian Ministry of Justice. In the women's prison in Vechta it was started on 15 April 1996 and in the men's prison in Lingen I, Dept. at Groß Hesepe the project was launched on 15 July 1996 (Meyenberg, Jacob, and Stöver, 1996).

Because of the rapid spreading of infectious diseases (HIV and hepatitis) among drug users in prison the Lower Saxonian Minister of Justice, Mrs. Heidrun Alm-Merk, set up a panel of experts on 25 November 1994. It was assigned the task to investigate if the availability of sterile injecting equipment in prisons which had already turned out to be effective outside prisons is a suitable means to induce drug using inmates to change their behaviour by taking less risks and to improve their physical condition in general. The commission comprised prison directors, practitioners familiar with the penal system, representatives of privately maintained drug- and AIDS-relief organisations, a physician and a co-ordinator in charge of drug abuse and AIDS prevention programmes in Lower Saxony.

The recommendations of this expert commission provided the basis for the cabinet decision to start a two-year model project in the two prisons mentioned above under which sterile injecting equipment is made available to imprisoned drug users. The project will be complemented by educational services for inmates and prison staff on HIV and hepatitis, on 'safer use' techniques for injecting drug use and 'safer sex' techniques inside and outside prisons.

The penitentiary staff of the individual prison will develop the concept for implementation of the project in the respective prison and will orient by the experience gained in the women's prison in Hindelbank (Bern) and in the men's prison in Oberschöngrün (Solothurn) in Switzerland where sterile injecting equipment has been made available since 1994 (Nelles, 1995).

Women's prison in Vechta

On 15 April 1996 the first machines supplying sterile injection needles were set up in the women's prison in Vechta. Prior to this the issue had been discussed extensively at all levels: in prisons, in the ministries in charge, at prison authorities and at drug abuse and AIDS relief organisations. The concept to be implemented in Vechta was developed by an interdisciplinary working group inside the prison and is based on the report issued by the Lower Saxonian Panel of Experts on Prevention of Infectious Diseases. It complements the already existing support services.

The great non-homogeneity of the inmate population requires different counselling and treatments. Moreover 'protection areas' for inmates without addiction and for those who intend to stop using drugs must be created. Therefore the exchange of unsterile for sterile injecting equipment is interlinked with extensive educational and counselling services, also provided for prison staff.

Counselling focuses on inducing inmates to lead a life without drugs and to avoid negative effects of imprisonment. Since these are the ultimate goals to be achieved, it becomes clear that the exchange of unsterile for sterile needles is only an intermediate step that has to be taken because only 40–50 per cent of drug addicted inmates can be reached by methadone or abstinence-oriented programmes

Implementation of the Model Project

As part of the admission procedure at the beginning of incarceration every inmate is informed in good time by means of a multilingual information paper about the modalities of a participation in the needle exchange project. Further pertinent information (safer use, safer sex) is given in the admission unit by experts on support for addicts. Needles can be exchanged in all sections of the prison, apart from the 'leave' section, in the home for mothers and children, or in the admission unit. The dummy of a syringe which must be inserted into the machine in order to obtain a sterile syringe is only handed out to drug-addicted inmates who have been examined by the prison doctor and whose addiction has been documented in their medical record. Inmates participating in a methadone programme are excluded from the needle exchange because they contracted for renouncing any additional consumption of drugs. Minors require their parents declaration of consent.

The machines were set up in four easily accessible places in the prisons. The dummy can be exchanged for a functioning syringe and after use can be exchanged for another sterile one. The machines also contain heat-sealed alcohol swabs and ascorbic acid in adequate portions, filters, plaster and ampoules holding a sodium chloride solution. The machines are emptied and refilled daily by trained staff of the health care unit. The information meetings for inmates complementing the exchange of syringes are designed to provide extensive information about the risks involved in injection drug use, to reduce health-damaging forms of consumption and to practise safer use techniques for the time after imprisonment. The drug addicts are also educated about behavioural patterns that are in agreement with the goals of the project: they should only have a syringe on them when it needs to be exchanged, prohibition of lending or selling syringes, each inmate may only possess one syringe, the syringe must remain in the prison if the inmate is transferred to another prison. Moreover 'safer sex' and 'safer use' training is offered once a week to all interested inmates.

At the beginning of the project the prison staff were given the opportunity to participate in a one-day information seminar. In addition to this, special information meetings are offered which the staff may attend during working hours in order to keep them informed about the latest in first aid, prophylaxis of infections, pharmacology and the handling of drug-addicts.

Possession of drugs is still prosecuted. Therefore the project cannot be considered a liberalisation of drug consumption in detention but must be viewed as a dealing with the reality of drug consumption in prison. Owing to the legal frame of the model project it seems unlikely that increased controls of cells or extended urine controls will be conducted.

Men's Prison in Lingen I, Dept. at Groß-Hesepe

After extensive discussions of the concept underlying the health-promoting project, of basic questions and of its implications for detention, the exchange of syringes started on 15 July 1996.

Contrary to the method applied in Vechta, no machines were set up in the prison of Groß Hesepe. Here the staff of the drug counselling service and of the health care unit of the prison hand out sterile syringes to inmates producing used ones during fixed hours (daily) in a tea-room. The tea room is located next to the drug counselling service and it is difficult to see into it. The inmates can reach it via the recreational ground. Prisoners intending to exchange syringes in the tea-room may spontaneously use the opportunity to also obtain counselling if they wish to do so. The participants in the exchange project have been assured that the provision of syringes is anonymous. The staff handing out the syringes have the duty to maintain confidentiality. All drug-addicted inmates may participate in the project. Prisoners participating in a methadone programme may not participate in the needle exchange project because they have contracted for renouncing any additional consumption of drugs.

In addition to the exchange of syringes further support services will be offered:

— individual counselling on HIV/AIDS provided by the staff of the health care unit and of the drug counselling service and the regional AIDS support group
— handing out of multilingual information papers on HIV/AIDS, safer sex and safer use
— information meetings on HIV/AIDS and hepatitis.

Support measures like training courses on First Aid will also be offered for the prison staff to brush up and deepen already existing knowledge. Information meetings will be organised at irregular intervals by the drug counselling service and the AIDS support group. Extensive discussions prior to the implementation of the project which were designed to render the project transparent, helped staff to develop a great deal of sensitivity for the drug problem and its medical and psycho-social implications. Thus a solid basis and the acceptance required for a successful realisation of the project was created. The great readiness of the prison staff to actively participate in the project was also reflected in the great number of staff who co-operated with the researchers involved in collecting the initial data.

Selected Evaluation Results

Most prisoners follow the rules regarding the supply of sterile needles, apart from a few cases of inadequate storage of syringes in cells. There was no threatening of staff or other inmates. During the study period the number of drug finds did not increase. For staff, the needle exchange programmes quickly became part of everyday life. Inmates reacted in different ways: while the drug using women were very accepting of the needle exchange programme, the drug using men seemed very reserved and cautious, fearing negative consequences of becoming known and registered as drug users. Staff drug counsellors are aware of medical confidentiality and participation in the project is recorded in neither personal nor health files, but prisoners still do not want to become known by the other staff members who potentially decide about drug testing and relaxation of cell controls. It will take time to reduce this mistrust of the programme. Absolute anonymity, however, is not possible in prison. At the beginning of the project participants were informed that syringes must be stored at a clearly specified site, not to control prisoners, but to avaoid staff searching cells coming into contact with used needles. In both prisons exclusion from the needle exchange project of prisoners who are taking part in methadone programmes is practically impossible, because they are, justifiably, not isolated. There are some indications of needles being used by these prisoners, obtained from participants of the needle exchange projects. The medical evaluation shows that the number of absecesses dramatically, and no sero-conversion could be observed during the 2-year pilot phase for those participants permanently in the exchange scheme.

Provision of Sterile Injection Equipment in Hamburg — Vierlande Prison

Since 26 June 1996 the inmates of the open detention unit of one the prisons in Hamburg (Vierlande, 370 places) may provide themselves with sterile needles which are available in machines set up at six different places in the prison. This exchange is also complemented by information and education services which inform inmates about the risks involved in injection drug use and train them in safer use techniques. Training and information is also offered for prison staff in order to help them handle drug-related situations adequately. The project is running until the end of 1997.

The method applied in Vierlande does not differ from the one used in Vechta (i.e. provision via machines, a dummy is needed for the first exchange). However, in contrast to Vechta participants in methadone programmes in Vierlande also have access to the needle supplying machines. Additionally, inmates who are permitted to leave the prison for a fixed period of time may receive syringes at the main gate. Planning and implementation of the project was assigned to an inter-disciplinary working group.

METHADONE PROGRAMMES

Since 1991 methadone treatments are covered by the health insurance plan. Methadone treatment has been and still is controversial as to its appropriateness and efficiency. Since it has been introduced in Germany, significant results have been achieved. Several evaluations established at the local and regional level (cf. Raschke, 1994) reveal the far-reaching improvements that have been reached in the area of health care and social stabilisation.

Methadone treatment of drug-addicted prisoners cannot be discussed without considering the legal and financial frame as well as the standards applied outside prisons. Contrary to all other European countries and to the USA, in Germany methadone treatment is not an established method of treatment in case of drug-addiction. Only if secondary diseases occur will a methadone treatment be started which is then covered by the health insurance plan.

In view of the situation of drug addicts in detention described at the beginning of this chapter it seems to be imperative to make methadone treatments available in prisons. Regrettably, representatives of traditional medicine do not yet consider it an established method of treatment for drug addicts in Germany. Although the Prison Act of 1977 provides that medical care of inmates must orient by the regulations of the national health insurance plan and although the World Health Organisation requires that medical care provided outside prisons should not differ from the one provided inside prisons (because inmates are not to be punished by deprivation of liberty *and* poor medical care), methadone treatments in prison are currently limited to a few prisons in Germany where committed prison doctors have fought for their implementation.

In some states in Germany it is possible to continue a methadone treatment that has been started prior to imprisonment and will be continued after detention. However, this is restricted to short-term detainees in order to 'bridge' the time in prison. Long-term methadone treatments are rejected by all prison doctors in Germany. Some penal institutions offer a 'gradual withdrawal'. Sometimes drug-addicted inmates who are assumed to become heroin users again after imprisonment and for whom a treatment outside prison has been planned, are permitted to start a methadone treatment shortly before their prison sentence is completed in order to prepare them for the time after detention and to improve their chances.

By starting methadone treatments in detention it is hoped that the treatment will help to:

— reduce the demand for opiates in detention;
— reduce the number of crimes in prison;
— to stabilise drug-users physically and socially in order to increase their motivation for participation in further support programmes.

In order to meet the requirement that drug-addicts in prison should have access to the same treatments offered outside prison, inmates falling into the following groups should be permitted to participate in methadone treatments in detention:

— those who had already started a methadone treatment prior to imprisonment;
— those who apply for participation in a methadone treatment after incarceration, while in prison and who meet the requirements for this treatment.

After detention, methadone treatments must be continued without interruption. Thus inmates/drug counsellors should have the opportunity to make the necessary arrangements prior to completion of the prison sentence.

Inside and outside prison psychosocial care is a useful addition to the project and is crucial for opening up new prospects. Furthermore, prisoners should have access to working and educational programmes and discussion groups to stabilise them socially and prepare them for the time after detention. The psychosocial care provided should be adjusted to the situation and requirements of the individual prisoner.

Bossong (1995) considers the prison setting to be comparatively suitable for this method of treatment:

> In prison the 'classic' target group for methadone treatments (therapy drop-outs, offenders who are reluctant to live abstinently, who are physically and socially incriminated) is great. The drug addicts can be reached

at any time so that handing out of methadone at regular intervals and the urine tests required can be carried out without any problem. The ultimate goal of imprisonment 'to induce offenders to lead their life without committing further crimes' (which must not necessarily be equated with abstinence!) corresponds to the goals to be achieved by the methadone treatment.' (Bossong, 1995, pp. 14–15).

It must also be assumed that inmates participating in a methadone treatment will become more receptive to services provided in detention. The treatment not only helps offenders to break away from the drug scene, to avoid other forms of addiction, but also helps them do without the very risky use of injection equipment.

Methadone treatment is a medically founded method of treatment which must be pursued irrespective of the patient's whereabouts. Reasons for interrupting the treatment should only arise from the medical or psychosocial context, not from control or punitive measures. The treatment is not a 'special treatment' granted to those who have behaved well, but a treatment for sick people which is used in more or less the same way as outside prison. Given a medical indication the offender is entitled to the treatment; the prison management may not refuse to grant it (Commission, 1995).

PROVISION OF ORIGINAL SUBSTANCES IN PRISONS

Since 1995, another remedial service — in addition to the methadone treatment — has been offered to injection drug users at the men's prison of Oberschöngrün: controlled provision of opiates. The requirements for participation in the programme are similar to the high-level admission requirements for participation in the first methadone treatment in Germany 10 years ago. Minimum age: 20, a 2-year provable opiate consumption, unsuccessful treatments, medical-psychological and/or social deficits, minimum sentence: 9 months. Because of these 'obstacles' therapeutic facilities are not used to full capacity (only 7 in 8). The programme is designed as a feasibility study of medically controlled provision of opiates in prison. The benefits and disadvantages of prescribing heroin are to be assessed, particularly the triple supply of heroin per day (maximum dosage 250 mg., on average 125–200 mg. for 100 Swiss Francs to be paid by the offender per month) which must be done under supervision, needs to be incorporated in everyday routine. It will also be interesting to look at the possible changes in the interactions between prison staff and inmates which might result from the prescription of heroin because, unlike methadone, heroin is not a medicine. Despite the limited conditions under which the study is carried out (including the small number of participants, and the unique conditions in a penal institution) which relativise the generalisability of the findings, the project in Switzerland will give fresh impetus to the expert discussion of whether the supply of original substances is a suitable means to prevent the spreading of infections and if it is an effective measure of harm reduction among imprisoned injection drug users.

INFECTION PROPHYLAXIS AS A COMPREHENSIVE METHOD OF HEALTH CARE PROMOTION IN PRISON

It has become clear that injection drug use among prisoners has become part of every-day routine in penal institutions, despite contrary political efforts and corresponding attempts to prevent drug use and addiction. The current conditions under which drugs are consumed in prison increase spreading of viral infections like HIV and hepatitis. High infection rates among inmates not only entail diseases and emergencies at the individual level, but in the long run they will also lead to rising demands on social and medical service providers. Recognising these correlations as facts it becomes clear that new priorities need to be set in the assessment of possible infectious diseases among injection drug users in prison. Only by focusing the efforts to be taken on new lines will it be possible to advance an effective and practical infection prophylaxis and to promote health care in penal institutions in general.

A responsible handling of these facts requires a reorientation in working with drug addicts in detention, in the medical care provided to inmates, in the co-operation with outside drug service providers as well as in the safeguarding of personnel-related and financial resources. The spectrum of the outlined possibilities of infection prophylaxis is aimed at uncovering the individual inmate's potential for improvement through instrumental and cognitive measures. In another step prophylaxis aims to extend the health care and disease preventing competence of action of the individual prisoner.

Changes in attitude and behaviour at the individual level, which are crucial for minimising the risks of infections cannot be treated separately. The scope for effective preventive work is not very wide if the correlations between individual actions and habits (patterns of drug consumption, sexual activities) and structural conditions (detention, drug policy pursued) are disregarded or neglected.

SUMMARY

There is a growing number of injecting drug users in German prisons. The risks they take reveal the close correlation between imprisonment and the spreading of infectious diseases like HIV and hepatitis. Despite this provable correlation prison administrators and the politicians in charge do not recognise that it is imperative to take measures for preventing the spreading of communicable diseases arising from drug use in prison. It has become clear that the standards applied inside and outside prisons differ. Differences occurred with respect to methadone treatments, testing procedures, counselling services, preventive programmes, the availability of condoms and of sterile injecting equipment.

Ten years after this has been acknowledged for the situation outside prisons, practitioners working inside prisons have also realised that there is a great need for harm reduction strategies inside prisons. Gradually programmes that have been successfully implemented outside prisons have become a matter of discussion and in part have already been adopted in prison, including methadone treatments and needle exchange programmes. The traditional goals of imprisonment and wide-spread attitudes towards addictions have been challenged.

NOTES

[1] Particularly studies of sero prevalence in penal institutions focusing on social-scientific parameters like behavioural pattern and attitudes, and socio-demographic parameters, analysis of medical records,biographical records. Also, it must be considered if anonymously conducted studies of sero-prevalence and follow-up examinations of inmates should be taken into account as well.

[2] Cases registered with judicial authorities by 31.12.93 and 31.3.94 respectively: 406 men and 55 women were HIV positive and 42 men and 15 women were ill with AIDS (BMG/BMJ 1995:6).

[3] In the test series an average of 10.8 per cent of the inmates refused to undergo repeated tests.

[4] e.g. as stipulated in the Prison Act: §3, para 1 stipulates that living conditions in detention must be adjusted to those outside prison, as far as this is possible. On the other hand the demand to provide adequate aid for drug addicted inmates must also be met. §3, para 2 of the Prison Act stipulates that harmful impacts of detention must be counteracted. This also means that any form of drug consumption or increase in drug use is contrary to the original goal to be achieved through imprisonment.

References

Albota, M. (1993) Erhebung zur HIV-Prävalenz intravenöser Drogenabhängiger im Hamburger Strafvollzug (Ms.).

Albota, M.u.a. (1995) HIV-Prävalenz intravenös Drogenabhängiger im Hamburger Strafvollzug im Jahresvergleich 1992–1993. *In: AIFO, H. 3/95, S. 127–132.*

AMSEL-*Forschungsprojekt, Projektgruppe Rauschmittelfragen, Abschlußbericht Bd. 1 Jugendberatung und Jugendhilfe,* Frankfurt: (Selbstverlag).

BMG/BMJ (1995) Dokumentation der Expertenanhörung zu dem Thema 'Drogen und HIV-Prävention im Justizvollzug'. Bonn (Ms.), 22.2.1995.

Borkenstein, Chr. (1994) Drogenarbeit im Vollzug: Künftig eine gemeinsame Aufgabe der Drogenhilfe? In: *Bewährungshilfe* 1/94.

Bossong, H. (1992) Möglichkeiten und Grenzen der Methadonsubstitution. Eine Übersicht über Forschung, Praxis und bundeseutsche Diskussion. In: *Bossong, H./Stöver, H. (Hrsg.): Methadonbehandlung.* Frankfurt/New York: Campus, S. 17–42.

Bossong, H. (1995) Methadon-Substitutionsbehandlung. In: *Das Grüne Gehirn — Der Arzt im öffentlichen Gesundheitswesen.* 36. Erg., Starnberg, Nov. 1995.

Bundesamt für Justiz (1995) Informationen über den Straf — und Massnahmenvollzug 1/95. CH-3003 Bern.

Driesch, D. von den, Kawamura, G. (1995): Straffällige Frauen — Lebenslagen und Hilfeangebote. In: *Neue Kriminalpolitik,* H. 1/1995, S. 33–36.

Hämmig, R. (1996) Heroinverschreibung und AIDS. In: *AIDS und HIV-Infektionen–17* Jäger, H., ed.. Erg.Lfg. 4/96.

Jacob, J., Schaper, G., Stöver, H. (1996) Verhalten und Verhältnisse: Präventionstheoretische und — praktische Aspekte der Infektionsprophylaxe im Strafvollzug. In: *Sozial Extra,* H. 7/8.

Justizministerium Baden-Württemberg (1994) AIDS-Prävention bei i.v. — drogengefährdeten Gefangenen. Brief an die Herren Leiter der Justizvollzugsanstalten, **21**, 2.

Keppler, K.-H.; Nolte, F.; Stöver, H. (1996) Übertragungen von Infektionskrankheiten im Strafvollzug — Ergebnisse einer Untersuchung in der JVA für Frauen in Vechta. In: *Sucht, H.* 2/96, S. 98–107.

Kleiber, D. (1995) Drogen und AIDS:Risikoverhalten und Prävention. In: *Landesstelle gegen die Suchtgefahren für Schleswig-Holstein* (Hrsg.), Kiel: (Selbstverlag), S. 10–27.

Kleiber, D. (1996) *HIV —Needle Sharing — Sex: Eine sozialepidemiologische Studie zur Analyse der HIV-Prävalenz und riskanten Verhaltensweisen bei i.v. Drogenkonsumenten/Dieter Kleiber und Anand Pant* (Hrsg.: Das Bundesministerium für Gesundheit). Baden-Baden: Nomos Verl.-Ges.

Kleiber (1991) Die HIV/AIDS-Problematik bei i.v. Drogenabhängigen in der Bundesrepublik Deutschland — unter besonderer Berücksichtigung der Situation hafterfahrener Drogenabhängiger. In: Busch, M., Heckmann, W., Marks, E. (Hrsg.): *HIV/AIDS und Straffälligkeit. Eine Herausforderung für Strafrechtspflege und Straffälligenhilfe.* Bonn: Forum-Verlag, S. 25–40.

Koch, U./Ehrenberg, S. (1992) Akzeptanz AIDS-präventiver Botschaften: Evaluation der Aufklärungs- und Beratungsarbeit bei i.v. Drogenabhängigen in der Bundesrepublik Deutschland. In: *Deutsche AIDS-Hilfe e.V. (Hg.): AIDS und Drogen II. Evaluation AIDS-präventiver Botschaften.* AIDS-Forum D.A.H., Bd. IX, Berlin, S. 27–101.

Kommission zur Entwicklung eines umsetzungsorientierten Drogenkonzeptes für den Hamburger Strafvollzug (1995) Abschlußbericht der vom Justizsenator der Freien und Hansestadt eingesetzten Kommission. Hamburg (Ms.), Febr. 1995.

Laufs, R. et al. (1994) Was bedeutet der Befund 'HCV-Antikörper positiv'? In: *Dt. Ärzteblatt* 91, H. 5, 4.2.94, S. B-238–240.

Müller, R., Stark, K., Guggenmoos-Holzmann, I., Wirth, D., Bienzle, U. (1994) Imprisonment: a risk factor of HIV infection, counteracting education and prevention programmes for intravenous drug unsers. *AIDS,* 9, 183–190.

Müller, R. u.a. (1995) Imprisonment: a risk factor for HIV infection counteracting education and prevention programmes for intravenous drug users. **AIDS** , 9, 183–190.

Nelles, J. et al. (1995) Pilotprojekt Drogen- und HIV-Prävention in den Anstalten in Hindelbank. Evaluationsbericht im Auftrag des Bundesamtes für Gesundheitswesen. Bern, Sept. 1995. Siehe auch: Pilotprojekt HIV-Prävention in den Anstalten in Hindelbank. Schlußbericht zu Handen des Bundesamtes für Gesundheitswesen, Sept. 1995.

Raschke, P. (1994) *Substitutionstherapie — Ergebnisse langfristiger Behandlung von Opiatabhängigen.* Freiburg: Lambertus.

Rieger-Ndakorerwa, G. u.a. (1994) Infektionsepidemiologie — Analyse der Zunahme der infektiösen Hepatitis in Hamburg. In: *Gesundh.* Wes 56, S. 132–136.

Stark, K. *et al.* (1994) *HIV-Infektion bei i.v. Drogenkonsumeten. Unveröff. Abschlußbericht an das BMFT.* Berlin.

Stöver, H. (1994) *Infektionsprophylaxe im Strafvollzug. Deutsche AIDS-Hialfe,* Berlin.

Tomasevski, Katarina (1992) *Prison Health. International Standards and National. Practices in Europe.* Helsinki: Helsinki Institute for Crime Prevention and Control, affiliated with the United Nations. Publication Series No. 21.

WHO (1993) WHO-Richtlinien zu HIV-Infektion und AIDS im Gefängnis. WHO/GPA/DIR/93.3. Übersetzt in: *Stöver (1994).* a.a.O. S. 119–12.

Chapter 5

SUBSTANCE ABUSE TREATMENT IN US PRISONS

Roger H. Peters and Marc L. Steinberg

US federal and state prisons have grown dramatically in the last decade, and now include over a million male inmates and 68,000 female inmates (US Department of Justice, 1996). During the 1980s, state prisoner populations increased by 237 per cent and federal prisoner populations increased by 311 per cent. Due to prison overcrowding, many states have begun to house prisoners in local jails, including eight states that currently hold more than 10 per cent of their prison population in jails. Prison populations are expected to continue growing by 24 per cent from 1995 to 2000 (US General Accounting Office, 1996), a figure that does not include more than 500,000 state and federal inmates held in local jails. Rates of prison incarceration (number of prisoners per 100,000 US residents) have also been rising steadily. From 1980 to 1995, incarceration rates increased by 191 per cent for state prisoners and 245 per cent for federal prisoners. The prison incarceration rate in 1995 was 428 inmates per 100,000 US residents (US General Accounting Office, 1996), and 600 per 100,000 US residents for incarceration in either jails or prisons, which is the highest rate for any developed country in the world.

Several factors contributing to the rapid increase in the US prison population include changes in law enforcement practices, sentencing law and policy, and in policies regarding release from incarceration. An increase in drug-related crime has also been linked to the surge of cocaine use that began in the mid-1980s and that has continued steadily since that time. Major law enforcement practices that have influenced arrest and incarceration rates include drug 'stings' and 'reverse sting' operations that target street-level users and sellers.

Several legislative changes have also contributed to the rise in US prison populations. The Sentencing Reform Act of 1984 abolished parole for federal offenders and limited time off for good behaviour to 54 days per year. Many state and federal prisoners incarcerated for drug offences (e.g., drug sales) are no longer eligible for parole and must serve mandatory minimum sentences as a result of legislation such as the Anti-Drug Abuse Act passed in 1986. Mandatory minimum sentences have led to increases in time served in federal prisons for drug offences from an average of 22 to 33 months (US Department of Justice, 1995a). Changes in legislation and law enforcement strategies have led to an increase in the proportion of prisoners incarcerated for drug-related charges, from 8 per cent in 1980, to 26 per cent in 1993. Significantly more federal prisoners are drug offenders than state prisoners (60 per cent *vs.* 22 per cent; US General Accounting Office, 1996).

THE RELATIONSHIP BETWEEN DRUGS AND CRIME

There is also mounting evidence that substance abuse increases the likelihood for criminal behaviour and incarceration (Leukefeld, 1985; US Department of Justice, 1992). One clear link between substance abuse and crime is that drug users have more extensive criminal records than non-users, and report greater criminal involvement than non-users (Ball, Shaffer, and Nurco, 1983; Ball, 1986; Collins, Hubbard, and Rachal, 1985; Johnson, Lipton, and Wish, 1986; Wexler and Lipton, 1993; US Department of Justice, 1992). The level of substance abuse appears to moderate the frequency and severity of criminal behaviour (Chaiken, 1986; Speckart and Anglin, 1986). Individuals with criminal records are also more likely to have a history of substance abuse than those without criminal records. Findings from the Drug Abuse Reporting Programme (DARP) and Treatment Outcome Prospective Study (TOPS) indicate that reductions in substance abuse resulting from involvement in treatment are also associated with reductions in criminal activity (Hubbard *et al.*, 1989; Simpson, Joe, and Bracy, 1982; US Department of Justice, 1992). Other evidence supporting the link between substance abuse and crime comes from surveys of prison and jail inmates, surveys of substance abusers in treatment, and offender drug testing programmes, which indicate that many offences are committed while under the influence of drugs or alcohol (US Department of Justice, 1988; 1992; 1995b), or in attempts to support a drug habit (US Department of Justice, 1992).

PREVALENCE OF SUBSTANCE USE DISORDERS IN US PRISONS

As shown in Table 5.1, the prevalence rates of substance abuse and dependence for US prisoners are significantly greater than for the general population. According to data from the Epidemiological Catchment Area study (ECA; Robins and Regier, 1991), the majority of prisoners have a diagnosable drug use disorder, and a quarter of all prisoners have an alcohol use disorder. A more recent study conducted

Table 5.1 A comparison of prevalence rates for substance abuse/dependence among prisoners and the general population.

	Prisons[a]	General population
Alcohol Abuse/Dependence	26%[b]	5.9%[b]
Drug Abuse/Dependence	56%[c]	7.6%[c]

a. Statistics were compiled from results of the Epidemiological Catchment Area (ECA) study conducted by the National Institute of Mental Health (NIMH). Data was collected from 5 sites during 1980–1984. In 3 of the 5 sites, state correctional facilities were sampled. In the remaining 2 sites (New Haven, Connecticut; St. Louis, Missouri), samples included both jail and state prison inmates. Jail inmates in Connecticut were housed in state-operated correctional facilities. As a result, the state correctional facility sampled at the New Haven site included both jail and prison inmates. At the St. Louis site, 4 jails and 10 state correctional facilities were sampled.
b. One-year prevalence rate (Robins and Regier, 1991).
c. Lifetime prevalence rate (Robins and Regier, 1991).
Source: Peters and Hills, 1993.

within the Texas prison system found similar results, using equivalent diagnostic procedures to those used in the ECA study (Peters *et al.*, 1998). Lifetime prevalence of alcohol abuse or dependence disorders in this study was 54 per cent, including 37 per cent for alcohol dependence. Lifetime prevalence of drug abuse or dependence disorder was 58 per cent, including 46 per cent for drug dependence. For the 30 days prior to the most recent incarceration, 56 per cent of inmates were found to have a diagnosable substance use disorder.

Given the significant number of inmates with substance use disorders and lengthy periods of incarceration, it appears that prison treatment programmes would provide a potentially viable strategy for reducing subsequent drug use and recidivism. The period of jail or prison incarceration is seen by many as an opportune time to provide therapeutic interventions pursuant to major lifestyle changes (Lipton, 1995). Despite the significant need for substance abuse treatment services among prisoners, treatment services in US prisons have not kept pace with the growing number of prison inmates with substance use disorders. At the present time only 10 per cent of prisoners receive any form of drug treatment (Simpson, Knight, and Pevoto, 1996). Many of these treatment programmes are not comprehensive in scope, including those that rely on peer counselling approaches such as AA and NA. The following section describes the history and evolution of substance abuse treatment services in US prisons. This is followed by a review of standards and guidelines for prison treatment services, and a description of several treatment programmes in state and federal prisons.

HISTORY OF SUBSTANCE ABUSE TREATMENT IN US PRISONS

As a result of the growing numbers of opiate addicts sentenced to federal prisons in the late 1920s, the US Congress passed the Porter Narcotic Farm Act in 1929, establishing the first formal system of prison-based substance abuse treatment for federal prisoners (Wexler, 1993). The Act created several treatment farms (later referred to as hospitals) in Lexington, Kentucky and Fort Worth, Texas, operated by the US Public Health Service (O'Donnell and Ball, 1966). Relatively few prison treatment programmes were developed during the 1950s and 1960's in the US (Wexler, 1993). The few programmes that were developed during this time were designed primarily for male opiate addicts, and included approaches used in community settings, such as methadone detoxification and maintenance, group therapy, and therapeutic communities. During the 1960s states such as California and New York passed legislation providing for civil commitment of narcotic addicts. Under these programmes, addicts could be court-ordered to enter treatment for up to 7 years without being convicted of a crime.

Federal inmates with a substance abuse history (primarily opiates) received treatment at either the Lexington or Fort Worth hospitals until the Narcotic Addict Rehabilitation Act (NARA) of 1966 was passed. NARA mandated in-prison treatment of narcotic addicts who were convicted of a federal crime. Under NARA, inmates with drug involvement were separated from the general prison population and housed in special treatment units.

In the mid to late 1970s the focus in the criminal justice system had shifted to punishment and deterrence, with less emphasis on rehabilitation or alternatives to incarceration (Palmer, 1996). A report issued by Martinson in 1974 summarised findings from 231 correctional studies that had been completed during the previous 20 years (Lipton, Martinson, and Wilks, 1975), and was highly influential in promoting the doctrine that treatment for substance-involved offenders was ineffective. Although Martinson (1974) conceded methodological flaws in the research, many policymakers used the 'nothing works' premise to reduce financial support for prison-based treatment programmes, believing that their constituents were more interested in punishment of drug-involved offenders, and that their support of treatment efforts would leave them vulnerable to being perceived as 'soft' on crime (Lipton, 1995).

During the 1970s, prison substance abuse treatment in the US was characterised by instability and transition. Several new therapeutic community programmes were implemented in New York, Connecticut, Nevada, and other states, and were supported by Federal block grants from the Law Enforcement Assistance Administration (LEAA; Wexler, 1993). However, most of these new programmes were eliminated or reduced in size over the next decade, due to elimination of LEAA block grants, budget cuts, administrative and treatment programmes staff turnover, and the emergence of the 'nothing works' doctrine resulting from Martinson's (1974) paper.

By the mid-1980s, increases in cocaine and other drug use were accompanied by increases in crime, thus focusing greater attention to efforts to remedy the drug problem. The 'war on drugs' promised by Presidents Reagan and Bush during the 1980s included new funds for law enforcement. By 1988, 'zero tolerance' policies were implemented by law enforcement, courts, and community corrections, thereby re-focusing anti-drug efforts on drug users instead of drug suppliers and dealers (Inciardi, 1993; US Department of Justice, 1997a). One result of strict drug laws was a dramatic increase in the number of drug arrests and convictions, followed by overcrowding of jails and prisons (Inciardi, 1993; US Department of Justice, 1996). Financial and legal interests related to jail and prison overcrowding, coupled with rapid cycling of drug offenders through the criminal justice system led to a renewed interest in correctional substance abuse treatment (Lipton, 1995), and increased state and federal funding for these treatment programmes.

Several federal initiatives in the past 10 years have supported the growth of US correctional substance abuse treatment programmes. In the area of training and implementation of prison treatment programmes, Project REFORM was funded by the US Department of Justice, Bureau of Justice Assistance (BJA) to help state corrections programmes implement, expand, or otherwise improve their substance abuse treatment programmes (Lipton, 1995).

Following the expiration of Project REFORM, responsibility for in-prison treatment efforts shifted from BJA to the Office for Treatment Improvement (OTI), which was subsequently renamed the Centre for Substance Abuse Treatment (CSAT). Project RECOVERY was funded by CSAT to provide the same type of support for prison treatment efforts that had begun under Project REFORM. Project RECOVERY continued to provide training and technical assistance to selected prison-based substance abuse treatment programmes, and encouraged sharing of information and approaches between correctional treatment programmes through professional conferences and workshops. Following the completion of Project RECOVERY, CSAT has continued to support the development of correctional treatment programmes through the Model Programmes for Correctional Populations initiative. This initiative has provided funding from 1990–1997 for demonstration programmes and technical assistance in both jails and prisons.

Support of correctional treatment programmes shifted once again in 1996, reverting back to the US Department of Justice under the auspices of the Residential Substance Abuse Treatment (RSAT) Formula Grant Programme. This programme will provide $270 million during 1996–2000 for the development of treatment programmes within state and local correctional and detention facilities (US Department of Justice, 1997b). Another major source of funding that has recently supported development of treatment programmes for prisoners and other offenders is the Byrne Formula Grant Programme, administered by the US Department of Justice, Bureau of Justice Assistance.

STANDARDS AND GUIDELINES FOR PRISON TREATMENT SERVICES

The following section reviews the legal contours and professional standards that have emerged over the last 20 years to guide the development of substance abuse treatment services in prisons. As described in this section, the courts have been reluctant to prescribe specific aspects of correctional substance abuse treatment services, but have been much more active in identifying required areas of correctional mental health services. As a result, it is the professional rather than legal standards that have provided the most guidance to prison-based substance abuse treatment programmes in the US

There are currently no legal mandates for providing a broad scope of substance abuse treatment services in jails or prisons (Peters, 1993). In Marshall vs. United States (1974), the Supreme Court ruled that a prisoner did not have a constitutional right to drug treatment. In Pace vs. Fauver (1979), a district court in New Jersey found that the Eighth Amendment was not violated by failing to provide treatment for alcoholism in a corrections setting. In this case, the court interpreted the Estelle vs. Gamble (1976) ruling to mean that the relevant medical condition must be of sufficient seriousness, and must be easily recognisable by a lay person or diagnosed by a physician.

The US Supreme Court has determined that prisons cannot ignore the 'serious medical needs' of an inmate (see the 'deliberate indifference' requirement of Estelle *vs*. Gamble, 1976). The Fourth Circuit Court of Appeals also ruled that there is no distinction between the right to medical treatment for prisoners and the right to mental health treatment (Bowring *vs*. Godwin, 1977). Another Court of Appeals (McGuckin *vs*. Smith, 1992) determined that a 'serious medical need' would exist if non-treatment of the condition could result in further significant injury or unnecessary infliction of pain, impairment in daily activities, or presence of chronic and substantial pain. Substance use disorders would not ordinarily fit these court-described conditions unless there were acute and life-threatening consequences (e.g., acute withdrawal symptoms, suicidal behaviour, or other acute physical conditions related to alcohol or drug toxicity; Cohen, 1993). Thus, constitutionally required substance abuse services for prison inmates appear to be quite circumscribed, and include screening, assessment, and treatment (e.g., crisis intervention, medically supervised detoxification) of acute and life-threatening physical symptoms related to substance use.

In two separate cases, the Court of Appeals of New York (Griffin *vs*. Coughlin, 1996);[1] and the Seventh Circuit Court of Appeals (Kerr *vs*. Farrey, 1996) have recently restricted US prisons from creating special privileges (e.g., family visitation, placement in minimum security facilities, opportunity to earn parole) that are contingent upon participation in self-help programmes such as Alcoholics Anonymous (AA) or Narcotics Anonymous (NA). The courts determined that these programmes contained 'explicit religious content', and that mandatory involvement in such programmes violates constitutional provisions for separation of church and state. As a result of these rulings, and to encourage wider inmate participation in treatment services, many prison systems are exploring the use of alternative self-help programmes, such as Secular Organisation for Sobriety (SOS), SMART Recovery, and Rational Recovery (National Commission on Correctional Health Care, 1997).

In the absence of legal standards for providing substance abuse treatment in prisons, several sets of professional standards and guidelines have been developed. However, agencies that have developed these standards do not currently perform regulatory functions to insure that standards related to substance abuse treatment or other health care services have been implemented as intended. The American

Correctional Association (ACA; 1990a), in co-operation with the Commission on Accreditation for Corrections has developed several standards for correctional institutions that are relevant to substance abuse treatment services. The ACA recommends written policies and procedures for clinical management of inmates with substance use disorders in the following areas:

- Diagnosis of chemical dependency by a physician.
- Determination by a physician as to whether an individual requires non-pharmacologically or pharmacologically supported care.
- Individualised treatment plans developed and implemented by a multidisciplinary team.
- Referrals to specified community resources upon release when appropriate.

The ACA and NCCHC standards also identify several items related to the substance abuse history that should be included in preliminary screenings.

The Report of the National Task Force of Correctional Substance Abuse Strategies (US Department of Justice, 1991), the National Institute on Corrections (NIC) describes several general guidelines for substance abuse treatment services provided in prison and other correctional settings. In 1993, the Substance Abuse and Mental Health Services Administration, Centre for Substance Abuse Treatment published a set of guidelines for implementing correctional substance abuse treatment programmes, developed through Project RECOVERY (Wexler, 1993). The guidelines called for the creation of comprehensive state plans for substance abuse treatment services within corrections systems, and planning at the institutional level. Several components of correctional treatment programmes that are recommended by CSAT and NIC include the following:

- Standardised screening and assessment approaches.
- Matching to different levels or types of treatment services.
- Individual treatment plans.
- Case management services.
- Use of cognitive-behavioural/social learning and self-help approaches, including interventions that address criminal beliefs and values.
- Relapse prevention services.
- Self-help groups (e.g., AA, NA).
- Use of therapeutic communities.

- Isolated treatment units.
- Drug testing.
- Continuity of services, including linkages to parole and community-based treatment services.
- Programme evaluation.
- Cross-training of staff.

OVERVIEW OF THE CORRECTIONAL TREATMENT LITERATURE

Although Martinson long ago retracted his conclusion that 'nothing works' in correctional treatment (1979), this belief has persisted over time among policymakers and administrators. A significant number of studies conducted since the time of Martinson's work have provided consistent evidence of positive outcomes associated with correctional treatment programmes. Several literature reviews and meta-analyses have reviewed findings from these studies (Andrews, *et al.*, 1990; Gendreau, 1996; Gendreau and Goggin, 1997; Gendreau and Ross, 1984), and have identified principles of effective correctional treatment programmes. Although these reviews include several programmes that are not dedicated to substance abuse treatment, they are instructive in identifying common principles which are likely to enhance the effectiveness of correctional treatment settings. Across different types of therapeutic programmes developed and tested in correctional settings, those based on social learning, cognitive-behavioural models, skills training, and family systems approaches have proven to be the most effective (Cullen and Gendreau, 1989). Programmes based on non-directive approaches, the medical model, or involving a focus on punishment or deterrence have proven to be 'ineffective'. In reviewing the correctional treatment literature, Gendreau (1996) has identified eight key principles of effective programmes:

1. Intensive services are behavioural in nature. Services should occupy from 40–50 per cent of offenders time, and should be of 3–9 months in duration. Programmes should use token economies, modelling, and cognitive-behavioural interventions designed to change offender's 'cognitions, attitudes, values, and expectations that maintain antisocial behavior'.
2. Programmes should target the 'criminogenic needs of high-risk offenders' including substance abuse, antisocial attitudes and behaviours, peer associations, and self-control. Risk assessment measures should be provided to identify these 'criminogenic needs'.

3. Treatment programmes should be multi-modal, and should match services according to the learning style and personality characteristics of the offender, and to the characteristics of the therapist/counsellor.

4. Programmes should include a structured set of incentives and sanctions. This system must be developed and maintained by staff, with ongoing monitoring of antisocial behaviours within treatment units, and positive reinforcers exceeding negative sanctions by an approximate 4:1 ratio.

5. Therapists or counsellors should be selected on the basis of effective counselling and interpersonal skills. Staff should have at least an undergraduate degree or equivalent, training in criminal behaviour and offender treatment, and on-the-job training in use of behavioural interventions. Quality of counselling services should be monitored regularly.

6. Programmes should provide a prosocial treatment environment that reduces negative peer influences.

7. Relapse prevention strategies should be provided that provide skills in anticipating and avoiding problem situations, and rehearsing prosocial responses to these situations. Training should be provided to family and friends to reinforce prosocial behaviours, and booster sessions should be provided following release to the community.

8. Linkage and referral to community services should be provided.

These principles of effective correctional treatment reflect several key components of professional standards and guidelines that have been developed by ACA, CSAT, NCCHC, and NIC, including the need for treatment matching, staff training, cognitive-behavioural interventions, relapse prevention services, isolated treatment units, and linkage and referral to community services. However, these principles also point to several new areas that are not incorporated within the standards and guidelines, and/or that have not been implemented widely in prison treatment programmes. These new areas include the following: (1) targeting inmates with significant risk for recidivism and relapse, (2) use of cognitive-behavioural interventions, (3) a focus on criminal thinking, values, behaviours, and impulse control issues, and (4) minimum education requirements for staff of at least a college degree. A major challenge for US prison treatment programmes over the next several decades will be to closely examine principles of effective correctional treatment and to begin to implement these within the context of new or existing substance abuse treatment programmes.

PRISON-BASED SUBSTANCE ABUSE TREATMENT PROGRAMMES

The following section describes several new substance abuse treatment initiatives developed within US federal and state prison systems during the last 15 years. Several of the programmes described in this section have thrived over a long period of time, while several other programmes have just recently been developed (Chaiken, 1989; Lipton, 1995). Research findings from these programmes demonstrate the effectiveness of correctional substance abuse treatment programmes in reducing substance abuse and criminal recidivism following release from prison (Falkin, Wexler, and Lipton, 1992).

Federal Bureau of Prisons Drug Abuse Programmes

The Federal Bureau of Prisons was one of the first agencies to respond to the recent drug abuse epidemic by developing a comprehensive system of treatment services for prison inmates (Murray, 1992; 1996). The Bureau's Drug Abuse Programmes (DAP's) include four different levels of treatment services (Lipton, 1995; Federal Bureau of Prisons, 1996a,b; 1997). The first level includes a 40-hour drug education programme attended by all prisoners who meet admission criteria. The second level of treatment involves 'non-residential' drug abuse treatment, in which treatment participants are not isolated from the general prison community. Residential treatment services are provided in the third level, in which participants are isolated from the general inmate population. Thirty four of the Bureau's prisons have a residential treatment programme, which are of varying length (6, 9, or 12 months), and include a minimum of 500 hours of treatment services (Federal Bureau of Prisons, 1996b; Weinman and Lockwood, 1993).

The Bureau's programmes also include transitional services following release from prison. Inmates may be released either to the US Probation Office or to a Community Corrections Centre, which are privately contracted, supervised halfway houses. Transitional treatment services are similar to those obtained in prison, and include ongoing counselling, regular drug testing, and assistance to obtain employment. A comprehensive longitudinal study is underway to examine long-term treatment outcomes for participants in the Bureau of Prisons treatment programmes.

California's Amity Prison Therapeutic Community

California's Amity Prison Therapeutic Community is a 200-bed unit located at the R.J. Donovan Correctional Facility is based on the

Stay'n Out programme in New York. The prison treatment programme consists of three phases, including a 2 to 3 month orientation phase. In the second phase, participants assist in daily operations of the therapeutic community and act as role models to newer participants. The third phase of treatment lasts for 1-3 months and involves decision-making skills related to recovery, and developing a plan for re-entry to the community. Following release from the prison, graduates are offered up to one year of aftercare treatment in a therapeutic community programme that serves up to 40 residents.

A recent evaluation of California's Amity prison programme indicated favourable outcomes associated with participation in prison treatment (Lipton, 1995, 1996; Simpson *et al.*, 1996). Rates of reincarceration during a one year follow-up period after release from prison were 43 per cent for those who completed the treatment programme, compared to 63 per cent for prisoners not participating in the programme, and 50 per cent for those who dropped out of the programme (Lipton, 1995). Only 26 per cent of individuals who were placed in an aftercare programme following graduation from the in-prison treatment programme were reincarcerated during the same period. Similar patterns of follow-up outcomes were found in relation to participant drug use.

Delaware's Key-Crest Programme

The 'Key' Programme was established in 1987 by the Delaware Department of Corrections (Hooper, Lockwood, and Inciardi, 1993; Inciardi, 1996; Inciardi, *et al.*, 1992; Pan, Scarpitti, Inciardi, and Lockwood, D., 1993). One year of treatment services are provided for male prisoners in a 140-bed therapeutic community that is modelled after New York's Stay'n Out programme. The Key Programme is unique in that a 6 month transitional phase (Crest Outreach Centre) is provided following completion of the in-prison programme, which includes 'Key' participants and other offenders who are supervised in the community. In the Crest programme, prisoners may hold jobs in the community while residing in the therapeutic community programme (Inciardi, 1996). A six month aftercare component is included as the last phase of the Crest programme.

In a recent evaluation of the Key and Crest programmes, researchers compared four groups who had participated in varying levels of programme services: (1) Key programme only, (2) Crest programme only, (3) combined Key-Crest programmes, and (4) an HIV prevention/education 'control' programme. Six month follow-up results indicated that individuals participating in the Crest programme (only) and the combined Key and Crest programmes were significantly less likely to use drugs or to be arrested than participants in the Key (only) and the control group (Martin, Butzin, and Inciardi, 1995). Positive outcomes associated with the Crest (only) and combined Key/Crest programmes were still evident after controlling for the effects for time spent in treatment.

Florida's Tier Programmes

The Florida Department of Corrections (FDOC) has a long history of supporting innovative prison-based substance abuse treatment. In the early 1970s, with funding through the Law Enforcement Assistance Act (LEAA), FDOC developed several of the first prison therapeutic communities in the country, in addition to specialised treatment programmes for female inmates and youthful offenders (Chaiken, 1989; Florida Department of Corrections, 1995; 1996). Comprehensive Substance Abuse Treatment Programmes are provided in 46 major correctional institutions, 31 community correctional centres, and 7 community facilities.

Inmates are placed in several 'tiers' of treatment services. Tier I services consist of 40 hours of drug education services per week, including an orientation to the importance of substance abuse treatment, and group counselling. Tier II programmes provide treatment for approximately 40 inmates at a time over a period of 4–6 months. Tier III programmes provide 4 months of treatment in an intensive therapeutic community setting, and include orientation, treatment, and re-entry phases. Tier IV services include 6–12 months of treatment in a residential therapeutic community in 12 institutions, and in seven community-based facilities, including a 54-bed treatment programme for inmates placed on work release.

New York's Stay'n Out Programme

One of the longest operating correctional treatment programmes in the US is the Stay'n Out Programme in New York, which provides a highly structured therapeutic community (Wexler and Williams, 1986). In 1989, the New York legislature appropriated $1 billion to augment drug abuse treatment efforts in New York state prisons, which included one 750-bed and seven 200-bed substance abuse treatment facilities (Lipton, 1995).

Outcomes from the Stay 'n Out programme were compared to those from milieu treatment, short-term counselling services, a waiting list, and a no-treatment control group (Wexler, Falkin, and Lipton, 1990; Wexler, Falkin, Lipton, and Rosenblum, 1992). Significantly fewer Stay'n Out participants were arrested during follow-up on supervised parole (lasting an average of 3 years) in comparison to other groups (27 per cent *vs.* 35 per cent in milieu treatment, 40 per cent in group or individual counselling, and 41 per cent in a no-treatment comparison group). However, there was no evidence that the Stay'n Out programme delayed the time to arrest during follow-up. Positive outcomes were correlated with increasing time in treatment up to one year; but after this duration, positive outcomes began to decline.

Oregon Department of Corrections

Oregon's Cornerstone Programme opened in 1976, and was modelled after the Stay'n Out programme in New York, but with a higher proportion of professionals and trained correction officers (Lipton, 1994; 1995). The Cornerstone programme is housed in a 32-bed residential unit in the Oregon State Hospital. Four phases of treatment are provided over a period of 10–12 months, followed by 6 months of aftercare/transitional services while under parole supervision (Field, 1989).

Several other modified therapeutic community programmes have recently been developed by the Oregon Department of Corrections, including the Turning Point Alcohol and Drug Programme at the Columbia River Correctional Institution, and the Powder River Alcohol and Drug (PRAD) Programme at the Powder River Correctional Facility. The Turning Point programme provides a 50-bed unit for females and a similar unit for males, while the PRAD Programme provides a 50-bed male unit. The Turning Point treatment programme serves as a pre-release institution for female inmates. In 1989, the Parole Transition Release (PTR) Project was initiated by the Oregon Department of Corrections in Washington County, Oregon, with funding from several federal agencies. Treatment services are provided for 35 offenders over a period of approximately 9 months. Treatment begins prior to release from prison, and continues in the community (Field and Karecki, 1992).

An evaluation of the Cornerstone Programme indicates that treatment participants experience significant reductions in re-arrest and recommitment to prison, in comparison to other groups of inmates. Field (1989; 1992) found that rates of re-arrest and reincarceration during follow-up were inversely related to the time spent in the treatment programme. Only 26 per cent of Cornerstone Programme graduates were recommitted to prison during a three year follow-up period, as compared to 85 per cent of individuals who dropped out of the programme after less than 2 months of participation, 67 per cent of non-graduates who completed from 2–5 months of treatment, and 63 per cent of non-graduates who completed at least 6 months of treatment.

The Texas Criminal Justice Treatment Initiative

In 1991, under the stewardship of Texas Governor Ann Richards, legislation was enacted to create the Texas Criminal Justice Treatment Initiative, the largest state prison treatment programme in the country at that time. This initiative originally provided $95 million for development of Substance Abuse Felony Punishment (SAFP) programmes and In-Prison Therapeutic Community Treatment (ITC) programmes. The initiative also provided funding for alternatives to incarceration programmes and Transitional Treatment Centres, which are community-based facilities for offenders who have completed a SAFP or ITC programme.

As originally enacted, legislation in Texas authorised the development of 12,000 secure treatment beds within the SAFP programme and corresponding space in community residential and non-residential programmes. The scope of SAFP and ITC programmes have since been substantially reduced by the legislature (Texas Department of Criminal Justice, 1997).

The Substance Abuse Felony (SAFP) System allows those with substance abuse problems who are convicted of non-violent felonies to enter long term (6–12 months) substance abuse treatment as a condition of parole or probation. Programme graduates then participate in 15 months of transitional services. State prisoners are eligible to participate in the In-Prison Therapeutic Community Treatment (ITC) programme, which provides drug treatment services for inmates who are within 9–10 months of parole.

Knight *et al.* (1997) report that ITC graduates are significantly less likely to be involved in criminal activity (7 per cent *vs.* 16 per cent arrested; 28 per cent *vs.* 47 per cent reported drug-related offences; and 41 per cent *vs.* 55 per cent involved in criminal activity as determined by any source), are less likely to have a parole violation 6 months after leaving prison (29 per cent *vs.* 48 per cent), and were less likely to use alcohol or other drugs, in contrast to an untreated comparison group. ITC graduates who went on to complete the TTC aftercare programme within the 6 month follow-up time frame were found to have lower recidivism rates than non-completers and a comparison group consisting of parolees, and fewer ITC completers used cocaine than the untreated comparison group.

The National Treatment Improvement Evaluation Study

The National Treatment Improvement Evaluation Study (NTIES; Centre for Substance Abuse Treatment, 1997) was conducted by CSAT to determine the long range outcomes of individuals involved in federally funded treatment programmes. Outcome data were obtained for over 4411 individuals, including 709 individuals from the 'correctional' sample, which consisted of 56 per cent prison inmates and 44 per cent offenders from other criminal justice settings. Participants in correctional treatment experienced the greatest reductions in self-reported criminal behaviour (e.g., 81 per cent reduction in selling drugs) and in arrests (66 per cent reduction in drug possession arrests, 76 per cent reduction in all arrests) among all other types of treatment settings/modalities examined in the NTIES study. Reduced drug use and enhanced mental health and physical health functioning were also observed during follow-up among the correctional sample.

CORRECTIONAL TREATMENT OF SPECIAL NEEDS POPULATIONS

Co-occurring Mental Health and Substance Use Disorders

Rates of both mental health disorders and substance use disorders are significantly higher among offenders than in non-incarcerated populations in the community (Keith, Regier, and Rae, 1991; Weissman, Bruce, Leaf, Floria, and Holzer, 1992; Robins and Regier, 1991). For example, rates of mental health disorders are four times higher among prisoners than in the general population, and rates of substance use are four to seven times higher (Robins and Regier, 1991). In the absence of epidemiological data, it is estimated that 3–11 per cent of prison inmates have co-occurring mental health and substance use disorders (Peters and Hills, 1993). Over 600,000 US prison inmates have either a serious mental illness or a substance use disorder, and approximately 130,000 inmates have co-occurring disorders (National GAINS Centre, 1997).

As in community settings, co-occurring disorders are often undetected or untreated in correctional settings. One survey found that many correctional systems had not developed procedures for compiling information regarding the rates of co-occurring disorders in their institutions (Peters and Hills, 1993). Non-detection of co-occurring disorders often leads to misdiagnosis, overtreatment of mental health symptoms with medications, neglect of appropriate interventions, inappropriate treatment planning and referral, and poor treatment outcomes (Drake, Alterman, and Rosenberg, 1993; Hall, Popleis, Stickney, and Gardner, 1978; Teague, Schwab, and Drake, 1990). There are several reasons for the non-detection of mental health and substance use disorders within correctional systems. These include negative consequences perceived by inmates for disclosing symptoms, lack of staff training in diagnosis and management of mental health disorders, and cognitive and perceptual difficulties associated with severe mental illness or toxic effects of recent alcohol or drug use.

Inmates with co-occurring disorders present a number of challenges in correctional settings, and manifest more severe psychosocial problems than other inmates (Peters, Kearns, Murrin, and Dolente, 1992) related to employment, family relationships, and physical health. Offenders with co-occurring disorders are more likely to drop out of treatment or to be terminated from treatment, are more likely to be hospitalised, and are thought to be at greater risk for suicide and criminal recidivism (Peters and Bartoi, 1997). Individuals with co-occurring disorders often do not fit well into existing treatment programmes (Carey, 1991). Once involved in treatment, these individuals do not respond as well as others with single diagnoses (Bowers, Mazoure, Nelson, and Jatlow, 1990).

Integrated approaches should be used in screening and assessment of co-occurring disorders among prison inmates (Peters and Bartoi, 1997). Relevant criminal justice, mental health, and substance use information should be reviewed in both screening and assessment of co-occurring disorders. Screening is useful in determining the relationship between co-occurring disorders and prior criminal behaviour, the interaction of these disorders, and motivation for treatment. Because of the high rates of co-occurring disorders in prisons, detection of a single disorder (i.e. either mental health or substance use) should immediately 'trigger' screening for the other type of disorder. Screening and assessment should include an interview, use of self-report and diagnostic instruments as needed, and review of archival records. In the absence of integrated instruments for examining co-occurring disorders, screening and assessment in prisons should include a combination of mental health and substance abuse instruments.

A number of recent initiatives in jails and prisons have been developed to address the treatment needs of this population, including several programmes developed within state prisons in Alabama,

Colorado, Delaware, Oregon, and Texas, and one programme in the Federal Bureau of Prisons (*et al.*, 1997). The in-prison dual diagnosis programmes share several features. First, programme staff have experience and training in both mental health and substance abuse treatment. Second, although the disorders were not always addressed simultaneously, both are treated as 'primary' disorders. In addition, each of the programmes utilise psychopharmacological and self-help services, and individual counselling is provided to supplement prisoners' involvement in several standard 'phases' or 'levels' of treatment. Lastly, each of the correctional treatment programmes provide a long-term focus, and recognise the importance of continued treatment following release from prison.

Most programmes for dually diagnosed inmates include a set of structured 'phases' or 'levels' of treatment, which are progressively less intensive over time. Phases of treatment often include an orientation phase focusing on motivation and engagement in treatment, intensive treatment, and relapse prevention and transition services. Aftercare, or linkage to other services is especially important to dually diagnosed prisoners due to their increased vulnerability to relapse (Peters and Hills, 1993). Most existing correctional dual diagnosis programmes provide re-entry services to facilitate the transition to aftercare treatment services, work release programmes, or halfway houses (Edens *et al.*, 1997). Several modifications made to correctional dual diagnosis programmes include smaller client caseloads, use of psycho-educational groups, shorter duration of treatment sessions, and more streamlined content of didactic and process group sessions. These programmes also tend to provide less peer confrontation than in most substance abuse treatment programmes (McLaughlin and Pepper, 1991; Sacks and Sacks, 1995).

TREATMENT OF FEMALE INMATES

From 1986 to 1991, the population of female prisoners increased by 75 per cent (Kline, 1993). The growth rate of female prisoners has exceeded that of males, rising at a rate of 12 per cent per year since 1980 (Bureau of Justice Statistics, 1994). This growth reflects a substantial influx of individuals arrested for drug-related crimes. According to the Bureau of Justice Statistics (1994), more than half of incarcerated females committed their crimes under the influence of drugs or alcohol.

Female offenders were found to have higher scores on several scales of the Addiction Severity Index (ASI; McLellan *et al.*, 1992; Peters, Strozier, Murrin, and Kearns, 1997), reflecting significantly more impairment than males related to drug use, employment, legal status, and psychiatric/psychological functioning (males were more impaired on the scale related to alcohol use). Female offenders were also more likely to report psychiatric problems such as serious depression and anxiety (Peters, *et al.*, 1997).

Fewer than 11 per cent of female offenders are involved in substance abuse treatment (Wellisch, Anglin, and Prendergast, 1993a), although a recent survey (American Correctional Association, 1990b) of state prisons indicated that over 40 per cent of female inmates needed substance abuse treatment. Specialised and intensive services for female offenders are less likely to be offered in programmes that serve both men and women, in comparison to those serving female inmates exclusively (Wellisch, Prendergast, and Anglin, 1994). Correctional treatment programmes for women are often of limited intensity and duration, do not assess the full range of psychosocial problems among substance abusing female inmates, and do not have sufficient resources to treat the majority of these problems (e.g., sexual abuse, domestic violence; Wellisch, Prendergast, and Anglin, 1994).

Several recommendations for developing correctional substance abuse treatment programmes for women are provided by Wellisch, Anglin, and Prendergast, (1993b). These include: (1) developing support for specialised female treatment programmes within the corrections system and in the community, (2) providing a continuum of care, (3) transition planning prior to release from prison, (4) ongoing supervision following release to the community, and (5) procedures for data collection and programme evaluation. Some have called for adoption of a 'co-occurring disorders' treatment model in developing services for substance abusing female inmates, based on the multiple and interrelated psychosocial problems manifested by this population (Peters, *et al.*, 1997). The authors recommend that several key principles in treating co-occurring disorders be considered in developing substance abuse services for female inmates. These principles include the following:

- Mental health services should be a central component of treatment, and not isolated from correctional substance abuse services for women.
- When multiple psychosocial problems are present, each should be treated as equally important as the foci of clinical interventions.
- Co-occurring problems should be treated simultaneously rather than sequentially.

- Integrative assessment and treatment approaches should be used that consider the interactive nature of different problems.
- The sequence of treatment services for female inmates should be determined by areas of more severe functional disturbance. These areas should be addressed earlier in the course of treatment.
- An extended assessment 'baseline' should be provided, reflecting the complexity of psychosocial problems among substance abusing female inmates.
- Correctional and treatment staff should receive training regarding the nature of co-occurring problems/disorders, and their interactive effects.

As with other correctional substance abuse treatment services, programmes for female inmates should be geographically isolated from the general prison population, whenever possible. Roles of correctional officers and treatment staff should be easily distinguishable to reduce conflicts regarding security and treatment issues, and to enhance confidentiality of clinical information shared with staff during treatment. Wellisch *et al.* (1993b) describe the importance of clearly defining staff roles for dealing with particular rule infractions. Flexibility should be provided in responding to these situations. Correctional treatment programmes should be staffed by females with professional training, and who can serve as role models.

Optimally, correctional treatment programmes for females should include means for participants to maintain contact with their children, since separation from children may greatly influence recovery goals and engagement in treatment (Wellisch *et al.*, 1993b). Female prisoners often are released to the community as the primary financial provider for their children, yet often do not have adequate job training. Vocational training and job readiness services should be a major component of correctional substance abuse programmes for women. Proper health care is also especially important for female inmates, since many have histories of physical or sexual abuse. They may also have recently given birth, or may be pregnant at the time of incarceration (Wellisch *et al.*, 1993a, 1993b).

One exemplary substance abuse treatment programme for female inmates is the Passages Programme for Women, developed by the Wisconsin Department of Corrections (Wellisch, *et al.*, 1993b). This programme was created in 1988, through funding by the US Department of Justice. The Passages Programme is a 12 week pro-

institutional violence, (3) at least moderate substance abuse problems, and (4) sufficient time remaining on the sentence to complete the in-prison treatment programme (and in some cases, sufficient time on parole to complete an aftercare programme).

Most of the existing US correctional treatment programmes include different phases of treatment. An orientation phase, followed by an intensive treatment phase and transition phase are common to many of these programmes. Within the various phases of treatment, there are several common types of treatment activities offered, including drug and alcohol education, individual and group counselling, life skills training, job training, and relapse prevention. Several pro-grammes offer cognitive-behavioural interventions and activities designed to reduce criminal thinking errors. Transition services are also a central component to many correctional treatment programmes, and include development of a re-entry plan, linkages with aftercare treatment providers, parole, and other community services.

Evaluations of correctional substance abuse treatment programmes provide consistent support for the effectiveness of these initiatives. Conclusions from several recent empirical reviews of the correctional treatment literature (Gendreau, 1996; Gendreau and Goggin, 1997) depart significantly from the 'nothing works' doctrine that emerged from Martinson's earlier work. These 'meta-analyses' indicate consis-tently positive outcomes associated with correctional treatment pro-grammes, with more favourable results obtained from programmes that address criminogenic needs of 'high-risk' offenders, that use cog-nitive-behavioural techniques, that provide relapse prevention activi-ties, that provide a focus on linkage and referral, and that are intensive, of lengthy duration, and multi-modal in approach.

Findings from the large multi-site NTIES study conducted by the Centre for Substance Abuse Treatment (1997) also support the efficacy of correctional treatment, and indicate that participants in these pro-grammes experience greater post-treatment reductions in criminal behaviour than non-offenders enrolled in several different types of community-based programmes. Controlled treatment outcome studies conducted in five state prison systems surveyed in this chapter all point to significant reductions in post-treatment criminal behaviour and improvements in other areas of psychosocial functioning (e.g., reduced drug use, employment). Length of treatment has also been found to be directly related to treatment outcome in these studies, although there appears to be diminishing effects of treatment beyond one year.

Inmates who participate in prison treatment that is followed by an aftercare programme in the community have significantly better outcomes (e.g., lower rates of re-arrest and reincarceration) than inmates who receive only the in-prison treatment. Additional research is needed to examine correctional treatment outcomes among samples that include untreated inmates. Moreover, this research should provide extended follow-up periods, and should examine substance abuse, unreported criminal activity, sanctions received while under community supervision, employment, and use of community services, in addition to more traditional measures of arrest and recommitment to prison.

NOTE

[1]   In Couglin v. Griffin (1997), the US Supreme Court subsequently denied certiori, allowing the decision to remain standing

References

American Correctional Association. (1990a) *Standards for adult correctional institutions, 3rd edition.* Washington, D.C.: St. Mary's Press.

American Correctional Association. (1990b) *The female offender: What does the future hold?* Washington, D.C.: St. Mary's Press.

Andrews, D.A., Zinger, I., Hoge, R.D., Bonta, J., Gendreau, P., and Cullen, F.T. (1990) Does correctional treatment work? A clinically relevant and psychologically informed meta-analysis. Criminology, 28, 369–404.

Ball, J.C. (1986) The hyper-criminal opiate addict. In B. D. Johnson and E. Wish (Eds.), *Crime rates among drug abusing offenders. Final Report to the National Institute of Justice* (pp. 81–104). New York: Narcotic and Drug Research, Inc.

Ball, J.C., Shaffer, J.W., and Nurco, D.N. (1983) Day-to-day criminality of heroin addicts in Baltimore: A study of the continuity of offense rates. *Drug and Alcohol Dependence,* 12, 119–142.

Bowers, M.B., Mazure, C.M., Nelson, C.J., and Jatlow, P.I. (1990) Psychotogenic drug use and neuroleptic response. *Schizophrenia Bulletin,* 16, 81–85.

Bowring v. Godwin, 551 F.2d 44 (4th Cir. 1977).

Carey, K.G. (1991) Research with dual diagnosis patients: Challenges and recommendations. *The Behavior Therapist,* 14, 5–8.

Center for Substance Abuse Treatment (1997) *NTIES: The National Treatment Improvement Study–Final Report.* Substance Abuse and Mental Health Services Administration, US Department of Health and Human Services. Rockville, MD.

Chaiken, M. (1986) Crime rates and substance abuse among types of offenders. In B. Johnson and E. Wish (Eds.), *Crime rates among drug-abusing offenders,* 12–54. *Final Report to the National Institute of Justice.* New York: Narcotic and Drug Research, Inc.

Chaiken, M. (1989) *In-prison programmes for drug-involved offenders.* Issues and Practices series, National Institute of Justice. Washington, D.C: US Department of Justice.

Collins, J.J. Hubbard, R.L., and Rachal, J.V. (1985) Expensive drug use in illegal income: A test of explanatory hypotheses. *Criminology*, 23,(4), 743–764.

Cohen, F. (1993) Captives' legal rights to mental health care. *Law and Psychology Review*, 17, 1–39.

Coughlin v. Griffin, 117 US 681 (1997).

Cullen, F.T., and Gendreau, P. (1989) The effectiveness of correctional rehabilitation. In L. Goodstein and D. MacKenzie (Eds.), *The American prison: Issues in research policy* (pp. 23–44). New York: Plenum.

Drake, R.E., Alterman, A.I., and Rosenberg, S.R. (1993) Detection of substance use disorders in severely mentally ill patients. *Community Mental Health*, 29, (2), 175–192.

Edens, J.F., Peters, R.H., and Hills, H.A. (1997). Treating prison inmates with co-occurring disorders: An integrative review of existing programmes. *Behavioural Sciences and the Law*, 15, 439–457.

Estelle v. Gamble, 429 US 97 (1976).

Falkin, G.P., Wexler, H.K., and Lipton, D.S. (1992) Drug treatment in state prisons. In Gerstein, D.R., and Harwood, H.J. (Eds.), *Treating drug problems, volume II* (pp. 89–131). Washington, DC: National Academy Press.

Federal Bureau of Prisons (1996a) [On-line] Federal Bureau of Prisons Quick Facts. Available: http://www.bop.gov/facts.html#population.

Federal Bureau of Prisons (1996b) *Drug abuse programme options in the Federal Bureau of Prisons: Third annual report to Congress*. Washington, D.C: US Department Justice.

Federal Bureau of Prisons (1997). *Federal Bureau of Prisons Drug Abuse Treatment Programmes*. Washington, D.C: US Department Justice.

Field, G. (1989). *A study of the effects of intensive treatment on reducing the criminal recidivism of addicted offenders*. Salem, Oregon: Oregon Department of Corrections.

Field, G. (1992) Oregon Prison Drug Treatment programmes. In C. Leukefeld and F. Tims (Eds.), *Drug abuse treatment in prisons and jails* (pp. 142–155). Research Monograph Series, Vol. 118. Rockville, MD: National Institute on Drug Abuse.

Field, G., and Karecki, M. (1992) *Outcome study of the Parole Transition Release project*. Salem, Oregon: Oregon Department of Corrections.

Florida Department of Corrections (1995*) Substance Abuse Programme Services Office: Comprehensive report, 1995*. Tallahassee, Florida.

Florida Department of Corrections (1996) *1995–96 annual report: The guidebook to corrections in Florida*. Tallahassee, Florida.

Gendreau, P. (1996) The principles of effective intervention with offenders. In A. Harland (Ed.), *Choosing correctional options that work*. Newbury Park, CA: Sage Publications.

Gendreau, P., and Goggin, C. (1997) Correctional treatment: Accomplishments and realities. In P. VanVourhis, M. Braswell, and D. Lester (Eds.), *Correctional counseling and rehabilitation*. Cincinnati, Ohio: Anderson.

Gendreau, P., and Ross, R.R. (1984) Correctional treatment: Some recommendations for successful intervention. *Juvenile and Family Court Journal*, 34, 31–40.

Griffin v. Coughlin, 88 N.Y. 2d 674 (1996).

Hall, R.C., Popleis, M.K., Stickney, S.K., and Gardner, E.E. (1978) Covert outpatient drug abuse. *Journal of Nervous and Mental Disease*, 166, 343–348.

Hooper, R.M., Lockwood, D.L., and Inciardi, J.A. (1993) Treatment techniques in corrections-based therapeutic communities. *Prison Journal*, 73, 290-306.

Hubbard, R.L., Marsden, M.E., Rachal, J.V., Harwood, H.J., Cavanaugh, E.R., and Ginzburg, H.M. (1989) *Drug abuse treatment: A national study of effectiveness*. Chapel Hill: University of North Carolina Press.

Inciardi, J.A. (1993). Introduction: A Response to the War on Drugs. In J. Inciardi, (Ed.), *Drug treatment and criminal justice*. Newbury Park, CA: Sage Publications.

Inciardi, J.A. (1996) The therapeutic community: An effective model for corrections-based drug abuse treatment. In K. Early (Ed.), *Drug treatment behind bars: Prison-based strategies for change*. Westport, CT: Praeger Publishers/Greenwood Publishing Group.

Inciardi, J.A. (1996) *A corrections-based continuum of effective drug abuse treatment*. National Institute of Justice. Research Preview. Washington, D.C: US Department of Justice.

Inciardi, J.A., Martin, S.S., Lockwood, D.L., Hooper, R.M., and Wald, B.M. (1992) Obstacles to the implementation and evaluation of drug treatment programmes in correctional settings: Reviewing the Delaware KEY experience. In C. Leukefeld and F. Tims (Eds.), *Drug treatment in prisons and jails* (pp. 176–191). Research Monograph Series, Vol. 118. Rockville, MD: National Institute on Drug Abuse.

Johnson, B.D., Lipton, D.S., and Wish, E.D. (1986) *Facts about the criminality of heroin and cocaine abusers and some new alternatives to incarceration.* New York: Narcotic and Drug Research, Inc.

Keith, S.J., Regier, D.A., and Rae, D.S. (1991) Schizophrenic disorders. In L.N. Robins and D.A. Regier (Eds.), *Psychiatric disorders in America.* New York: MacMillan.

Kerr v. Farrey, 95 F.3d 472 (1996).

Kline, S. (1993). A profile of female offenders in state and federal prisons. In M.D. Laurel, (ed.), *Female offenders: Meeting needs of a neglected population.* American Correctional Association.

Knight, K., Simpson, D.D., Chatham, L.R., and Camacho, L.M. (1997) An assessment of prison-based drug treatment: Texas' in-prison therapeutic community programme. *Journal of Offender Rehabilitation,* 2(3/4), 75–100.

Leukefeld, C.G. (1985) The clinical connection: drugs and crime. *International Journal of the Addictions,* 20(6/7), 1049–1064.

Lipton, D.S. (1994) The correctional opportunity: Pathways to drug treatment for offenders. *The Journal of Drug Issues,* 24(2), 331–348.

Lipton, D.S. (1995) *The effectiveness of treatment for drug abusers under criminal justice supervision,* National Institute of Justice Research Report.

Lipton, D.S. (1996) Prison-based therapeutic communities: Their success with drug abusing offenders. *National Institute of Justice Journal,* 12–20.

Lipton, D.S., Martinson, R., and Wilks, J. (1975) *The effectiveness of correctional treatment.* New York: Praeger Publishers.

Marshall v. United States, 414 US 417 (1974).

Martin, S.S., Butzin, C.A., and Inciardi, J.A. (1995) Assessment of a multistage therapeutic community for drug-involved offenders. *Journal of Psychoactive Drugs,* 27,(1), 109–116.

Martinson, R. (1974) What works? Questions and answers about prison reform. *The Public Interest,* 35, 22–54.

Martinson, R. (1979) New findings, new views: A note of caution regarding prison reform. *Hofstra Law Review,* 7, 243–258.

McGuckin v. Smith, 974 F.2d 1050 (9th Cir. 1992).

McLaughlin, P., and Pepper, P. (1991) Modifying the therapeutic community for the mentally ill substance abuser. *New Directions for Mental Health Services,* 50, 85–93.

McLellan, A.T., Kushner, H., Metzger, D., Peters, R., Smith, I., Grissom, G. Pettinati, H., and Argeriou, M. (1992) The fifth edition of the Addiction Severity Index. *Journal of Substance Abuse Treatment,* 9, 199–213.

Murray, D.W. (1992) Drug abuse treatment programmes in the Federal Bureau of Prisons: Initiatives for the 1990's. In C. Leukefeld and F. Tims (Eds.), *Drug treatment in prisons and jails* (pp. 62–83). Research Monograph Series, Vol. 118. Rockville, MD: National Institute on Drug Abuse.

Murray, D.W. (1996). Drug abuse treatment in the Federal Bureau of Prisons: A historical review and assessment of contemporary initiatives. In K. Early (Ed.), *Drug treatment behind bars: Prison-based strategies for change.* Westport, CT: Praeger Publishers/Greenwood Publishing Group.

National Commission on Correctional Health Care (1997) *CorrectCare,* 11,(2), 1–17.

National GAINS Center (1997) *The prevalence of co-occurring mental and substance abuse disorders in the criminal justice system. Just the Facts series.* Delmar, New York: The National GAINS Center.

O'Donnell, J.A., and Ball, J.C. (1966) *Narcotic addiction.* New York: Harper and Row.

Pace v. Fauver, 479 F. Supp. 456 (D.N.J. 1979).

Palmer, T. (1996) Growth-centered intervention: An overview of changes in recent decades. In K. Early (Ed.), *Drug treatment behind bars: Prison-based strategies for change*. Westport, CT: Praeger Publishers/Greenwood Publishing Group.

Pan, H., Scarpitti, F.R., Inciardi, J.A., and Lockwood, D. (1993) Some considerations on therapeutic communities in corrections. In J. Inciardi (Ed.), *Drug treatment and criminal justice*. Newbury Park, CA: Sage Publications.

Peters, R.H. (1993) Substance abuse services in jails and prisons. *Law and Psychology Review*, **17**, 86–116.

Peters, R.H., and Bartoi, M.G. (1997) *Screening and assessment of co-occurring disorders in the justice system*. Delmar N.Y: The National GAINS Center.

Peters, R.H., and Greenbaum, P.E., Edens, J.F., Carter, C.R., and Ortiz, M.M. (1998) Prevalence of DSM-IV substance abuse and dependence disorders among prison inmates, *American Journal of Drug and Alcohol Abuse*, **24**(1), 573–587.

Peters, R.H., and Hills, H.A. (1993) Inmates with co-occurring substance abuse and mental health disorders. In Steadman, H.J., and Cocozza, J.J. (Eds.), *"Providing services for offenders with mental illness and related disorders in prisons"* (pp. 159–212). Washington, D.C.: The National Coalition for the Mentally Ill in the Criminal Justice System.

Peters, R.H., Kearns, W.D., Murrin, M.R., and Dolente, A.S. (1992) Psychopathology and mental health needs among drug-involved inmates. *Journal of Prison and Jail Health*, **11**(1), 3–25.

Peters, R.H., Strozier, A.L., Murrin, M.R., and Kearns, W.D. (1997) Treatment of substance-abusing jail inmates: Examination of gender differences. *Journal of Substance Abuse Treatment*, **14**(4), 339–349.

Robins, L.N., and Regier, D.A. (1991) *Psychiatric disorders in America: The Epidemiologic Catchment Area Study*. New York: Free Press.

Sacks, S., and Sacks, J. (1995) *Recent advances in theory, prevention, and research for dual disorder*. Paper presented at the Middle Eastern institute on Drug Abuse, Jerusalem, Israel.

Simpson, D.D., Joe, G.W., and Bracy, S. (1982) Six-year follow-up of opioid addicts after admission to treatment. *Archives of General Psychiatry*, **39**, 1318–1323.

Simpson, D.D., Knight, K., and Pevoto, C. (1996) *Research summary: Focus on drug treatment in criminal justice settings*. Ft. Worth, TX: Institute of Behavioural Research, Texas Christian University.

Speckart, G., and Anglin, D.M. (1986) Narcotics use and crime: A causal modeling approach. *Journal of Quantitative Criminology*, **2**, 3–28.

Teague, G.B., Schwab, B., and Drake, R.E. (1990) *Evaluating services for young adults with severe mental illness and substance use disorders*. Arlington, VA.: National Association of State Mental Health Programme Directors.

Texas Department of Criminal Justice (1997) *Department of Criminal Justice*. [On-line]. Available: http://www.lbb.state.tx.us/lbb/members/reports/fiscal/fspscj/FS696.htm.

US Department of Justice (1988) *Drug use and crime: Special report* (NCJ-111940). Washington, D.C: Bureau of Justice Statistics.

US Department of Justice (1991) *Intervening with substance-abusing offenders: A framework for action. Report of the National Task Force on Correctional Substance Abuse Strategies*. Washington, D.C: National Institute of Corrections.

US Department of Justice (1992) *A national report: Drugs, crime, and the justice system*. Washington, D.C: Bureau of Justice Statistics.

US Department of Justice (1994) *Women in prison*. Washington, D.C: Bureau of Justice Statistics.

US Department of Justice (1995a) *Prisoners in 1994*. Washington, D.C: Bureau of Justice Statistics.

US Department of Justice (1995b) *Drugs and crime facts, 1994*. Rockville, MD: Bureau of Justice Statistics.

US Department of Justice (1996a) *Prison and Jail Inmates, 1995*. Washington, D.C: Bureau of Justice Statistics.

US Department of Justice (1996b) *Crime in the United States, 1995: Uniform Crime Reports*. Washington, D.C: Federal Bureau of Investigation

US Department of Justice (1997a) *Violent Crime Control and Law Enforcement Act of 1994*. [On-line]. Available: http://gopher.usdoj.gov/crime/crime.html

US Department of Justice (1997b). *Grant Programmes for 1995*. [On-line]. Available: http://gopher.usdoj.gov/crime/ojp_brf.html

US General Accounting Office. (November, 1996) *Federal and State Prisons: Inmate Populations, Costs, and Projection Models*. Report to the subcommittee on Crime, Committee on the Judiciary, House of Representatives. Washington, D.C.

Weinman, B.A. and Lockwood, D. (1993) Inmate drug treatment programmeming in the federal bureau of prisons. In J. Inciardi (Ed.), *Drug treatment and criminal justice* (pp. 194–208). Newbury Park, CA: Sage Publications.

Weissman, M.M., Bruce, M.L., Leaf, P.J., Florio, L.P., and Holzer, C. (1992) Affective disorders. In L.N. Robins and D.A. Regier (Eds.), *Psychiatric disorders in America* (pp. 53–80). New York: Macmillan.

Wellisch, J., Anglin, M.D., and Prendergast, M.L. (1993a) Numbers and characteristics of drug-using women in the criminal justice system: Implications for treatment. *Journal of Drug Issues*, **23**,(1), 7–30.

Wellisch, J., Anglin, M.D., and Prendergast, M.L. (1993b) Treatment strategies for drug-abusing women offenders. In J. Inciardi (Ed.), *Drug treatment and criminal justice* (pp. 5–29). Newbury Park, CA: Sage Publications.

Wellisch, J., Prendergast, M.L., and Anglin, M.D. (1994) *Drug-abusing women offenders: Results of a national survey*. Washington, D.C.: Office of Justice Programmes, National Institute of Justice: Research In Brief, US Department of Justice.

Wexler, H.K. (1993) *Establishing substance abuse treatment programmes in prisons: A practitioner's handbook*. Rockville, MD: Center for Substance Abuse Treatment.

Wexler, H.K., Falkin, G.P., and Lipton, D.S. (1990) Outcome evaluation of a prison therapeutic community for substance abuse treatment. *Criminal Justice and Behavior*, **17**(1), 71–92.

Wexler, H.K., Falkin, G.P., Lipton, D.S., and Rosenblum, A.B. (1992) Outcome evaluation of a prison therapeutic community for substance abuse treatment. In C. Leukefeld and F. Tims (Eds.), *Drug abuse treatment in prisons and jails* (pp.156–175). Research Monograph Series, Vol. 118. Rockville, MD: National Institute on Drug Abuse.

Wexler, H.K. and Lipton, D.S. (1993) From reform to recovery: Advances in prison drug treatment, in J. Inciardi (Ed.), *Drug treatment and criminal justice* (pp. 209–227). Newbury Park, CA: Sage Publications.

Wexler, H.K., and Williams, R. (1986) The Stay'n Out therapeutic community: prison treatment for substance abusers. *Journal of Psychoactive Drugs*, **18**, 221–330.

Chapter 6

DRUG USE AND HIV/AIDS IN SUB-SAHARAN AFRICAN PRISONS

Jude U. Ohaeri

The term sub-Saharan Africa refers to some 41 independent multi-tribal nations, constituting about 400 million of Africa's estimated (1990) population of 661 million, separated from their Arab-Berber North African neighbours by the Sahara desert, and home to the predominantly Negroid 'Black Africans'. Island nations off the coast of Africa, such as Madagascar and Comoros (in the Indian Ocean) are not included, as the populations there are not indigenous 'Black Africans'.

As a political block, they have socio-economic organisations that group them into West Africa (e.g. ECOWAS, ECOMOG), Central Africa, East Africa and Southern Africa (e.g. Southern African Development Community). While there are marked differences in cultural, socio-economic and political circumstances (even within sub-regions), there are interesting continental trends that justify dealing with them together for this review exercise. The common trends appear to have been made possible by the similar experiences of all African nations in the political, social, economic, and cultural realms.

For instance, all have recently undergone devastating colonial experiences. By the time Western European colonialists left Africa (mostly in the 1960s), serious developmental problems had been created that affected all areas of endeavour, especially health care (Rodney, 1972). There is a general lack of a democratic culture, with a frequent resort to military coups, authoritarianism, inter-tribal warfare and religious unrest. Hence the region has the greatest number of refugees in the world.

Economically, excluding the Republic of South Africa, the estimated total industrial manufacturing output in the region is a meagre 12 per cent of the gross domestic product, and its population growth rate is high (about 3 per cent) compared with Europe's (about 1 per cent) (Encyclopaedia Britannica, 1985). This places African nations firmly in the developing world, which has serious implications for health care delivery in general and development of services in prisons in particular.

It is these common trends that have justified previous reviews of mental health care delivery in the region (German, 1972, 1987a, 1987b, Odejide, Oyewunmi and Ohaeri, 1989). Taking its cue from the previous reviews, this chapter will:

(i) highlight the general prison conditions from medical and human rights perspectives;

(ii) present an overview of psychoactive drug use and HIV/AIDS prevalence rates in the general population and in prisons, using representative countries from West, Central, East, and Southern Africa;

(iii) discuss the differences between the patterns in this region and those of developed countries;

(iv) examine remedies for the drug use / HIV situation in prisons.

Relevant literature was acquired from Medline, Index Medicus and the Internet. In addition, colleagues in Africa who have researched into psychoactive substance abuse, HIV/AIDS and prison populations were contacted by post for help in the literature review. This chapter attempts to improve on the limitations of previous works, by examining data from not only the English speaking countries, but also the French and Portuguese worlds of Africa.

Firstly, none of the above sources revealed a single published work on the topic from Arab North Africa. Indeed, the only papers on prisoners from the larger Arab world were from Kuwait (Fido *et al.*, 1992, 1993; Al.-najjar *et al.*, 1996).

Secondly, it appears that researchers in Black Africa have paid scant attention to the medical condition of prisoners; so that, whereas there is an impressive body of reports on human rights in pre-democratic Republic of South Africa (i.e. before 1992), reports on medical conditions and drug use are few and far between. Not surprisingly, most reports have emanated from countries where governments have invested greatly in education, namely, Nigeria, Kenya and Republic of South Africa.

PRISON CONDITIONS

Perhaps it is understandable that prison conditions are inhuman in war torn countries, such as Burundi, Rwanda and Somalia in East Africa, and Congo in Central Africa. The Penal Lexicon Home Page of the Internet cites shocking reports of prison conditions in these countries. In Burundi, for instance, the PRI chairperson, Ahmed Othmani visited the prisons of the country's three main cities, from 29 April to 7 May 1996, accompanied by the International Prison Watch and the Local League of Human Rights (ITEKA). It was noted that the Gitenga prison was holding 215 per cent of its recommended capacity, the Bujumbura (capital city) prison 219 per cent, and the Ngozi men's prison 373 per cent. Official statistics showed that Nuyinga and Ruyigy prisons, each designed for 100 prisoners, were accommodating 567 and 390 respectively. The prisons suffered from a chronic shortage of money, and conditions were very bad: prison guards were untrained and there were not enough of them. Moreover, disease was rife — a typhoid epidemic caused the deaths of 98 prisoners at Ngozi men's prison between October 1995 and March 1996, and the victims of the epidemic were kept together with other prisoners. Of the total prison population of 6159, 80 per cent — 5046 people — were still awaiting trial. Many of those held on remand were suspected of being involved in ethnic cleansing (PRI Newsletter, June 1996).

In neighbouring (i.e. just north) Rwanda, Medicins Sans Frontieres revealed that the conditions in the Gitarama prison were so bad that doctors had to amputate inmates' feet made gangrenous through standing in filth all day and night because there was not enough room to lie down. The prison was reported to hold 7000 prisoners in a space designed to hold 400. Nearly 1000 prisoners died in the disease ridden prison between September 1994 and May 1995.

The Congolese Observatory for Human Rights (1996) has published a report on the living conditions in Congolese prisons. The report described serious problems with food, health, environment, and buildings. According to the report, the prisons were not secure and prisoners come and go at will. However, this situation was necessary for them to get food and medicines in order to survive. The prisons were alleged to be 'dying places and gangsters training centres' (Les Conditions de Detention Dans les Maisons D'Arret du Congo, observatoire Congolais des Droits de L'Homme, Brazaville, February 1996).

What is more difficult to understand is that fairly similar reports emanate from relatively peaceful countries such as Nigeria, Niger, Senegal (West Africa), Kenya (East Africa) and Malawi (South Africa).

In Nigeria, a report from the popular press noted that on average, ten prisoners a week die in two of the main prisons in Lagos (former capital), many of malnutrition (The Independent, 30 January, 1996). In the scientific literature, Olubodun, Jaiyesini, Olasode and Sobowale

(1991), reported on the case of a 22-year old Nigerian prisoner who, within two years of confinement, developed features of malnutrition, with severe sensory and motor neuropathy of the lower limbs and pulmonary tuberculosis. Despite intensive nutritional rehabilitation, this patient did not regain the use of his lower limbs. In another report of the same prison (Olubodun, 1996), it was noted that, compared with a general population sample, the prisoners had significantly higher blood pressure, and lived in overcrowded conditions. Other Nigerian workers have highlighted the issue of overcrowding (Ihezue Okonkwo and Okereke, 1993) and high mortality rates (Mba, 1989; Akinnawo, 1993) in Nigerian prisons.

A most worrisome issue in the popular press is the Nigerian military government's use of prisons for human rights abuses and the large number of people awaiting trial in prisons. Official reports in February 1996 revealed that of the 143 prisons nationwide, 35,750 persons (or 65 per cent of total prison inmate population) were said to be awaiting trial (Adesanya *et al.*, 1997).

In Niger, workers in the field have noted that the prisons are overcrowded. For example, the Central Prison in Niamey (capital) is meant for 300 prisoners, but now accommodates 1200 persons (Ousseini, 1997). In addition, the poor prison conditions have led to filth, tuberculosis is rife, and there is lack of finance, materials and personnel to improve the situation. The women and children are not segregated from the other prisoners.

In Senegal, the Observatoire International des Prisons and allied local groups have published a report on the uprising which took place at the Maison centrale d'Arret in Dakar, Senegal on 29 November 1996. The authors stated that the following factors contributed to the uprising:

(i) very poor relationships between staff and prisoners;
(ii) overcrowding — with 928 prisoners being held in a prison which had space for 475;
(iii) the fact that over 70 per cent of those held in the prison were pre-trial prisoners, the majority of whom had been held for two to four years, without adequate information about their case, or having seen a lawyer;
(iv) very poor hygiene and sanitation;
(v) very low quality food and medical care;
(vi) very limited opportunities for work or education
(Penal Reform International Newsletter, No. 28, March 1997).

From Kenya, reputable newspapers have given some account of prison conditions. The Kenyan Assistant Minister for Home Affairs, when replying to a question in parliament, stated that the Kenyan prison system contains 41,064 prisoners, which represents an overcrowding rate of 30 per cent. Of these, 12,039 (29.3 per cent) were on remand. This Member of Parliament claimed that Kenya's prisons had 'become the most notorious in the world' (East African Standard and Daily Nation, 23 October 1996).

In Southern Africa, in the apartheid era (i.e. up to 1992), while the world was inundated with information about human rights abuses (London and Dowdall, 1993), there was relative silence on the goings on in the so called free African states, such as Malawi under Kamuzu Banda (1964–1993). Peltzer (1995) has given a detailed account of the degrading prison conditions in Malawi in that 30-year period. This was a follow up to earlier reports by Amnesty International (1992, 1994) and other workers (Grotrian et al., 1992, Lwanda, 1993). In a country of 8.5 million people, it is estimated that well over 250,000 persons had been detained without trial; so that no village had been left untouched by detention or disappearances. Amnesty International reported that 285 people were packed into a single cell, prisoners were chained and beaten and tortured by use of electric shocks, as well as a frightening unexplained pattern of death while under custody. It was noted that the poor conditions in the prisons were caused by over-crowding, Malawi's poverty, and the culture of punishment which pre-vailed under Banda. Detainees and prisoners (sharing accommodation) suffered from the denial of reading and recreational materials and the denial of medical treatment was the norm. It was also stated that women prisoners faced frequent rapes and pregnancies, for example at Zomba prison.

The ex-detainees whom Peltzer interviewed reported that priests were banned from visiting them. The latest arrival slept next to the bucket for the toilet. 'After twenty two people had emptied their urine and something else into it, your first job in the morning would be to carry the bucket outside for emptying. The only consolation was that there were so many new arrivals that one did not sleep next to the bucket for more than two days' (Peltzer, p. 231). Also in some prisons, 'the cell was 3 × 2 metres, just bare floor, no toilet facilities, not even a bucket, one had to urinate on the floor' (Peltzer, pg. 237). Peltzer com-mented that, 'in comparison in Malawi 62 per cent interviewees had a history of physical torture and 50–70 per cent a history of severe mental torture.' London and Dowdall (1993) reviewed three studies of torture victims in South Africa where a history of physical torture was found in 72–89 per cent of the cases and history of mental torture in 78–83 per cent of the cases (Peltzer, pg. 240).

It appears that similar prison conditions existed in the West African state of Chad, where Jaffe (1992) found in a study of treating torture victims in Chad that 34 per cent presented with symptoms related to post traumatic stress disorder.

In democratic Republic of South Africa, a recent report (Puppets in Prison Project, 1996) indicated that, whereas accommodation exists for 95,000 prisoners, there were 120,000 prisoners occupying this space. It was alleged that South African prisons were not only over-crowded, but also were rife with gangs and violence. The report claimed that 'sex is often a chip that is bargained for by prisoners in return for favours or protection from a particular gang or cell boss. It is therefore likely, that the prevalence of HIV in prisons will be at least equal to that in society generally'. The authors stated that prisoners' grievances included forced segregation, inadequate medical care, breaches of confidentiality and denial of access to work and recreational facilities. They claimed that phenomena such as rape, prostitution, sodomy and sexual violence occur and are extremely difficult to control inside prison.

PRISON MEDICAL SERVICES

From the foregoing, it is clear that governments in Black Africa have conceived of prisons as a place for punishing criminals and deterring their political opponents. It is, therefore, not surprising that in the face of scarce funding for providing essential social services to the general population, scant attention has been paid to the development of medical services in prisons. Even in the potentially more economically affluent nations such as Nigeria, health care allocation has stagnated at two per cent of the national budget, far less than the five per cent recommended by the World Health Organisation. The problem with health care in prisons is further compounded by the fact that Ministries of Health have no direct input in health care delivery in prisons.

Coupled with the well known problem of shortage of medical doctors, the vast majority of these countries do not even have a separate prison medical service. What seems to prevail is that prison authorities liase with nearby hospitals for the treatment of sick inmates, who are then brought to the out-patient clinic in handcuffs. Alternatively, the mentally ill who have offended against the law are admitted compulsorily in psychiatric hospitals at state capitals; many of these psychiatric hospitals do not have psychiatrists, and certainly no facility for secure detention.

The situation of medical services in prisons in the Republic of South Africa is an understandable exception to the rule, and the standards are fairly comparable to the situation in the developed countries of Europe and North America. However, in response to a recent damning report on prison health care at South Africa's Polismoor Prison, it was noted that, compared with the situation when the prison was opened over two decades ago, the authorities were now having to care for twice as many inmates, with half as many doctors and 21 per cent fewer nurses and orderlies (Aginsky and Craven, 1996).

Nigeria provides an example for understanding prison medical services in the few countries that have developed such a service. In Nigeria, all prisons are under Federal control. There is a well established administrative structure for prison medical services, headed by a medical doctor of the rank of Assistant Controller of prisoners, who reports directly to the Controller General of prisons. However, many prisons have no medical doctors, none have regular psychiatric service and there is chronic shortage of medication in the dispensaries (Asuni, 1986). In the south-eastern town of Enugu, although a hospital located within the prisons should cater for those with mental disorders, there is no resident or regular psychiatric cover (Ihezue et al., 1982, 1993). Prisoners with severe mental disorders are usually treated as in-patients in nearby psychiatric hospitals. Curiously, formal psychiatric services in Nigeria owe their origin to the need to cater for criminals with psychotic disorders (Boroffka, 1975). Hence Nigeria has the skeletal structure upon which a credible prison medical service can be built; and in spite of the noted inadequacies, it is unfortunately in advance of the situation in the vast majority of countries in the region (except South Africa and Zimbabwe). For example, in Niger, the hospital in the Central Prison is said to be badly equipped with only one nurse, poor hygienic conditions and poor ventilation, which has been responsible for the outbreak of tuberculosis of a strong virulent strain requiring hospitalisation (Ousseini, 1990).

It appears that a comparative standard (with Nigeria) of prison medical services exists in Kenya and Tanzania. In Kenya, offenders with severe mental disorders are hospitalised at the Mathari Mental

Hospital (Muluka and Acuda, 1978). In Tanzania, such patients are treated at a special hospital, Isanga Institution, modelled along special hospitals in England, such as Rampton Hospital (Mbatia and Ferguson, 1993).

MENTAL DISORDERS IN PRISONS

In order to have a deeper understanding of drug abuse problems in prisons, it is useful to firstly consider the situation with the broader group of mental disorders under which addictive behaviour is classified. Earlier reviews of psychiatric problems in the region, which made no reference to prison conditions, had come to the following conclusions (German, 1972, 1987; Odejide *et al.*, 1989):

(i)   the broad group of mental disorders described in European and North American cultures are also seen in Black Africa, except eating disorders (e.g anorexia nervosa and bulimia), which seem to be culture-bound to the Caucasian world and related groups;
(ii) in the clinical psychiatric setting, the commoner forms of depression seen are of mild-moderate severity, with relative uncommoness of symptoms of severe depression, and preponderance of somatic symptoms;
(iii) also in the clinical setting, there is relative uncommoness of personality disorders;
(iv) schizophrenia is the commonest cause of psychiatric hospitalisation, followed by mania. In the case of mania, many patients show the unipolar form instead of the bipolar (manic-depressive) variety (Makanjuola, 1985).

However, there are some reports from Uganda (Orley and Wing, 1979) and Zambia (Rwegellera, 1981) which indicate patterns of depressive symptomatology similar to Caucasian cultures. Also from Uganda, Assael and German (1970) reported on a comparative study of psychiatric morbidity among University students from Makerere in Uganda, Belfast and Edinburgh in the UK. They found the following prevalence rates for personality disorders: 7.4 per cent for Uganda, 7.0 per cent for Belfast, and 5.2 per cent for Edinburgh. It would be interesting to see how this general population situation is reflected in prisons.

This review is limited by the virtual lack of published works on psychiatric morbidity in prison populations, outside of Nigeria. Even in South Africa with a generous presence of psychiatric researchers, the available papers in this regard are mostly concerned with mental disorders among former political detainees who suffered from denial of human rights during the apartheid era.

On the other hand, there is an impressive number of works from Nigeria. However, most of these studies are based on psychiatric evaluation of either criminals referred to hospitals for treatment (Makanjuola and Olaomo, 1981; Baiyewu, 1988; Abiodun, 1986; Ihezue *et al.*, 1993; Akinnawo, 1993; Udofia, 1997), homicide cases in prisons (Asuni, 1969; Agomoh, 1993), or retrospective reviews of forensic cases in long-stay units of hospitals (Odejide, 1981; Ogunlesi, 1988). Less commonly, there have been systematic assessments of prison populations for personality disorders (Enyidah, 1993), general psychiatric morbidity (Agbahowe *et al.*, 1998) and drug abuse (Adesanya *et al.*, 1997), using modern standard instruments. In the studies that focused on hospitalised mentally ill offenders, schizophrenia (mostly of the paranoid type) was the commonest diagnosis (43 per cent to 75 per cent); and other diagnostic categories were epilepsy (6 per cent to 18.5 per cent), personality disorders (15 per cent) and drug abuse (19.5 per cent). Of the studies that assessed homicide cases in prisons, schizophrenia (27 per cent to 50 per cent) was again the commonest diagnosis. When personality disorders were systematically assessed in a maximum security prison, it was found that 52 per cent (of 213 males) fulfilled ICD-10 criteria for personality disorders. However assessment for personality disorders among patients compulsorily admitted in hospital by the courts suggested that there were no 'psychopaths' in one study (Baiyewu, 1988); while a second study diagnosed only 1.1 per cent (out of 354) as having psychopathy, which was significantly higher than the figure for a control group of psychiatric patients (0.3 per cent) (Udofia, 1997). In the most recent study of 100 inmates of a medium security hospital, six subjects were diagnosed as having antisocial personality disorder, using DSM-III-R criteria (Agbahowe *et al.*, 1998).

Reports from Kenya and Tanzania support the Nigerian findings. In a study of a group of criminal patients at Kenya's main mental hospital, Mathari Mental Hospital, no single case of 'psychopathic disorder' was found (Muluka and Acuda, 1978).

However, Mbatia and Ferguson (1995–1996), in a comparative study of mentally ill offenders at Isanga Institution (a special hospital in Tanzania for criminals) with patients in a similar special hospital in England (Rampton Hospital), reported the following prevalence rates: of 75 subjects assessed at Isanga, 44 (58.7 per cent) had schizophrenia/paranoid states; 7 (9.3 per cent) had affective psychoses; 9 (12 per cent) had transient organic psychotic conditions; 8 (10.7 per cent) had neurotic disorders; 2 (2.7 per cent) had alcohol and drug psychoses; 5 (6.7 per cent) had a primary diagnosis of personality disorders (all ICD-9 diagnoses).

However, on the whole, 55 per cent had personality disorder because 54 per cent of the schizophrenic patients had co-morbid personality disorder (using the Personality Assessment Schedule — Tyrer and Alexander, 1979). In the English sample, 30 (40 per cent) had primary diagnosis of personality disorders. Of the English sample, 79 per cent of them had personality disorder, because 60 per cent of the schizophrenics were thought to have co-morbid personality disorder.

In Southern Africa, references to the condition of political detainees in Malawi (Peltzer, 1995–96) and the Republic of South Africa (Forster and Sandler, 1985; Solomons, 1989) indicate high levels of psychic distress and frank mental disorders among prisoners in these countries. In particular, post–traumatic stress disorder was diagnosed in at least 30 per cent of political detainees (Peltzer, 1995–1996).

PSYCHOACTIVE SUBSTANCE USE DISORDERS IN PRISONS

It will be useful to view drug problems in prisons from the broader perspective of substance use disorders in the general population. Surprisingly, the many studies on substance abuse in the general population have paid scant attention to the situation in prisons. For instance, in a recent edition of the journal, 'Drugs: Education, Prevention and Policy' (1996) devoted to the situation in sub-Saharan Africa, none of the papers made any mention of prison populations. However, the papers from English speaking (Gureje and Obikoya, 1992; Ohaeri and Odejide, 1993) and French speaking (Facy et al., 1995, 1996) West Africa, as well as East Africa (Mwenesi, 1995) and Southern Africa (Thony and Sethna, 1995; McDonald, 1996), give the reviewer enough materials to indicate general patterns of drug use in the region's general population :

(i) Although the absolute use of psychoactive products is increasing, the data provided by African countries to specialised agencies of the United Nations reveal a fairly low level of drug abuse (Facy et al., 1995, 1996).

(ii) While the lowest alcohol consumption rates are in the former British West African colonies (Nigeria, Ghana, etc.), alcohol abuse in East, Central, and Southern Africa is a major cause of health and social problems (McDonald, 1996). In Swaziland for instance, it is estimated that the per capita consumption in the country's 'urban corridor' is in excess of 20 litres of pure alcohol per annum among the area's 85,000 residents (Malepe, 1989). In South Africa, there are reportedly over one million alcoholics, representing 5.8 per cent of South Africans over 15 years of age.

(iii) Even allowing for rates of alcohol problems, cannabis is the drug most responsible for drug-related admissions in psychiatric hospitals (Ohaeri and Odejide, 1993). South Africa has the dubious distinction (according to a 1995 report by the commission on narcotics of the UNO's Economic and Social Council) of being the largest producer of cannabis in the world, apart from Mexico and Morocco (McDonald, 1996). Cannabis is reportedly more popular than alcohol among addicts in Kenya, a country with high drinking rates (Beckerleg, Telfer and Sizi, 1996).

(iv) While Nigeria's city of Lagos was the leading port of entry for heroin and cocaine in Africa in the 1980s and early 1990s, stiff checks by the drug enforcement agency have drastically curtailed the situation by the mid 1990s, and now attention has shifted to countries such as Senegal, Cote D'Ivore, Benin (in West Africa), Kenya's coastal towns (e.g Mombasa) and South Africa. Although the use of heroin and cocaine has penetrated disadvantaged communities, it is still more likely to be limited to high income users. Even in relatively high income South Africa, the UNDCP (1993) estimated that cocaine abuse is not yet manifest as a major problem. Although there are allegedly growing problems of heroin use in East and Southern Africa (but no hard data), heroin abuse is perceived as on the low side throughout the region. A unanimous finding is the lack of available data suggesting that intravenous injecting is a preferred method of use, although isolated cases have been reported. Rather, sniffing or smoking (chasing the dragon) is the most common ingestion method. For instance, Kenya's national profile of 383 drug abusers found only 24 who used heroin, and only two of those who injected (Mwenesi, 1995).

In another report from Kenya, Beckerleg *et al.* (1996) noted that in a town where they instituted a rehabilitation programme for heroin users (Watamu), heroin was not injected there, and nor was it injected in the neighbouring town. Heroin use in these towns was by young people associated with the tourist industry. They attributed the absence of IV injecting to the difficulty of obtaining injecting equipment and lack of knowledge about how to use syringes. Van Burgh (1996) concluded that although South Africa has not yet reached the level of substance abuse evident in Europe and the Americas, there is undoubtedly much cause for concern. Indeed, recent press reports from Cape Town (October, 1997) indicate that vigilante groups (mostly Muslim youths) in settlements outside the town have engaged drug dealers in street battles.

In reflection of the general population situation, the available reports and the responses of the workers in the field to this author's enquiries indicate the following pattern in prisons:

(i) abuse of psychoactive substances is on a far lower scale than that reported from Western Europe and North America (Maden, Swinton and Gunn, 1991, 1992; Covell, 1993).
(ii) Cannabis is the most common drug abused by prisoners.
(iii) The use of heroin and cocaine is very rare.
(iv) Intravenous injecting of drugs is virtually unknown in prisons.

Offenders referred for assessment in psychiatric hospitals predominantly use cannabis. Of 146 offenders seen over a period of 10 years at Nigeria's Neuropsychiatric Hospital, Aro, Abeokuta, 'drug abuse and dependence' (not rigorously defined) was evident among 29 subjects, all of whom used cannabis (Ogunlesi et al., 1988). Also, armed robbers at the prison in the Nigerian mid-western town of Benin City were found to have commonly used cannabis and alcohol on daily basis before the commission of crime (Adamson and Malomo, 1991).

Out of those who used drugs among the prisoners interviewed in 84 prison facilities in the French speaking African states of Benin, Madagascar, and Cote D' Ivoire, 80 per cent used cannabis, while 11 per cent used heroin: compared with 54 per cent (cannabis) and 9 per cent (heroin) for abusers in general hospitals and psychiatric facilities (Facy et al., 1995–1996). However, occasional users were more common than regular users of these drugs.

In comparing the socio-demographic characteristics of drug abusers in prisons with those of drug abusers in general and psychiatric hospitals in these French speaking African States, it was found that:

(i) Gender distribution was similar, with women being under-represented by about 13 per cent, and more so in the prison group.
(ii) Marital status was similar in both groups, with single people more numerous (75 per cent) among imprisoned subjects than in hospital patients (65 per cent; $p > 0.05$).

(iii) Whereas 68 per cent of prison drug abusers were under 30 years of age, the corresponding percentage in hospital group was 48 per cent ($p = 0.005$)

(iv) Illiteracy was more frequent among prison drug abusers (21.7 per cent) than in hospital patients (2 per cent) ($p = 0.00001$).

(v) Heroin abuse in prison was found only in Benin and Cote D'Ivore, not in Madagascar.

In a maximum security prison at Ibadan (Nigeria), 36 per cent (of 213 males) were said to be abusers of drugs, all of whom were using cannabis (Enyidah, 1993). In a recent systematic study of another prison population in Nigeria (all males, the majority of whom were awaiting trial), using DSM-III criteria, cannabis was the only drug regularly used in the past month by 6.6 per cent (of 395 subjects), out of whom eleven (42.3 per cent of 26) satisfied criteria for dependence. Use of intravenous drugs was not evident. The majority of cannabis users had been in prison for less than six months and were on charges of theft and armed robbery. In the past month, none of the subjects had used heroin and cocaine. The subjects (one each) who admitted using volatile hydrocarbons, 'Chinese Capsule', and diazepam in the past month, reported only occasional use of these substances (Adesanya et al., 1997).

In a similar systematic assessment of 100 convicted inmates of another Nigerian prison, it was found that 25 inmates had only past histories of drug abuse prior to imprisonment, including cannabis (11 per cent) and alcohol (13 per cent). None admitted current use of illicit drugs (Agbahowe et al., 1998).

From Tanzania (East Africa) Mbatia and Ferguson (1995–1996) reported that of 75 inmates assessed at a prison mental hospital only two (2.6 per cent) were labelled as having 'alcohol and drug psychoses'.

From the reported experiences of political detainees in Malawi one gets the impression that cannabis use is probably high among prisoners in Southern Africa. One of the ex-detainees interviewed by Peltzer (1995–1996) remarked that they smoked 'Indian Hemp so as to distance ourselves from reality; we used to satisfy ourselves sexually during the long night'. Apparently, drug use was so rampant that, when they were called for release (after 15 months of detention), they thought they were going to be punished for tobacco smuggling.

HIV/AIDS AND SEXUAL PRACTICES IN PRISONS

It is in the area of HIV/AIDS that prison populations have received appreciable attention in sub-Saharan Africa. The surprising thing among these investigators is that whereas HIV has been strongly associated with drug abuse in developed countries and unprotected sex in Africa, (Power, Markova and Rowlands, 1991; Bird *et al.*, 1992), they paid no attention to drug use problems. For instance, of the factors listed to be responsible for the spread of HIV in Mozambique, drug abuse was not even mentioned (Vaz, Gloyd, and Trindale, 1996).

The interest in HIV studies in African prisons has been in response to the widely reported high rates in European and American countries, and also partly due to the dubious claim of HIV originating in Central Africa. In Britain, it was reported that, according to Her Majesty's Prison Service about 35 prisoners are known to be HIV positive at any one time (BMJ News, February, 1995). Elsewhere, HIV prevalence in prisons was reported as being 23 per cent in New York, US (Floria *et al.*, 1992); 16.5 per cent in Sao Paulo, Brazil (Lorence *et al.*, 1992); and 16.1 per cent in Genoa, Italy (Icard *et al.*, 1992). In the US, the incidence of AIDS is 14 times higher in State and Federal prisons (202 cases per 100,000) than in the US general population (14.65 cases per 100,000), and this difference is thought to be due to the over representation of persons with histories of high-risk behaviour, especially intravenous drug abuse (American College of Physicians, *et al.*, Position Paper, 1992).

In the midst of the AIDS scare in Africa, especially with the alarming reports from Ivory Coast, (De Cock *et al.*, 1990), a US based group mounted a broad based study in major urban areas in six West African States in 1985–87, involving 4,248 individuals (Kanki, *et al.*, 1987). Participants were categorised into control group (healthy people, pregnant women, prisoners, hospital patients), those at risk (prostitutes, STD patients) and those with disease associated with AIDS (e.g. tuberculosis). The prison population consisted of 55 inmates from Burkina Faso and 282 from Ivory coast. Total HIV seroprevalence rates were as follows :

(i) Senegal: 0 per cent (0/426) for the control population, 0.7 per cent (3/422) for the risk group, and 1.1 per cent (2/178) for the disease group.

(ii) Guinea: 0.6 per cent (2/314) for the control group, 0 per cent (0/13) for the risk group, and 0.8 per cent (1/131) for the disease group.

(iii) Guinea Bissau: 0 per cent (0/151) for the control population; 0/39 for the risk group, and 0/273 for the disease group.

(iv) Mauritania: 0 per cent (0/140) for the control group, 0 per cent (0/9) for the risk group and 5.7 per cent (2/35) for the disease group.

(v) Burkina Faso: 0.5 per cent (2/416) for the control group, 13.2 per cent (45/340) for the risk group, and 4.5 per cent (1/22) for the disease group.

(vi) Ivory Coast (Cote D'Ivore): 3.7 per cent (38/1067) for the control group, 19.8 per cent (46/232) for the risk group, and 10 per cent (4/40) for the disease group.

In particular, the HIV seroprevalence among prisoners was, 1.8 per cent in Burkina Faso, and 6.7 per cent in Cote D'Ivore.

The investigators found only five cases of diagnosed AIDS among the 4248 individuals. They concluded that HTLV-4 is the more prevalent than the T-lymphotropic virus in West Africa.

Another group from Western Europe studied the trends in the prevalence of HIV infection in different populations in Gabon (Central/West Africa) from 1986 to 1994, involving 7082 individuals in Libreville (the capital) and 1657 (771 pregnant women, 886 healthy) individuals from Franceville, another town. The study involved 1808 prisoners, of which 650 were tested in 1986 and 1,158 in 1994. It was found that HIV prevalence was relatively low and remained stable (0.7–1.6 per cent in pregnant women, 2.1–2.2 per cent in the general population). The prevalence was also stable among prisoners, 2.1 per cent in 1986 and 2.7 per cent in 1994, which was similar to the general population rates. However, there were marked increases in HIV rates for infectious diseases and tuberculosis patients suggesting that the HIV epidemic in Gabon is still in its early stages and may not yet have reached a plateau. The authors stated that their findings were similar to those of workers in Cameroon, a nearby West African country.

Another country that has received media attention on AIDS is Zaire (now Democratic Republic of Congo) following recognition of AIDS there in 1983. By the time Belgian and American researchers came to carry out their study in October, 1984, it was noted that about 15 AIDS cases were being diagnosed at the Mama Yemo Hospital weekly (a 2000-bed hospital in Kinshasha). However, of 2384 hospital workers investigated, 152 (6.4 per cent) were found to be seropositive, indicating low risks for occupational transmission of HIV (Mann, *et al.*, 1986). When the tests were repeated in 1986 among 2002 workers from the same hospital, HIV seroprevalence was found to be 8.7 per cent, indicating a cumulative incidence of new HIV infection of 3.2 per cent (N'Galy *et al.*, 1988). The same group reported HIV rates among pregnant women and blood donors from 1984 to 1986 which were similar. Among pregnant women aged 20–30 years, HIV rates increased from 8.9 per cent (of 1,281) to 9.2 per cent (of 3339) participants; and in those aged over 30, the increase was 6.3 per cent (of 300) to 6.7 per cent (of 1551). Among blood donors aged over 30 years, there was actually a decrease from 6.2 per cent (of 247) to 5.9 per cent (of 2416).

In a study of 340 men attending an STD clinic in Kenya, at which the HIV seroprevalence rate was 11.2 per cent, it was concluded that heterosexual genital intercourse was the only likely route by which sexually active men in Nairobi acquire HIV infection. (Simonsen *et al.*, 1988).

However, along with these relatively low prevalence rates, high prevalence rates have been reported in other large towns, such as Kampala (Uganda), Lusaka (Zambia) and Blantyre (Malawi), where HIV prevalence levels in pregnant women is said to be well above 20 per cent (Mertens *et al.*, 1994; Buve *et al.*, 1995). According to recent information, from World Health Organisation Global Programme on AIDS (WHO, 1995), in 1994 Zimbabwe and Botswana (in Southern Africa) had the highest per capita incidences of AIDS cases in Africa. The latest figures from Botswana (NACP, 1995), where it is acknowledged that HIV/AIDS data are more reliable than in many other African countries, show that 34.8 per cent of all females aged between 20 and 24 are now HIV infected.

Unfortunately, we have little data on HIV in prison populations from these African countries where high seroprevalence rates have been reported. For example, in Zambia, the HIV seroprevalence among prisoners was 16.1 per cent at a time when the HIV prevalence among pregnant women in Lusaka was 11.6 per cent (Maboshe, *et al.*, 1989; Torrey and Way, 1990).

The data available on HIV in prisons are from countries where, according to available empirical as opposed to impressions from the media, the HIV rates are relatively low. Kebede *et al.* (1991), in a study of 450 prisoners from Ethiopia's Dire Dawa District prison in 1988, reported that HIV-1 antibody was detected in 39 (6.0 per cent) of prisoners, while 141 (31.6 per cent) had a positive VDRL titre. Older prisoners were 2.5 times more likely to be HIV seropositive, and a shorter stay in prison (less than three months) was significantly associated with HIV-1 seropositivity. Prisoners with prostitute contact before prison were 2.5 times more likely to be HIV-1 seropositive than those prisoners who denied such contact, although this did not reach statistical significance. None of the prisoners reported homosexuality, and there was no mention of drug use problems. However, seropositivity rates of 16 per cent to 60 per cent were reported among high risk groups in Ethiopia, such as prostitutes (Ayehunie *et al.*, 1987), and the general HIV seroprevalence rate in Ethiopia was two per cent among blood donors (National AIDS Prevention and Control Unit, 1990). By January 1990, 285 AIDS cases had been reported in that nation. Between 1987 to 1989 in Bophuthatswana, South Africa (population 1–9 million), a sentinel network was mounted of all the eleven hospitals, and three prisons to assess the degree of endemicity of HIV, involving 19,941 persons of all ages. In April to August 1989, a stratified multistage random sample of the resident population aged 15 years and older, was conducted, involving 1553 subjects. In the first study of hospitals and prisons, HIV rates were: 0.07 per cent for 1987, 0.16 per cent for 1988, and 0.24 per cent for 1989. Overall, 34 blood samples were positive yielding a rate of 0.17 per cent (of 19,941). Of particular note was the fact that of the 3875 prison inmates involved, none was HIV positive (Tshibangu, 1993).

In the larger Republic of South Africa, the authors of the 'Puppets in Prison Project'(1996) noted that the country's Department of Correctional Services reported the existence of only 722 HIV/AIDS cases on 30 June 1996, out of a total prison population of 118,597 (i.e. 0.61 per cent). They commented that since compulsory HIV testing was stopped in 1994, it was impossible to determine how many prisoners were carrying the virus. In spite of this standpoint, the authors went to claim (without any supporting data) that current HIV infection rate estimates ranged between 15 per cent to 30 per cent. Accordingly, the Minister of Correctional Services was successfully lobbied to announce a change in policy on the issue of condoms in prison and the isolation of HIV positive prisoners. A declaration of intent was made in May 1996 that condoms were now to be freely issued in South African prisons, and prisoners infected with HIV were no longer to be isolated from the general prison population. It is noteworthy that, in this fairly voluminous report, no mention was made of the role of drug abuse and IV injecting in HIV rates in the prisons of South Africa.

In Mozambique, which has recently emerged from a protracted civil war, a cross-sectional study was carried out among 1,284 male and 54 female prisoners in three prisons and one jail in Maputo, from September 1990 to February, 1991, to assess the prevalence of and risk factors for syphilis and HIV. The authors noted that there was no reported intravenous drug use (Vaz *et al.*, 1995). One hundred and four (7.8 per cent) inmates had positive serological tests for syphilis, while 8 (0.6 per cent) had HIV antibodies. The HIV positive cases were all males, six of whom were positive for HIV-1, one for HIV-2 and one for both viruses; all had previous STD diagnoses, and five had been in prison for less than 90 days. Seventy men (5.5 per cent) reported having had sexual intercourse while in prison, and in all but one instance, this involved sex with another man. The first case of AIDS was reported in Mozambique in 1986. Seroepidemiological studies carried out in Maputo province in 1990 demonstrated a HIV prevalence of 0.9 per cent among blood donors, 4 per cent among war displaced persons, and 3.7 per cent among soldiers. Again, of the factors thought to be responsible for HIV in Mozambique, there was no mention of drug abuse. Cannabis use while in prison was reported by 379 (26 per cent) men and 9 (17 per cent) women, but was not significantly associated with syphilis.

Based on the above findings, the Mozambiqan workers selected 300 inmates from the largest prison (Machava prison) and put them through a period of health education from July to December, 1993. It was found that a large proportion of the prisoners had high risk behaviours for HIV (65 per cent had two or more sexual partners per month and 39 per cent had a history of STD) and low AIDS knowledge at incarceration (Vaz et al., 1996). Statistically significant increases in knowledge occurred after the intervention.

Similarly in West African states, relatively low levels of HIV seroprevalence has been reported among prison inmates. The HIV seroprevalence (0.4 per cent) among male inmates in Dakar, Senegal, was not significantly different from Dakar blood donors in the same period (Samb et al., 1989; Torrey and Way, 1990). At the central prison in Niamey (Niger) Ousseini (1990) studied 660 inmates. He noted that drug use by intravenous injection was non existent, but that homosexual practices probably occurred. It was found that 3 (0.45 per cent) of the prisoners were HIV positive. One each had HIV-1 and HIV-2 respectively, while a third subject had HIV-1 and HIV-2. This rate was similar to the general population rate of 0.5 per cent. He noted that, in the badly equipped medical room, the nurse boils the necessary hospital equipment for at least half an hour, thus making transmission from injections almost non existent. Hence, the impression is that homosexual practices are the cause of HIV transmission, although there are no available data to support this. A supply of condoms has, therefore, been given by the authorities, but the condoms are not accepted in a strongly religious country where over 95 per cent are Muslims.

CONCLUSION

It is not surprising that the poor prison conditions highlighted above are a reflection of the political instability and low socio-economic indices in Black Africa. It appears that African governments are too preoccupied with political survival to be seriously concerned with the situation in prisons. The implication of this is that resourceful individuals and non-governmental organisations (NGOs) should intervene.

The problem with the better known NGOs is that they seem to be more concerned with the human rights of detained politicians and other high profile persons. There is a need for enterprise by NGOs in the area of improving the actual material living circumstances of prisoners. Another problem is that of the large number of people who are interminably awaiting trial in African prisons. Studies have shown that their self-concept is significantly more impaired than controls (Onyeneje and Eyo, 1996). These are the most urgent needs of prisoners in the region. It is such enterprise that will persuade governments to organise credible prison medical services.

In a way one could say that the prisons in the region are fortunate to have such a relatively low level of drug abuse and HIV prevalence rates, for the available resources would not be able to cope with the magnitude of drug abuse and HIV problems found in the prisons of developed countries. However, in keeping with the observation that the prison situation is a reflection of events in the outside, the HIV prevalence rate was relatively high in Zambian prisons, a country with one of the highest HIV rates. The trend is that we should expect relatively high HIV seroprevalence rates in the prisons of Uganda, and Malawi. In view of the fact that HIV is a problem that tends to grow if unchecked, workers in the countries with relatively low prevalence rate cannot afford to take things for granted. Considering the widely reported sexual practices in these prisons, even the relatively low prevalence rates could escalate if control measures are not taken.

It is, therefore, gratifying to see that NGOs and researchers in Mozambique (Vaz et al., 1996) and South Africa (Puppets in Prison, 1996) have pioneered efforts aimed at the prevention of spread of HIV in prisons. These methods of health education using inmate peers appear to be much more culturally appropriate than the Caucasian model of condom distribution, as the experience in Niger has shown (Ousseini, 1990).

In marked contradistinction to the situation in developed countries, the drug abuse problem in African prisons is mainly related to cannabis use. The problem is greater in maximum security prisons than in medium security ones. This is an area where NGOs that have interest in psychological services can do fruitful work, as is being attempted in Nigeria and South Africa (Solomons, 1989). One problem with cannabis use is that it tends to fuel the psychotic symptoms which are quite common among prisoners in Africa. One way to safeguard the mental health condition of those with mental disorders is that prison warders should be specifically delegated to see that such inmates do not get involved in the use of cannabis. But the question really is whether drug abuse could be rife in prisons where the workers do not collaborate. Hence attention to the training and welfare of workers, as well as establishment of adequate staffing positions, among other things, can enhance efforts geared towards controlling the spread of drug abuse and HIV in prisons.

References

Abiodun, O. (1986) *A study of mentally ill offenders in a Nigerian prison psychiatric unit.* Unpublished thesis submitted to the Nigerian Postgraduate Medical College, Lagos.

Adamson, T.O. and Malomo, I.O. (1991) Psychological profiles of some armed robbers in Bendel State, Nigeria. *Nigerian Medical Journal*, 21, 41–44.

Adesanya, A. ; Ohaeri, J.U., Ogunlesi, A.O. Adamson, T.A. and Odejide, A.O. (1997) Psychoactive substance abuse among inmates of a Nigerian prison population. *Drug and Alcohol Dependence*, 47, 39–44.

Africa: In: The New Encyclopedia Britanica, Vol.13, Macropaedia: knowledge in Depth. Chicago, Encyclopaedia Britanica, 1985. Rodney, W. (1972). How Europe Underdeveloped Africa. Bogle-L'Ouverture Publications, London.

Agbahowe, S.A., Ohaeri, J.U. ; Ogunlesi, A.O. and Osahon, R. (1998) The prevalence of psychiatric morbidity among convicted inmates in a Nigerian prison community. *East African Medical Journal*, 75 (1), 16–23

Aginsky, M. and Craven, S.A. (1996) Prison health care. *South African Medical Journal*, 86 (6), 691 (letter).

Agomoh, A. (1993) *A comparative study of the psychopathology of homicidal offenders and non-violent offenders in a maximum security prison in Lagos State.* Unpublished Fellowship Thesis submitted to the Nigerian Postgraduate Medical College.

Akinnawo, E.O. (1993) Prevalence of psychopathological symptoms in a Nigerian prison. *Psychopathologie Africaine*, 25(1), 93–104.

Al.-najjar, M., and Clarke, D.D. (1996) Self-esteem and trait anxiety in relation to drug misuse in Kuwait. *Substance Use and Misuse*, 31, (7), 937–943.

American College of Physicians, *et al.* (1992) The crisis in Correctional Health Care: The Impact of the National Drug Control Strategy on Correctional Health services. *Annals of Internal Medicine*, 117, (1), 71–77.

Amnesty International (1992) *Malawi: Prison conditions, cruel punishments and detention without trial*. London: Amnesty International

Amnesty International (1994) *Malawi: a new future for human rights*. London: Amnesty International.

Asuni, T. (1969) Homicide in Western Nigeria. *British Journal of Psychiatry*, 115, 1105–1110.

Asuni, T. (1986) Mental health in prisons: the African perspective. *International Journal of Offender Therapy and Comparative Criminology*, 30, (1), 22–??.

Ayehunie, S., Britton, S., and Yemane Berman, T. (1987) Prevalence of Anti-HIV antibodies in prostitutes and their clients in Addis Ababa, Ethiopia (Abstract), *Scandinavian Journal of Immunology*, 26, 304.

Baiyewu, O. (1988) Compulsory admission of psychiatric patients in Yola. *Nigerian Medical Journal*, 18, (1), 303–357.

Beckerleg, S., Telfer, M., and Sizi, A.K. (1996) Private Struggles, public support rehabilitating heroin users in Kenya. *Drugs: Education, Prevention and Policy*, 3, (2), 159–169.

Bird, A.G., Gore, S.M., Jolliffe, D.W., and Burns, S.M. (1992) Anonymous HIV surveillance in Saughton Prison, Edinburgh. *AIDS*, 6, 725–733.

Boroffka, A. (1975) The provision of psychiatric services in developing countries: Nigeria an example. *African Journal of Psychiatry*, 13, 1–7.

British Medical Journal (1995): News, 310, 4th February, p. 278.

Buve, A., Carael, M., Hayes, R., and Robinson, N. (1995) Variations in HIV prevalence between urban areas in Sub-Saharan and Africa: do we understand them? *AIDS*, 9, (suppl. A), S103–S109.

Covell, R.G., Frischer, M., Taylor, A., Goldberg, D., Green, S., Mokegarey, N. and Bloor, A.L. (1993) Prison experiences of injecting drug users in Glasgow. *Drug and Alcohol Dependence*, 32, 9–14.

De Cock, K.M., Barrere, B., and Diably, Y. (1990) AIDS — the leading cause of death in the West African city of Abidjan, Ivory Coast. *Science*, 249, 793–796.

Delaporte, E., Janssens, W., Pecters, M., Buve, A. *et al*. (1996) Epidemiological and molecular characteristics of HIV infection in Gabon, 1986–1994. *AIDS*, 10, 903–910

Enyidah, SN (1993) *Personality disorder in a Nigerian prison community*. Unpublished Fellowship Thesis submitted to the West African Postgraduate Medical College.

Facy, F., Gueye, M., Ahyi, R.G., and Kalasa, B. (1995/96) Enquetes epidemiologiques sur l'Usage de drogues on Afrique: (Epidemiological Studies on Drug use in Africa) Benin, Cote-D'Ivoire, Madagascar, Senegal. *Psychopathologie Africaine*, 27 (2–3), 177–202.

Fido, A.A. and Al.-Jabally, M. (1993) Presence of Psychiatric Morbidity in Prison Population in Kuwait. *Annals of Clinical Psychiatry*, 5, 107–110.

Fido, A.A., Razik, M.A., Mizra, I., and El-Islam, M.F. (1992) Psychiatric Disorders in Prisoners Referred for Assessment: A Preliminary Study. *Canadian Journal of Psychiatry*, 37, 100–103.

Forster, D. and Sandler, D. (1985) *A study of detention and torture in South Africa: Preliminary Report*, Cape Town: Institute of criminology, University of Cape Town, South Africa.

German, G.A. (1972) Aspects of clinical psychiatry in sub-Saharan Africa. *British Journal of Psychiatry*, 121, 461–479.

German, G.A. (1987a) Mental health in Africa: I: the extent of mental health problems in Africa today. *British Journal of Psychiatry*, 151, 435–439.

German, G.A. (1987b) Mental health in Africa, II: the nature of mental disorder in Africa today. *British Journal of Psychiatry*, 151, 440–446.

Grotrian, A., Deighton, J., Bowring, B., Harris, P., Mehta, S., and Robertson, G. (1992) *Human Rights in Malawi*. Report of a joint delegation of the Scottish Faculty of Advocates and Law Society of England and Wales, September, 17–20.

Gureje, O. and Obikoya, O. (1992) Alcohol and drug abuse in Nigeria: a review of the literature. *Contemporary Drug Problems*, 19, 491–504.

Ihezue, U.H., Ebigbo, P. O., and Onuora, A.N. (1982) The origin and function of the Enugu Asylum with comments on the historical development of medico-legal care of mentally abnormal offenders. *Nigerian Journal of Psychiatry*, 1, 18 –28.

Ihezue, U.H., Okonkwo, K.O., and Okereke, E.N.C. (1993) Long Stay patients in a Nigerian prison mental hospital: Survey of psychosocial problems.. *Psychopathologie Africaine*, 25, (1), 77–93.

Jaffe, H. (1992) New regime in Chad: a French mission has treated torture victims in the former French colony in Africa. *Torture*, **2**, 7–9.

Kanki, P.J., M'Boup, S., Ricard, D. et. al. (1987). Human T-lymphocyte virus type 4 and HIV in West Africa. *Science*, **236** (4803), 827–831.

Kebede, Y., Pickering, J., McDonald, J.C., Wotton, K., and Zwede, D. (1991) HIV infection in an Ethiopian prison. *American Journal of Public Health*, **81**(5), 625–627.

London, L. and Dowdall, T.L. (1993) Evidence of torture: political repression and human rights abuses in South Africa. *Torture*, **3**, 39–40.

Lwanda, J.L. (1993) *Kamuzu Banda of Malawi: a study in promise, power and paralysis*. Glasgow: Dudu Nsomba Publications.

Maboshe, N.N., Sinuooya, O., and Chimfwembe, E. (1989) Sexual practices and HIV infection in some Zambian prisons. In: *Program and Abstracts. V International Conference on AIDS*, Montreal Canada.

Maden, A., Swinton, M., and Gunn, J. (1991) Drug dependence in prisoners. *British Medical Journal*, **13**, 302–305.

Maden, A., Swinton, M., and Gunn, J. (1992) A survey of pre-arrest drug use in sentenced prisoners. *British Journal of Addiction*, **87**, 27–33.

Makanjuola, R.O.A. (1985): Recurrent unipolar manic disorder in the Yoruba Nigerian: further evidence. *British Journal of Psychiatry*, **147**, 434–437

Makanjuola, R.O.A., and Olaomo, M. (1981) Psychiatric morbidity in a Nigerian prison. *Nigerian Medical Journal*, **11**, 111–120.

Malepe, T.B. (1989) Alcohol-related problems in Swaziland. *Contemporary Drug Problems*, **16**, 43–58.

Mann, J., Francis, H., Quinn, T.C., Bila K., *et al.* (1986) HIV seroprevalence among hospital workers in Kinshasha, Zaire. *Journal of American Medical Association*, **256**, 3099–3102.

Mba, J. (1989) Living in Hell: life in Nigerian prisons is nasty, brutish, inhuman. *Newswatch Weekly Magazine*, June, 1989.

Mbatia, J. and Ferguson (1995) Camparison of personality status between British and Tanzanian abnormal offenders. *Psychopathologie Africaine*, **27**, (1) 5–24.

McDonald, D. (1996) Drugs in Southern Africa: an overview. *Drugs: Education, Prevention, Policy*, **3**, (2), 127–144.

Mertens, T., Burton, A., stoneburner, R. (1994) Global estimates and epidemiology of HIV infections and AIDS. *AIDS*, **8**, (suppl.1) S361–S372.

Muluka, E.A.P., and Acuda, S.W. (1978) Crime and mental illness: a study of a group of criminal patients in Mathari Mental Hospital. *East African Medical Journal*, **55**, (8), 360–365.

Mwenesi, H.A. (1995) *Rapid Assessment of Drug Abuse in Kenya: a national report*, Nairobi; UNDCP.

NACP (1995) *Fourth HIV Sentinel Surveillance in Botswana* (Draft Copy). National AIDS Control Programme, Ministry of Health, Government of Botswana, Gaborone.

N'Galy, B., Ryder, R.W., Bila, K. *et al.* (1988) HIV infection among employers in an African hospital. *The New England Journal of Medicine*, **319**, 1123–1127.

Odejide, A.O. (1981) Some clinical aspects of criminology. A study of criminal psychiatric patients at the Lantoro psychiatric institution. *Acta Psychiatrica Scandinavica*, **63**, 208–224.

Odejide, A.O., Oyewunni, L.K., and Ohaeri, J.U. (1989) Psychiatry in Africa: An Overview. *American Jounral of Psychiatry*, **146**, (6), 708–716.

Ogunlesi, O.A., Makanjuola, J.D., and Adelekan, M.F. (1988) Offenders admitted to the Neuropsychiatric Hospital, Aro, Abcokuta: a ten-year review: *West African Medical Journal*, **7**, 210–215.

Ohaeri, J.U., and Odejide, A.O. (1993) Admissions for drug and alcohol–related problems in Nigerian psychiatric care facilities in one year. *Drug and Alcohol Dependence*, **31**, 101–109.

Olubodun, J.O. (1996) Prison life and the blood pressure of the inmates of a developing community prison. *Journal of Human Hypertension*, **10**, 235–238.

Olubodun, J.O., Jaiyesimi, A.E., Olasode, O.A., and Sobowale, A.B. (1991) Severe clinical nutritional neurological damage in a young Nigerian detainee. *Tropical and Geographical Medicine*, **43**, (1–2), 231–233.

Onyeneje, E.C., and Eyo, I.E. (1996) Custodial Status and self concepts of Nigerian inmates remanded to prison custody. *Perceptual and Motor Skills*, **82**, 209–210.

Ousseini (1994) Seroprevalency of the HIV infection at the Central Prison of Niamey (Niger). *Bull. Soc. Path*, Ex. **87**, 190.

Peltzer, K. (1995) Psychosocial Effects of political dention in Malawi from 1964 to 1993. *Psychopathologie Africaine*, **27**, (2–3), 221–244.

Power, K.G., Markova, I., and Rowlands, A. (1991) Sexual behaviour in Scottish prisons. *British Medical Journal*, **302**, 1507–1508.

Puppets in Prison (1996) *Proposal to the South African Department of Health for the funding of Research and Production of a four-year Programme of Educational Workshops and Live Performances in South African Prisons*, Johannesburg: Gary Friedman Productions.

Samb, N.D., Boys, C.S., and Diouf, G. (1989) HIV-1 et HIV-2 on millieu carceral a Dakar, Senegal. In: *Program and Abstracts: V International Conference on AIDS (Montreal) Canada*.

Simonsen, J.N., Cameron, W.D., Gakinya N. *et al.* (1988) Human immunodeficiency virus infection among men with STD. Experience from a center in Africa.*The New England Journal of Medicine*, **319**, 274–278.

Solomons, K. (1989) The dynamics of post-traumatic stress disorder in South African political ex-detainees. *American Journal of psychotherapy*, **Vol. XLIII**, (2), 208–217.

Torrey, B. and Way, P. (1990) Seroprevalence of HIV in Africa: Winter 1990. Washington center for International Research. US Bureau of the Census: 55.

Tshibangu, N.N. (1993) HIV infection in Bophuthatswana: Epidemiological surveillance, 1987–1989. *South African Medical Journal*, **83**, 36–39.

Tyrer, P. and Alexander, J. (1979) Classification of personality disorder. *British Journal of Psychiatry*, **135**, 165–167.

Udofia, O. (1997) Mental illness and crime in South Eastern Nigeria. *Nigerian Journal of Psychiatry*, **1**, (4), 209–217.

Van Der Bugh, C. (1996) Substance Abuse in a Democratic South Africa: current and future education and prevention policies and strategies. *Drugs ; Education, Prevention and Policy*, **3**, (2), 153–157.

Vaz, R.G., Gloyd, S., Folgosa, E., and Kreiss, J. (1995) Syphilis and HIV infection among prisoners in Maputo, Mozambique. *International Journal of STD and AIDS*, **6**, 42–46.

Vaz, R.G., Gloyd, S., and Trindale, R. (1996) The effects of peer education on STD and AIDS knowledge among prisoners in Mozambique. *International Journal of STD and AIDS*, **7**, 51–54.

WHO (1995) *The current Global situation of the HIV/AIDS Pandemic. Global Programe on AIDS*. World Health Organization, Geneva.

Chapter 7

HIV, HEPATITIS AND DRUGS EPIDEMIOLOGY IN PRISONS

Sheila M. Gore and A. Graham Bird

In the autumn of 1990, the visionary then-governor of Edinburgh Prison, Mr. John Pearce, invited us on behalf of the Scottish Prison Service to devise a methodology which would be acceptable to prisoners and which would allow unbiased estimation of HIV prevalence and related risk behaviours in Scottish prisons. John Pearce was concerned because the HIV epidemic in Edinburgh had an injecting drug user focus, then of unknown size (Burns *et al.*, 1996), and there is an association between injecting drugs and imprisonment he needed to plan for when, and how many of, his prisoners would experience severe HIV-related immunodeficiency.

Willing Anonymous Salivary HIV [WASH] surveillance was the methodology that we devised (Bird *et al.*, 1992; Bird and Gore, 1994; Gore and Bird, 1995). Briefly, after advance publicity organised by the prison, we outlined the study rationale to prisoners a week before the surveillance day. On the study day, we reiterated the rationale to groups of 20 prisoners immediately before they passed through the surveillance hall (usually the prison's gymnasium). All prisoners were invited to participate. They did so by giving a saliva sample to be tested for HIV antibodies and self-completing an anonymous risk-factor questionnaire. Saliva sample and questionnaire were then linked by a sealed number and enveloped pair chosen at random by the prisoner from a bag of 50 envelopes. She or he then put one sealed label on the completed questionnaire, folded it into the envelope provided, and deposited the envelope in a blue collection bin as she or he exited the surveillance area. The other sealed label was fixed to the prisoner's saliva sample which was then deposited in the red collection bin as the prisoner exits.

WASH surveillance works primarily because it delivers 'demonstrable anonymity'. Prisoners themselves link saliva sample and questionnaire but the number under the seals is unknown both to them and to others so that the pair can never be attributed back to an individual prisoner. Moreover, prisoners themselves physically separate their saliva sample and questionnaire into different collection bins before exiting the surveillance area so that it is impossible for anyone to retrieve them and add any covert attribution after the prisoner has left. Prisoner-scrutineers, who are present in the surveillance area throughout the study day, are a further guarantee of *bona fides* by the research team and prison staff present to escort prisoners to and from the study area.

WASH surveillance works also because prisons and prisoners want it to work, and because prison staff can organise the escort of groups of 20 prisoners every 15 minutes with supreme efficiency and *esprit de corps*. Crucial to the high compliance has been extensive pre-study briefing to allay suspicion and anxiety and the rapid reporting back of the general results to inmates within one month of the study. Inmates learn the results from us at the same time as do the prison's governor and staff. Individual studies have had an important educational role and have intensified HIV awareness. Parallel availability of named confidential HIV tests, usually by prison medical staff but not always (Bird *et al.*, 1995), is an ethical pre-requisite in our view; and in some institutions demand for this facility has been extensive (Bird *et al.*, 1993; Bird *et al.*, 1995).

WASH surveillance has been scientifically and cost efficient. Because prisons are enriched for injecting drug users (Covell *et al.*, 1993; Shewan *et al.*, 1994; Gore and Bird, 1995) who commit crimes to finance their illegal drugs' spend (Hutchinson *et al.*, 1999), they are therefore a convenient venue for learning about the risk behaviours, including inside prisons, and HIV prevalence of injectors. Prisons also bring together in one location inmates from different parts of the country and so are an efficient single venue for making regional comparisons about the prevalence of injecting drug use by prisoners who reside, say, in Glasgow or Edinburgh. The cost of WASH surveillance studies from 1991–96 has been of the order of £10 per eligible prisoner, or £50,000 pounds in total, and has been borne variously by the Scottish Prison Service, the Scottish Centre for Infection and Environmental Health, the Office of the Chief Scientist for Scotland, the Medical Research Council, the EC Network for HIV/Hepatitis Prevention in Prisons, and Murex Diagnostics.

WASH methodology achieved its objectives sufficiently well that it has been taken up by an EC Network for HIV/Hepatitis Prevention in Prisons and in 1997 was being implemented in eight EC countries: Belgium, England, France, Germany, Italy, Portugal, Spain and Sweden.

The research programme on 'HIV Epidemiology in Prisons' which we put forward in 1990 had three other goals besides WASH surveillance. The second goal — to measure immunological progression in HIV-infected prisoners if there was substantial undisclosed HIV prevalence — has fortunately been unnecessary because none of our WASH surveillance studies in Scottish prisons to date has discovered a substantial level of HIV infection unknown to the prison's medical staff. The third goal was to measure the role of prisons in HIV transmission. A new WASH design for measuring HIV or Hepatitis C seroconversion in prison, which also delivers 'demonstrable anonymity', has since been published (Gore et al., 1996 Gore and Bird, 1998). Fourthly, we aimed to test whether immunological or clinical progression of HIV disease was affected (favourably or unfavourably) by periods of incarceration. A study plan to establish all periods of incarceration in Edinburgh Prison during 1983–94 for men in the Edinburgh City Hospital HIV Cohort, who were mainly injectors, was devised which protected both medical and prisoner confidentiality. It received research and ethical clearance, and answers to the fourth question will first appear in a University of Cambridge doctoral thesis to be examined in 1999.

The WASH surveillance methodology was thus part of a 4-point research programme on 'HIV Epidemiology in Prisons', which was itself part of our 5-year plan for MRC-BIAS (Biostatistical Initiative in support of AIDS/HIV studies in Scotland). MRC-BIAS came into being in February 1992 in collaboration with consultants in infectious diseases (Dr. R.P. Brettle) and public health (Dr. D.J. Goldberg] as our co-grantholders.

From 1991 onwards, the data from WASH surveillance studies in Scotland have compelled us increasingly to address the harm reduction needs of prisoners who inject drugs. We have made a case, including to Chief Medical Officers in the UK, for major interventions to be evaluated in prison-based randomised controlled trials, such as placements on drug reduction programmes. Still other interventions have required not further research but immediate action on public health grounds, such as prisoners' access to sterilisation tablets. Yet others have required audit and action, such as to improve the rate of Hepatitis B vaccination of prisoners; and revision of how acute Hepatitis B infections are reported to national surveillance centres so that the role of prisons in Hepatitis B outbreaks (Gill et al., 1995) can be properly established, and followed-up (Gore et al., 1999).

In February 1995, random mandatory drugs testing (rMDT) of prisoners was introduced on a pilot basis to eight prisons in England (Gore and Bird, 1995). Without critical evaluation, it was extended to all establishments of the Prison Service in England and Wales by the end of March 1996, and throughout establishments of the Scottish Prison Service by March 1997.

Because of rMDT, which prompted the first author's resignation as a grantholder for WASH surveillance in England, cross-sectional WASH surveillance studies in England and Wales were delayed from February 1995 until January 1997. Is it mere coincidence that access for EC-funded WASH surveillance in establishments of the Scottish Prison Service was denied in 1997 after we had published in the British Medical Journal data on frequency of injecting inside prison from 1996 WASH surveillance studies at Lowmoss and Aberdeen Prisons (Bird *et al.*, 1997) and used them to estimate, *inter alia*, the inefficiency of rMDT at detecting prisoners who inject heroin inside?

rMDT was seen both as a weapon in the Home Office's 'war on drugs' and as 'a means of gathering information'. Doctors and scientists saw it differently. Journalists and politicians at first confused rMDT and WASH surveillance studies (Connor, 1995a, 1995b) but the former eventually realised what we as scientists had forewarned (Gore and Bird, 1995; Bennetto, 1996): that rMDT risked converting prisoners from cannabis to heroin use to avoid detection — because cannabis remains in the urine for three weeks, heroin for three days (Gore, Bird and Ross, 1996; Jurgens, 1996).

In the following section we briefly review what was written about blood-borne virus transmission in prisons, and associated risk behaviours, before 1991. Then we deal with intelligence from WASH surveillance studies in Scotland. In the next section we outline the range of our studies on HIV, hepatitis and drug use in prison which have come after WASH surveillance. The following section reviews rMDT. It shows how data from WASH surveillance studies in 1996 were used to elucidate the inefficiency of rMDT as 'a means of gathering information' about heroin use in prisons, and scans the statistics of offences against prison discipline in England and Wales in 1996 for evidence about rMDT's effectiveness in the 'war against drugs', and in particular, on violence in prisons.

BEFORE WASH SURVEILLANCE

There was already evidence that UK prisons were enriched for injecting drug users. For example, in 1988–89 Maden, Swinton and Gunn

(1991) interviewed a random sample of 1751 men serving a prison sentence in England, of whom 127 (8 per cent) reported injecting in the six months before arrest. A question about drug use within prison had to be dropped because of prisoners' suspicions, however. Power *et al.* (1991), on the other hand, invited for interview a 13.5 per cent stratified random sample of Scottish prisoners, 86 per cent of whom agreed to take part (559 interviewees), which included being asked about high risk sexual or injecting behaviour during incarceration. Eight per cent of respondents had injected (ever) in prison but only one male prisoner reported anal sex with another man in prison. Power *et al.* contrasted the low reported rate of anal sex in prison with the reporting of inside injecting, which inmates did not fear to acknowledge and was much the more prevalent risk behaviour.

Despite self-completion of anonymous questionnaires, recruitment biases and modest sample size made it impossible to draw unimpeachable inferences from other early studies (Carvell and Hart, 1990; Kennedy *et al.*, 1991) which inquired about the proportion of ex-prisoner injectors who had ever injected inside prison (33/50 and 14/56 respectively). None of the above studies measured HIV prevalence and therefore could not relate it to risk behaviours inside and out of prison.

In the US and in Sweden, mandatory or voluntary HIV testing of prisoners at reception is undertaken but linked information on risk behaviours was minimal or lacking; HIV prevalence in prisoners correlated with the prevalence in injectors in the outside community, however (see Bird *et al.*, 1992 for more detail and references).

The advent of HIV disease had brought prisons into a more prominent public health focus. However, the predilection of prison populations for blood-borne virus infections had been foreshadowed in the early 1980s when, for example, the UK Blood Transfusion Services had ceased donor sessions in prisons because of five to ten times higher prevalence of Hepatitis B infection and carriage rate in prison inmates (Barr *et al.*, 1981; Gore *et al.*, 1995). By this action, the UK's blood supply was thereby protected, but not its prisoners; nor were their risk-related behaviours inquired into (perhaps for fear of what might be revealed?) so that appropriate harm reduction measures were not introduced. It was not until March 1993 that WHO Guidelines on HIV Infection and AIDS in Prisons (1993) set a standard against which all prison services could, and should, measure their compliance with public health imperatives for prisoners.

Table 7.1 First WASH surveillance studies in 6 Scottish male prisons, Cornton Vale for women, and two young offender institutions (Polmont YOI in 1992 and Glenochil YOI in 1994).

Available inmates	Responders (%)	Valid Q	Injectors (%)	Injectors who ever injected inside (%)	HIV +ve salivas	Anal sex ever in prison
			PRISON and YEAR:			
Edinburgh 1991: 499	378 (76%)	363	66/358 (18%)	31/66 (47%)	17 [all IDU]	0
Perth 1995: 434	304 (70%)	282	82/278 (27%)	69/81 (85%)	6 [all IDU]	3
Aberdeen 1996: 157	146 (93%)	143	53/142 (37%)	39/53 (74%)	2 [0 IDU]	0
Glenochil 1994: 352	295 (84%)	284	75/278 (27%)	44/75 (59%)	7 [all IDU]	2
Barlinnie 1994: 1073	985 (92%)	928	327/918 (36%)	162/323 (50%)	9 [8 IDU]	3
Lowmoss 1996: 312	293 (94%)	286	116/282 (41%)	66/116 (57%)	2 [2 IDUs]	2
TOTAL: males: 2827	**2410 (85%)**	**2286**	**719/2256 (32%)**	**411/714 (58%)**	**43 [40 IDU]**	**10**
Cornton Vale female 1995: 145	**136 (94%)**	**132**	**58/127 (46%)**	**32/56 (57%)**	**0***	**Not asked**
TOTAL: YOs: 587	**583 (99%)**	**562**	**99/556 (18%)**	**27/99 (27%)**	**0**	**3**

* Footnote: two women in Cornton Vale on the surveillance day were known to be HIV infected and had chosen not to take part.

WASH SURVEILLANCE STUDIES IN SCOTLAND, 1991–96

Table 7.1 maps, by prison and year of surveillance, HIV prevalence for injector-inmates, since most HIV antibody positive saliva samples have been from injector-inmates (see Table 7.1). Glenochil Prison excepted, where HIV and Hepatitis B infections were transmitted in the jail in the first half of 1993, HIV prevalence for injector-inmates is substantially higher in prisons on Scotland's east coast than around Glasgow, its largest city.

Table 7.1 also details the major findings of the first WASH surveillance studies in six adult male prisons in Scotland (Bird *et al.*, 1992; Gore *et al.*, 1995; Bird *et al.*, 1995; Gore *et al.*, 1997; Bird *et al.*, 1997), and summarises those in young offenders' institutions (Bird *et al.*, 1993; Gore *et al.*, 1995) and at Cornton Vale for female prisoners (Gore *et al.*, 1997). Response rate, percentage of prisoners with a history of injecting drug use, proportion of injector-inmates who had ever injected inside prison, proportion of male prisoners who had ever had anal sex with another man in prison, number of HIV antibody positive saliva samples and related risk behaviour are shown.

Thirty-two per cent of adult male prisoners in Scotland had a history of injecting drug use (but there was regional variation in injector-prevalence, being twice as high in Glasgow as in Edinburgh residents). Over half the injector-inmates had injected inside prison at some time (58 per cent: 411/714). A highly variable proportion of injectors (as between establishments) reported they had started to inject inside prison: Edinburgh (not asked), Perth (25/80: 31 per cent), Aberdeen (10/52: 19 per cent), Glenochil (18/72: 25 per cent); Barlinnie (20/319: 6 per cent), Lowmoss (5/115: 4 per cent) and Cornton Vale for women (1/56: 2 per cent). Starting to inject inside prison was not a new phenomenon to the 1990s, but was reported also by injectors whose injecting career had begun in the early 1980s.

WASH surveillance studies in Scotland all pre-dated the introduction of rMDT in the establishments concerned. Before rMDT, we estimated that one in 60 first time prisoners who had never previously injected drugs is initiated into injecting drug use on his first incarceration. After rMDT, data are not available for Scotland; but an estimate should be derivable from 1997 WASH surveillance studies in England and Wales where, unfortunately, a pre-rMDT estimate is lacking.

A quarter of adult injector-inmates (198/766: 26 per cent) reported an attack (ever) of hepatitis or jaundice: Edinburgh (23/66: 35 per cent), Perth (18/80: 22 per cent), Aberdeen (7/53: 13 per cent), Glenochil

(20/74: 27 per cent), Barlinnie (86/323: 27 per cent), Lowmoss (27/114: 24 per cent), Cornton Vale (17/56: 30 per cent); but lower at Polmont YOI (8/67: 12 per cent). The adult acute hepatitis report rate was very significantly lower at Aberdeen ($p < 0.01$) where injecting had begun more recently: 61 per cent of Aberdeen's injectors (32/53) but only 30 per cent of Lowmoss's (35/116) had started to inject in 1992 or later.

Finally, Table 7.1 agrees with Power's earlier work (1991) on high risk sexual behaviour in prison in that less than 0.5 per cent of adult male prisoners in Scotland who participated in cross-sectional WASH surveillance reported having had anal sex with another man in prison. But 19 per cent, much higher than the 7.7 per cent found when Power *et al.* (1991), interviewed a stratified random sample of inmates, reported having at some time injected inside prison.

Clearly, injecting is by far the major risk factor for blood-borne virus transmission inside prisons rather than sexual risk: as both the behavioural and salivary HIV test data in Table 7.1 show. Sadly, Scotland has seen confirmation of this at Glenochil Prison in 1993 (Taylor *et al.*, 1995; Gore *et al.*, 1995; Yirrell *et al.*, 1997) and again in 1997: despite sterilisation tablets having been available to Scottish prisoners since December 1993 and evidence confirming their use from the 1996 WASH surveillance studies (Bird *et al.*, 1997).

Comparison of the 1991 and 1996 WASH questionnaires shows how the risk behaviour questions have evolved. The first major change came in 1994: the question about 'starting to inject inside' was included because it was relevant, and an issue of concern, for Glenochil Prison's medical team. We have since always also asked whether a prisoner had injected in Glenochil Prison during January to June 1993, because this is a proven HIV risk factor for Scottish injectors. Following the publication of 'Sexual Behaviour in Britain' (1994), we added the question about 'treatment (ever) for a sexually transmitted disease'. Since 1995, we have also asked about hepatitis C test uptake (ever) because this was an issue for prisoners and the medical team at Perth Prison.

In 1996, the EC Network pilot year, we added questions about hepatitis B vaccination of prisoners, about the frequency of injection inside prison in the last 4 weeks and of prisoners' use of sterilising tablets to clean needles and works, about proximity of last injecting drugs on the outside before coming into prison this time, and about tattooing in prison (cf. Dufour *et al.*, 1996). The question about frequency of injection inside prison, about which we were hesitant and so had paired with the question on frequency of use of sterilising tablets to clean needles and works, was answered successfully as Mr Bill Middleton, the governor of Lowmoss Prison, had anticipated, and by whose encouragement our hesitation was overcome.

From the above, it is clear that the content of 1991–96 WASH surveillance questionnaires evolved in response to specific issues that concerned the research team, the individual prisons which hosted WASH surveillance and, for 1996, in collaboration with the EC Network (although the Scottish questionnaire in 1996 had resisted many of the EC pilot innovations in the interest of brevity).

There was also epidemiological and prison rationale in the choice of establishments, as was also written into the WASH programme for England and Wales by the first author when she was a grantholder for this project. Geographically, surveillance in Scotland ranged from east to west; and then up the north east coast of Scotland from Perth to Aberdeen to elucidate injector/HIV prevalence; and periodically (in 1994 and 1996; access denied for 1997) to revisit the conundrum of high injector yet low HIV prevalence in Glasgow and the west of Scotland. Community salivary HIV surveillance of Dundee's injectors (Haw et al., 1996) following the model of Glasgow and Edinburgh shortly predated the WASH surveillance at Perth Prison, which is the local prison for Dundee. However, no such study had been undertaken in north east Scotland, so that WASH surveillance at Aberdeen Prison gave the first quantitative insight to injector/HIV prevalence in Grampian region.

In prison terms, the WASH surveillance programme in Scotland focused on large local prisons, establishments for longer-term prisoners (such as Glenochil and Shotts), Scotland's largest young offenders' institution (Polmont Young Offenders' Institution) and only female prison (Cornton Vale), but was sufficiently flexible to respond rapidly to HIV transmission in jail (which was what dictated the timing of 1994 WASH surveillance at Glenochil Prison and prompted its intended re-inclusion in 1997) and to intelligence from prisoners and staff.

The above questions would have been retained in 1997, with the addition of salient others, some of which were based on the EC Network's 1996 pilot questionnaire: to discover which medical services prisoners were most likely to have attended in the year before incarceration (to identify venues for more successful delivery of Hepatitis B vaccination outside prison); to ask about methadone treatment from a doctor in the year before incarceration and whether methadone was discontinued in prison, a topic which is much discussed in the columns of medical journals (Bath *et al.*, 1993; Farrell and Strang, 1994; Lush, 1994; Jurgens, 1996; Gruer and McLeod, 1997) and finally how many sex partners in the year before incarceration were injecting drug users or were HIV infected.

Was low/no cost — because EC-funded — WASH surveillance in 1997 censored to curtail accumulation of data on frequency of injecting inside prison? Suchlike data are essential for the interpretability of rMDT, that is: to translate from a) percentage testing positive for heroin in rMDT to b) percentage using heroin inside prison. Such censorship is not unique: for over two years, Strang has been delayed by the Home Office in the publishing of data for England and Wales on drug use inside prison. Intriguingly, by some strange poetic justice, these delayed data were first made public by Professor Strang at a November 1997 meeting of the Scottish Division of the Royal College of Psychiatrists on 'Drug Misuse and the Prison System: Clinical and Treatment Issues', at which the operation of mandatory drug testing in Scottish prisons was also discussed.

We trust that the setback to WASH surveillance in Scotland is temporary because, out of this contretemps, the Chief Medical Officer for Scotland, Sir David Carter, has forged an initiative in conjunction with the Scottish Prison Service to convene under his chairmanship a Working Party to deliberate key public health issues in relation to Scottish prisons and thereby to develop a 3 year programme of research on Drugs, HIV and Hepatitis. Scotland's Prison Service may thus again be in pole position by having agreed to a public and prisoners' health initiative that opens up a breadth of considerations to be evaluated by soundly academic and peer-reviewed methodologies.

WASH surveillance at Glenochil Prison in 1994 (Gore *et al.*, 1995), just over a year after the infection control exercise in June/July 1993 which followed an outbreak of HIV and hepatitis B transmissions in the jail (Taylor *et al.*, 1995), was particularly important. It vindicated in practice the epidemiological case we had set out in principle in July 1993 (Gore and Bird, 1993). In particular, WASH surveillance estimated that there had been over 20 HIV infections in Glenochil Prison in 1993, of which 14 had been diagnosed by the prison's medical officer or in the course of the infection control exercise. This finding has prompted further collaborative work to complete the epidemiological account of HIV and hepatitis B transmission at Glenochil Prison, as outlined in the next section.

AFTER WASH SURVEILLANCE: PRISON-RELATED HIV, HEPATITIS, AND DRUGS STUDIES IN SCOTLAND

Glenochil follow-up

A first task was to check the estimate of 'at least 20 HIV infections' associated with the Glenochil 1993 outbreak and to devise a methodology for doing so without breach of medical or prisoner confidentiality. This was done through collaboration between MRC-BIAS, the infection control team at the Scottish Centre for Infection and Environmental Health, the prison, and the Edinburgh University Centre for HIV Research. Molecular techniques had shown that 13/14 diagnosed Glenochil infections were the same virus and that neither of two putative sources identified at the time was the infector (Yirrell *et al.*, 1997). Briefly, the plan was to look for matches of the identifier 'first initial, soundex of surname, date of birth' for each of the 636 men who had been in Glenochil Prison at any time between January and June 1993 on the similarly indexed registers as follows: a) HIV antibody positive and deaths register, b) AIDS diagnoses and deaths register, c) CD4 count register, d) acute hepatitis B register and e) HIV test request register (for description of registers, see: HIV and AIDS Surveillance in Scotland, 1995). Date of HIV diagnosis was used to segregate matched identifiers into 'putative sources' (who were already HIV infected before 1993) and 'recent HIV diagnoses'. Molecular techniques could then be applied to determine: i) if any of the newly identified 'putative sources', of which there were four, was indeed the infector for the Glenochil cohort and ii) if any of the 'recent HIV diagnoses' shared the same virus as the Glenochil cohort (see Hutchinson *et al.*, 1999).

Attention in 1993 had focused mainly on the transmissions of HIV, but hepatitis B had also been transmitted among injectors. The opportunity was therefore taken via d) above, and in collaboration with Scotland's virologists, to reconstruct the extent of hepatitis B transmissions associated with Glenochil Prison in 1993. Eleven hepatitis B infections were discovered, only two of which had been reported to the Scottish Centre for Infection and Environmental Health and neither of these was obviously prison-related from the information available centrally (see Hutchinson *et al.*, 1998).

Meanwhile, AIDS diagnosis within two months of seroconversion in one of the Glenochil cohort (three other rapid HIV progression followed) led at the first author's suggestion to HLA typing of the Glenochil cohort because it was likely (Steel *et al.*, 1988; Mcneil *et al.*, 1996) that the patient diagnosed with AIDS would have the rapid disease progression phenotype HLA-A1, B8, DR3; and this was the case.

Two deaths within two years of HIV seroconversion out of the 20 estimated HIV infections (that is: 10 per cent mortality within two years of injection-related HIV infection when there was co-temporaneous transmission of hepatitis B) sparked another epidemiological investigation. The injection-related outbreak of HIV infection in Lothian region in Scotland in 1983–84 had also been co-incident with hepatitis B transmissions.

To derive a comparable estimate for Lothian of injectors' mortality within two years of HIV infection, we devised a methodology to determine deaths in 1983–86 of HIV infected but undiagnosed individuals in Lothian, particularly injecting drug users. In brief, we targeted individuals aged 15–55 years, who had tested positive (we took a 100 per cent sample: group A) for hepatitis B surface antigen in 1983–84, or had tested negative (we took a 50 per cent sample: group B) but were at high risk for blood-borne virus transmission according to their reason for testing. The death records of the Registrar General for Scotland were then consulted to identify deceased patients in groups A and B. Stored sera from 1983–84 for patients who had died early (1983–86) and who had not been diagnosed with HIV disease were then tested anonymously for HIV and Hepatitis C antibodies. As a result (Gore *et al.*, 1998), Lothian injectors' mortality within two years of HIV infection was estimated as 10 per cent (approximate 95 per cent confidence interval: from 6 per cent to 13 per cent), just as for Glenochil ten years later.

PRISONS NEED PROTOCOLS FOR HIV/HEPATITIS OUTBREAKS

As outlined above, a range of studies into the tragic transmissions during January to June 1993 of HIV and Hepatitis B infections in Glenochil Prison in Scotland has been reported (Taylor *et al.*, 1995; Gore *et al.*, 1995; Yirrell *et al.*, 1997; Hutchinson *et al.*, 1998a, Hutchinson *et al.*, 1999; McMenamin *et al.*, 1997). These were to control infection, and for ethnographic, molecular, immunological, and surveillance purposes. We ventured to propose the lessons that could be learned from this evidence; and put forward a protocol for use by public health and prison authorities in following-up any acute hepatitis B infection(s) or HIV seroconversion(s) which may relate to a period of incarceration (Gore *et al.*, 1999). Our recommendations are applicable also in the case of hepatitis C seroconversions in prison, which we believe have also occurred in UK prisons, only without publication thereon. In particular, since only two out of 10 acute Hepatitis B infections which related to a period of incarceration in Glenochil Prison during January to June 1993 were reported to the Scottish Centre of Infection and Environmental Health [SCIEH] and neither of these was identifiable by SCIEH as being prison-linked, we have recommended changes in the reporting of acute hepatitis infections. In particular, we have suggested that recent incarceration (and where) should be added as one of the questions which is routinely asked about every acute infection with hepatitis B or C, so that the national surveillance centres can more efficiently search for prison-related clusters in hepatitis infections which have occurred within six months of each other.

HEPATITIS C INCIDENCE AND PREVALENCE

In the longer term hepatitis C has the potential to cause a much larger burden of disease than HIV, including in Scottish prisons. Not only is hepatitis C at least 10-fold more easily transmitted than is HIV by contaminated needles and syringes (Dore, Kaldor and McCaughan, 1997), but the prospect of a protective vaccine is remote and a significant proportion of hepatitis C infected individuals will develop chronic liver disease (Poynard *et al.*, 1997) with attendant burden on local healthcare budgets.

Scotland has a culture of injecting drug use and so must concern itself with hepatitis C incidence, prevalence and progression. Prisons in Scotland and elsewhere need to measure the incidence of hepatitis C seroconversion in jail and the associated risk behaviours. A new WASH design to do this which links recruitment saliva sample (for example: on admission to prison or at cross-sectional WASH surveillance), discharge questionnaire about risk behaviours (including during current incarceration) and discharge saliva sample; monitors non-compliance; and affords demonstrable anonymity has been worked out for use when fully-validated salivary testing for hepatitis C antibodies becomes available (Gore, Bird and Burns, 1996; Gore and Bird, 1998; Gore *et al.*, 1999; McIntyre *et al.*, 1996).

No hepatitis C incidence studies have been reported from Scotland prisons to date. Crofts *et al.* (1994) conducted confidential voluntary testing of all prison entrants in Victoria, Australia for markers of exposure to blood-borne viruses with collection of minimal data on demography and risk factors over 12 months. Over 99 per cent of nearly 3700 prison entrants complied, of whom 344 entered prison and were tested more than once, whereby Crofts *et al.* estimated hepatitis C incidence rate (not necessarily inside prison, however) at 41 per 100 person years for injecting drug users aged less than 30 years. McBride, Ali and Clee (1994) called for antibodies to the hepatitis C virus to be determined in future studies of high risk behaviour in UK prisons (see Gore *et al.*, 1999 who have since used a fully validated salivary test for Hepatitis C on prisoners' stored saliva samples). A similar study to the new WASH design — but utilising voluntary anonymous finger prick blood samples — would be possible, but volunteer rates for blood sampling are likely to be lower than for provision of saliva samples. Goldberg *et al.* plan to conduct such a study in Scotland's prisons in the near future in which very large numbers of volunteers will need to be recruited for hepatitis C seroconversions assuredly to be documented, as Gore and Bird (1998) have shown based on prior estimates drawn from Scottish data.

Since the 1994 WASH surveillance study at Barlinnie Prison we have sought prisoners' permission for their saliva samples to be tested in due course for hepatitis C antibodies when a suitable salivary test came into being which would allow hepatitis C prevalence to be related to prisoners' self-reported history of injecting drug use. Hepatitis C antibody results on 1994–96 stored WASH saliva samples from Scottish prisoners have shown that half of Scotland's adult injector inmates were hepatitis C carriers, compared to only 3 per cent of non-injectors. Similar work is in hand for 1997 studies by EC Network on HIV/hepatitis in Prisons and in England and Wales.

The issue of hepatitis C prevalence is being tackled more generally in the context of Scotland's unlinked anonymous testing (UAT) programme for HIV (HIV and AIDS Surveillance in Scotland, 1995). In this, and its counterpart in England and Wales (Unlinked Anonymous Surveys Steering Group, 1996), blood samples given for another reason — including by pregnant women (for rubella testing), women undergoing termination of pregnancy (for rhesus testing), attendees at genito-urinary medicine (GUM) clinics (for syphilis testing), general hospital attendees (for serum urea) or Guthrie blood spots from newborns (who have the mother's antibodies) — are tested anonymously for HIV antibodies. This UAT programme is being extended gradually to include testing for hepatitis C antibodies.

UNLINKED ANONYMOUS DRUGS TESTING

The first author wrote to the Chairman of the UAT Steering Group on 24 September 1996 to suggest Unlinked Anonymous Drugs Testing (UADT) of the antenatal, GUM and general hospital samples to allow monitoring of 'current drug use' in sentinel groups, with analysis by age-group, gender, geographical area and sample source. Inferences about the percentage of users in the last month, say, would have to be qualified by taking into account the drug-specific half-life and also the frequency of use by users who belong to the above sentinel groups, although the latter could be elicited by distribution of anonymous self-completion questionnaires on randomly selected days at relevant clinics. From the outset, the army has appreciated that unattributable behavioural data were needed on frequency of use of different drugs for the army's interpretation of its random Mandatory Drugs Testing (rMDT) of soldiers. Such enlightenment has slowly dawned, after published data (Bird *et al.*, 1997) and personal tutorials, on the UK's prison services about the limited inferences they can draw from rMDT of prisoners, and this may be reflected in changes to rMDT in a revised 1998–2001 Prison Drugs Strategy.

HEPATITIS C PROGRESSION

Hepatitis C infection has a long, age-dependent natural history which is also influenced by level of alcohol consumption (Poynard, Bedossa and Opolon, 1997). Efficient study of hepatitis C progression cannot, therefore, be based on contemporary seroconverters because very few progressions to chronic liver disease occur within the first decade of follow-up. Instead, it requires the unbiased ascertainment of one or more cohorts of patients with prevalent hepatitis C infection, whose time of infection was at least a decade ago and for some of whom the seroconversion window can be narrowed, for example by eliciting the start of their injecting career.

For Lothian region in Scotland alone, Gore *et al.* (1998) have shown that a cohort of 600 patients who were already hepatitis C infected by 1983–84 and who have survived at least to 1 January 1995 can be established by testing now for hepatitis C antibodies the sera which were submitted to the Regional Virus Laboratory in 1983–84 for hepatitis B surface antigen testing. Only half of the cohort of 600 1995-survivors appeared to have a history of injecting drug use. The Lothian methodology could be taken up by other regional virus laboratories which have stored sera for over a decade from patients for whom hepatitis B surface antigen had been requested.

ECONOMIC IMPLICATIONS OF INJECTING DRUG USE

The economic implications of drug injecting in Glasgow have been studied by Hutchinson *et al.* (1999) who investigated the characteristics associated with the amount spent on drugs by 1,024 community injecting drug users in Glasgow who participated in voluntary anonymous salivary HIV surveillance in 1993 and 1994. Mean weekly drugs spend was reported to be £324. Higher weekly drugs spends were associated with respondents who had been in prison more often, and half of the injectors interviewed said that 93 per cent or more of their drugs spend was from illegal sources. Mean annual illegal drugs spend per injector was estimated to be £11,000. Accordingly, the retail value of goods acquired illegally by an estimated 8500 injectors in Glasgow (Frischer *et al.*, 1993) to pay for drugs was worked out to be in the range 187 to 467 million pounds per annum, depending upon whether black market value was taken optimistically as 50 per cent or, more realistically, as 20 per cent of retail value.

The Task Force to Review Services for Drug Misusers (Report of an Independent Review of Drug Treatment Services in England. Chairperson: Reverend Dr. John Polkinghorne, 1996) regarded the lack of existing UK research on drug treatment effectiveness as its single largest handicap. An observational National Treatment Outcome Study was initiated by the Task Force as a stop-gap but it also issued a clarion call for randomised controlled trials of drug treatment effectiveness.

In the absence of better data, Hutchinson *et al.* (1999) therefore suggested that their regression analysis of weekly drugs spend, after adjustment for other determinants, could be regarded as offering a tolerable estimate of the plausible impact of drug treatment programmes on drug expenditure. The impact was a modest 16 per cent reduction. Even so, Hutchinson *et al.* showed that substantial savings could be made if injectors had access to drug reduction programmes which cost less than £5,000 per injector per annum, of which there are several (see, for example, Gruer *et al.*, 1997) and which were modestly effective. Placements may be needed for up to half the injectors in a region: Gore *et al.* (1999), who invited inmates of two Oxford and Anglia prisons to self-complete an anonymous health needs questionnaire, found that half the prisoners with a history of injecting drug use wanted help with their drugs problem.

PRISON-BASED RANDOMISED CONTROLLED TRIALS

Prisons should not be overlooked as a venue for randomised controlled trial of drug reduction placements (Gore and Seaman, 1996; Gore, 1999), and such randomised trials have started in Australia and in prisons in the Netherlands. Prison-based drug reduction trials have advantages, as follows: firstly, while drug reduction places are limited in prisons, randomisation is an ethical, because fair, way of allocating scarce places among otherwise equally eligible injecting drug users who want them; secondly, the Scottish Prison Service, for example, has a national prisoner index, so that it would be easily possible to compare recidivism within one or two years of release from the index sentence (during which the prisoner was randomised) between men who were randomised to 'drug reduction placement' or not; thirdly, because most prisoners are registered with a general practitioner (Cassidy *et al.*, 1999), and with the prisoner's permission his general practitioner could be contacted one year after the prisoner's release for details about drugs-related problems (overdose, abscess) and other serious morbidity, and other hospitalisations such as admission to accident and emergency; and fourthly, because injecting drug users typically serve multiple short terms of imprisonment, the sort of drug reduction placement that prisons can offer to them is either of necessity limited by the person's tarriff, or requires outreach to be organised for a community drug reduction programme/general practitioner liaison to continue the prison's initiative.

Other prison-based trials might compare the effectiveness of more/or less costly interventions to reduce the risk of overdose death for recently released prisoners with a history of injecting drug use (Seaman, Brettle and Gore, 1998). More radically, a court-based randomised controlled trial could compare incarceration versus placement in a secure drug reduction centre for injectors who had been found guilty of non-violent crimes.

Gore (1999) has considered the ethics of randomisation, important outcomes both inside prison and during follow-up after release from index sentence, plausible effect sizes and hence the required numbers to be randomised (about 800 inmates) in prison-based drug reduction trials.

OVERDOSE DEATHS IN RECENTLY RELEASED INJECTOR-INMATES

Up to 30 September 1994, the Edinburgh City Hospital (ECH) HIV Cohort included 332 male injecting drug users. The great majority of any times spent in prison by these men will have been served in their local prison, Edinburgh Prison. Seaman *et al.* (1998) abstracted records of all periods spent in Edinburgh Prison during 1983–94 by the above cohort of male HIV positive injectors.

To protect medical confidentiality, the 332 names of male HIV infected injectors were embedded in an alphabetical list of 704 names (prepared by consultant in infectious diseases, Dr. R.P Brettle) which contained also the names of male injecting drug users (IDUs) who were not known to be HIV infected, HIV infected male non-IDUs, and male non-IDUs who were not known to be HIV-infected. The embedding guaranteed that neither Seaman and Gore (who did the abstraction from prison records), nor anyone accidentally seeing the list could identify individuals either as injectors or as HIV-infected: ethically, and hence methodologically, important. The inclusion of HIV-negative and non-IDU patients was designed also to enable prison history to be compared, controlling for injector and/or HIV status. In order to maintain prisoner confidentiality, individuals were listed on the prison terms' database, not by name, but by master index: initial of first name, Soundex of surname, gender and date of birth.

Objectives of this research project — which later linked on master index the prison and clinical histories of men in the Edinburgh City Hospital HIV Cohort, their HIV seroconversion intervals in particular — included retrospective estimation back to 1983 of HIV prevalence in Edinburgh Prison; the role of the prison in HIV transmissions in 1983–84 (on the basis of seroconversion interval and terms served in Edinburgh Prison, no male IDU in the ECH HIV Cohort could be shown *definitively* to have been infected in Edinburgh Prison but further work identified a putative transmission network, see 1999 University of Cambridge Thesis by Seaman); whether methadone maintenance reduced reoffending (the association was more with referral to the Edinburgh City Hospital Cohort; for review, see Ward, Mattick and Hall, 1992); and whether imprisonment affected HIV progression (further results on immunological progression and progression to AIDS will follow, but the two weeks following release from prison were associated with 8-fold higher risk of overdose death than at other comparable times at liberty: the recent-release rate was 1 overdose death per 1000 recently-released days).

The Chief Inspector for Prisons for Scotland, Mr. Clive Fairweather, surmised from his conversations with prisoners that overdose deaths in recently released prisoners far exceeded the number of suicides inside prisons in Scotland. Seaman, Brettle and Gore (1998) followed up this conjecture by HM Inspector of Prisons for Scotland and found it to be well-founded based on extrapolation from the ECH/Edinburgh Prison estimate cited above.

Further work by Gore and Hutchinson in collaboration with the medical adviser to the Scottish Prison Service, seeks to establish whether the above estimated recent-release overdose death rate applies for prisoners with a history of injecting drug use who were released from Scottish prisons in the immediate past, namely 1995–97. The methodology involves confidential matching of demographic details for ex-prisoners on SPIN (the Scottish Prison Service's national index of prisoners) against the death records held by the Registrar General for Scotland. Thereafter, the prison doctor will be asked whether the doctor was aware of a history of injecting drug use for a set of ex-prisoners released from the same establishment The set comprises the case (deceased) and two or more other prisoners (age and release matched to the deceased). The identity of the deceased is not to be revealed to the prison doctor, although s/he may know it for other reasons.

HEALTHCARE NEEDS ASSESSMENT FOR PRISONERS

Finally, attention is turning, not only in Scotland but elsewhere, to unattributable assessment of prisoners need for healthcare and their views about access to healthcare within their prison. The debate has been fired by HM Chief Inspector of Prisons in England and Wales, Sir David Ramsbotham (1996), in his discussion paper 'Patient or Prisoner?'. Cassidy (1999) is developing a new approach, based on self-completion questionnaires which also invite inmates a) to make suggestions for improving the healthcare of prisoners and b) to comment about drugs or the drugs problem in prison, and which has the potential to evolve into a needs assessment tool kit for use throughout the Prison Service in England and Wales. Besides the self-completion questionnaires, it also entails independent observations, for example, on the healthcare appointments system, the standard of prison medical records and on the qualifications of healthcare staff within the establishment. The views of prison officers could also be taken into account by asking them, again anonymously, to self-complete a proforma which invites them to score their degree of belief in a randomly ordered series of propositions including, for example: 'Anyone with mention of heroin on their prison file should be strip searched after every visit'; 'All prisoners should be offered hepatitis B vaccination'; 'Cannabis should be legalised'.

Already piloted in two prisons, at the second of which over 60 per cent of inmates completed the questionnaires which Cassidy distributed personally, further improvements, including streamlining of the issuing and collection of sealed completed questionnaires and in pre-briefing of inmates, should enable completion rates to equal those achieved in the 2-yearly prisoner survey (on generally less sensitive issues) which has been conducted in Scotland with Butler Trust recognition of its success.

COST AND EFFECT OF rMDT AS A WEAPON IN THE 'WAR AGAINST DRUGS' AND AS A MEANS OF GATHERING INFORMATION

In the absence of refusals, we have estimated the likely cost of random Mandatory Drugs Testing (rMDT) for a prison of 500 inmates where 35 per cent of inmates test positive, one tenth of them for class A drugs, as £16,000 per 28 days (Gore and Bird, 1996) the majority of this cost (over £13,000 pounds per 28 days) being the extra punishment days given to prisoners who test positive for cannabis. Costs decrease roughly in proportion to any decrease in punishment days.

Our calculations were based on 14 days punishment for cannabis and 21 days for class A positive in rMDT. However, governors may elect to suspend punishment, especially for a first rMDT offence, or otherwise vary the above tarriff. Punishment by additional days of unsentenced inmates is prospective in the sense that it takes effect only if the inmate is subsequently sentenced. Below we compare the rMDT-related 369,900 additional days which our calculations were predicated upon with Home Office data for 1996 concerning the punishment of drug-related unauthorised transactions, not all of which were discovered by rMDT (Statistics of offences against prison discipline and punishments, England and Wales, 1996).

In England and Wales, MDT was in place for at least the last nine months of 1996 in all establishments. The total number of drugs-related unauthorised transactions was about 21,000, or 38 per 100 average prison population, which was a vast increase on the number of proven drug use/possession offences previously (there were 2450 in 1994 before MDT pilots began and 5,650 in 1995, the transitional year) but this does not prove any difference in actual use. The figure of 38 per 100 average prison population includes the results of non-random mandatory drugs testing (Statistics of offences against prison discipline and punishments, England and Wales, 1996).

Additional days put back the date on which an inmate can be released and the amount given in 1996 added approximately 1280 to the annual average prison population (Statistics of offences against prison discipline and punishments, England and Wales 1996). Drugs-related offences, for which punishment by *unsuspended* additional days averaged 13 days, accounted for about 500 of the annual average population increase, and hence about 182,500 additional days. This represents only half our predication but in line with it when account is taken of the fact only 54 per cent of punishments with additional days in the Prison Service overall in 1996 were immediate punishments. [Please note: not all 'drugs-related offences' need have rMDT, or even MDT, connection.]

The average population in custody in 1996 was 55,300 and there-fore, in practice, the Prison Service's introduction of MDT to prisons throughout England and Wales coincided with an addition of just under 1 per cent to the average population, or one extra prison if the excess were not being absorbed as exacerbation of overcrowding.

We underline that the proportion of the 'one extra prison' require-ment that: a) relates strictly to rMDT and b) relates to rMDT-associ-ated punishment of cannabis use cannot be determined from the published statistical series which do not differentiate 'Unauthorised Transactions' by whether rMDT was involved or by class of drug. We can, however, be fairly certain that the entirety does not relate to rMDT. Also, because of prospective and suspended punishments, our predication over-estimated by a factor of two the punishment days actually served so that the caution written into our Lancet paper — 'Costs decrease roughly in proportion to any decrease in punishment days' was highly apposite.

Note also that in all prison establishments in England and Wales in 1996/97, as compared with rMDT pilot prisons in 1995, the percent-age testing positive in rMDT for cannabis was around 20 per cent and for heroin was 5.5 per cent (Gore and Bird, 1998).

VIOLENCE IN PRISONS

So much for the cost of rMDT and its likely impact on the average prison population. What effect has its introduction had on violence in prisons? At the Royal Statistical Society in November 1995, Gore (1996) called for evaluation of the policy of rMDT to include the monitoring of assaults on staff and other prisoners because violence in prisons is often associated with drug use.

Some 209 offences against prison discipline were punished per 100 average prison population in 1996 in England and Wales, 1 per cent more than in 1995. Excluding MDT-related offences, the number of offences punished per 100 average population fell by 14 per cent, the types of offence which mainly accounted for this fall being 'disobedience or disrespect' (down from 96 to 83 per 100 average prison population in 1996) and 'other offences, (down from 26 to 21).

Violent offences per 100 average prison population were: 22, 22, 23, 26, 26 in the five years before rMDT was introduced, 24 in 1995 (transitional year) and 23 in 1996 when there were 5300 assaults on any person and 7550 adjudications for fighting between prisoners (see Prison statistics, England and Wales 1996) representing an 8 per cent decrease in 1996 on 1992–94, but only a 3 per cent decrease on 1990–94. These temporal changes, albeit not large, are in MDT's favour. They are not necessarily due to MDT, however, because improvements in security were also being implemented.

The above decreases contrast with provisional assault figures for 1995 for the seven male prisons/young offenders' institutions in the rMDT pilot: assaults were 501 in 1993, 505 in 1994, and 603 in 1995, a highly significant 20 per cent increase (Gore, Bird and Ross, 1996).

The explanation may lie in conversion to a rate 'per 100 average male prison population'. The average male prison population in England and Wales rose from 43,005 in 1993, to 46,983 in 1994, and 49,068 in 1995. Using the 'All male establishment' totals to infer an adjustment for the seven male pilot establishments, population-corrected figures for assaults would read:

$$501, 462 \ [= 505 * (43005/46983)] \text{ and } 552.$$

Even 552, the prison population corrected figure, represents a 16 per cent increase on the assault rate in 1993–94. The Home Office should undertake further analyses to elucidate apparent contradictions between the 1995 pilot study and the 'roll out' of rMDT to all prison establishments in England and Wales by the end of March 1996.

Do Prisoners Switch from Oral Cannabis to Use of Heroin, Including by Injection, to Avoid Detection in rMDT?

Cannabis stays in the urine for three weeks, heroin for three days. Do prisoners convert from oral cannabis to the use of heroin in prison, including by injection, to avoid detection in rMDT? Has rMDT created a new market for heroin in UK prisons? How could we find out (see Gore, *et al.*, 1998)?

Firstly, had the rMDT pilot study in England and Wales been properly designed, with randomisation of prisons to unattributable or punished rMDT, the first of the above questions could have been answered definitively. The pilot study was not set up to provide an evidence-base for policy, however. The policy had already been determined: the pilot study was window dressing. Its main function was to refine the implementation of rMDT.

Gore, Bird and Ross (1996) analysed the performance of rMDT in 1995 within the pilot prisons by comparing the results of rMDT in two time periods. These were February to May 1995, when there were 1089 random tests of which 362 (33.2 per cent) were positive for cannabis, and 44 (4.1 per cent) for opiates or benzodiazepines, of which 29 were for opiates (2.7 per cent); and June to December 1995 when there were 2282 random tests of which 663 (29.1 per cent) were positive for cannabis, and 168 (7.4 per cent) for opiates or benzodiazepines, of which 100 were for opiates (4.4 per cent). The highly statistically significant 65 per cent increase in the percentage of inmates testing positive for opiates — up from 2.7 per cent to 4.4 per cent — signalled the need for urgent policy review. Several caveats applied to the above data: whether the refusal rate had decreased in the second period; whether there was a decrease between periods in the number of opiate positives who also tested positive for cannabis, as would be expected if conversion to heroin from cannabis was occurring because of rMDT; and whether availability of class A drugs in prison had increased because of, or despite, rMDT?

The second question could have been answered easily by inviting prisoners' anonymous observations on drugs and the drugs problem in prisons, as Gore *et al.* (1999) have now done to the indictment of rMDT.

rMDT: a Means of Gathering Information?

Turning now to rMDT as 'a means of gathering information', it is crucially important to realise that a) the percentage testing positive for heroin (opiates) in rMDT is a vast under-estimate of b) the percentage using heroin (opiates) inside prison. To translate from a) to b), we need to take account of how long heroin typically remains in the urine after its use in prison, and of the frequency of its use in prison by inmates who take it. The latter information can only be collected through the voluntary co-operation of prisoners.

Frequency of injection (of any illegal drug) in the last four weeks was asked for in the 1996 WASH surveillance questionnaire for Aberdeen and Lowmoss Prisons. Bird *et al.* (1997) summarised the answers as a mean of 6.0 injections in four weeks (s.d. = 5.7) by inside injectors. The two prisons together held 112 injector-inmates who had been in prison for more than four weeks, of whom 57 (51 per cent) had injected in the last four weeks.

We now illustrate, for Aberdeen and Lowmoss Prisons which hold just under 500 prisoners between them, the difficulty of inferring from a) percentage testing positive for heroin to b) percentage using heroin inside. We make the following basic assumptions:

A1. heroin remains in the urine for 3 days.

A2. mean frequency of injecting heroin is 6 times in four weeks.

A3. non-injection inside-users of heroin take heroin only as often as injectors do (that is: use is more dictated by availability than by route of administration).

A4. inside use of heroin is solely by injection OR solely by non-injection route (a simplification).

A5. Inside users of heroin = inside injectors of heroin, OR inside users are 1.5 times or 2 times as many as inside injectors of heroin.

In addition, we posit:

P1. If rMDT functions on 7 days per week, an inside-injector/user will test positive, on average, on 6*3 days = 18 out of 28 (64 per cent).

P2. If rMDT does not function at weekends, inside-injector//user may test positive on as few as 4*1 [injects/uses on Friday evening] + 2*3 = 10 days out of 28 (36 per cent).

P3. If rMDT functions 6 days per week, e.g. not on Sundays, or if inside-injector is only partially successful in exploiting non-operation of rMDT at weekends, then inside-injector [/user] may test positive, on average, on 4*2 [injects/uses on Friday evening, no rMDT on Sundays] + 2*3 = 14 days out of 28 (50 per cent).

Based on 1996 WASH surveillance data, assumptions A1. to A5. and posits P1. to P3., we show in Table 7.2 the number of heroin positives per 100 rMDT tests to be expected for Aberdeen and Lowmoss Prisons where 40 per cent of inmates had a history of injecting drug use, of whom half were current inside-injectors.

Whereas in England and Wales rMDT mainly did not operate at weekends, we were led to believe that in Scotland rMDT functions on

Table 7.2 Assumed numbers [based on A1. to A5.] of heroin positives per 100 rMDT tests at Aberdeen and Lowmoss Prisons. (Our preferred estimates in bold).

If % inside-users of heroin at Aberdeen and Lowmoss Prisons is:	P1. rMDT @ 7 days: 18/28	P2. rMDT @ 5 days: 10/28	P3. rMDT @ 6 days: 14/28
Assuming that 100% of inside-injectors inject heroin only			
40%: twice as many as WASH % inside-injectors [of any drug]	26	14	20
30%: 1.5 times as many as WASH % inside-injectors [of any drug]	**19**	11	**15**
20%: equals WASH % inside-injectors [of any drug]	13	7.1	10
Assuming that 50% of inside-injectors inject heroin only and 50% heroin never			
20%: twice as many as assumed % heroin only injectors	**13**	7.1	**10**
15%: 1.5 times as many as assumed % heroin only injectors	9.6	5.4	7.5
10%: equals assumed % heroin only injectors	6.4	3.6	5.0

TABLE 7.3   Number of heroin positives per 100 rMDT tests.

b) % Inside- users of heroin	Frequency of heroin use: 6 times in 4 weeks				Frequency of heroin use: 8 times in 4 weeks	
	Clearance time: 3 days		Clearance time: 2 days		Clearance time: 2 days	
	P1. rMDT @ 7 days [18/28]	P2. rMDT @ 5 days [10/28]	P1. rMDT @ 7 days [12/28]	P2. rMDT @ 5 days [4/28]	P1. rMDT @ 7 days [16/28]	P2. rMDT @ 5 days [8/28]
40%	26	14	17	**5.7**	27	11
30%	19	11	13	4.3	17	8.6
20%	13	7.1	8.6	2.9	11	**5.7**
15%	9.6	5.4	6.4	2.1	8.6	4.3
10%	6.4	3.6	4.3	1.4	**5.7**	2.9

the same basis at weekends and on weekdays. If confirmed, our preferred estimates would shift to those shown in italics. Testing at weekends is unconfirmed.

We contacted the Scottish Prison Service, to whom we showed Tables 7.2 and 7.3 and the associated text, and asked for the opiate results of rMDT for the first 6 to 8 months in which rMDT was operational in both Aberdeen and Lowmoss Prisons (at least 300 rMDT tests). Data were received as follows: in the period April to September 1997, 44/347 (12.7 per cent) prisoners tested positive for heroin in rMDT at Aberdeen and Lowmoss Prisons. This accords well with our a priori preferred interval: 10 per cent to 15 per cent.

Table 7.3 shows the discrepancy between a) the percentage testing positive for heroin in rMDT and b) the percentage using heroin inside prison according to whether rMDT functions @ 7 days per week or @ 5 days [that is: not at weekends]; according to whether clearance time for heroin is 3 days or 2 days; and according to whether the mean frequency for inside-use of heroin is 6 times or 8 times in four weeks.

Notice from Table 7.3 that the differential between operating rMDT @ 7 days versus rMDT @ 5 days is relatively greater at a lower average frequency of use: 3-fold if 6 injections in 4 weeks [12/28 versus 4/28] compared to 2-fold if frequency of use is 8 injections in 4 weeks [16/28 versus 8/28].

The main point of Table 7.3, however, is that unless one knows how rMDT operates, the clearance time for heroin as typically used in prison, and the frequency and organisation of heroin use in prison by inside-users, '5.7 heroin positives per 100 rMDT tests', could mean 40 per cent or 20 per cent or 10 per cent of inmates are inside-users of heroin.

As a means of gathering information about the percentage of inside-users of specific class A drugs such as heroin, rMDT is hopelessly, expensively and dangerously flawed (cf. Gore, Bird and Strang, 1999). As it currently operates, rMDT is likely to produce serious under-estimates of the scale of class A drug use and hence also of injection drug use with its attendant public health risks. Grave under-resourcing of prisoners' healthcare needs, both for infection prevention and for reduction of drug dependency, is the inevitable consequence. As such, rMDT represents a serious public health own goal for the UK's prison services, and is likely to perpetuate both an historic weak link in the community approach to the prevention of blood-borne virus transmission and inequality of access to treatment for drug dependent prisoners.

To remove the danger that to avoid testing positive for cannabis in rMDT prisoners are switching to the use of heroin inside prison, we must at least cease testing for cannabis, as the Swiss did; and so cut the market for heroin inside prisons that rMDT has almost surely created (Gore, Bird and Ross, 1996; Gore, *et al.*, 1998).

CONCLUSION

When the history of the outbreaks of blood-borne virus infections in the last three decades of this millennium is finally analysed, it is likely that the prisons will represent the section of the community where the opportunity for prevention has been cruelly overlooked by a combination of suppression of information, apathy and denial, together with a failure of co-ordination between public health services outside and medical services within prisons.

Voluntary surveys, such as WASH surveillance (but see also Bellis *et al.*, 1997; Dolan, Wodak and Penny, 1995; Mason, Birmingham and Grubin, 1997; Power *et al.*, 1991) have consistently demonstrated that prison inmates will co-operate fully and reliably in studies that are of enormous value not only to prisoners and the prisons but also to communities which they serve. The conduct of such surveys also uncovers a high level of concern and thirst for knowledge and ongoing search by prisoners for the tools for their own protection or rehabilitation during incarceration where access to healthcare has been and remains extremely limited (Ramsbotham, 1996).

Prisons thus represent both a threat and an opportunity (Bird *et al.*, 1993; Gill, Noone and Heptonstall, 1995; Dolan, Wodak and Penny,

1995): a literally captive population, heavily enriched for active drug users, and confronted by a life-event which presents the alternatives of a continued, or even prison-initiated, journey into drug use with all its attendant risks, or an opportunity for drug reduction and rehabilitation. Our pragmatic approach to evolution in information gathering, analysis and dissemination together with randomised and fully evaluated approaches to intervention strategies makes both humane and economic sense. It represents a public health imperative for the control of chronically progressive epidemics of blood-borne viruses. Protection of prisoners is also protection of the wider society to which they belong. Failure to do so places at risk of onward viral transmission not only this but subsequent generations. Failure indicts the society that tolerates it.

References

Barr, A., Houston, S.R., MacVarish, I.P., Dow, B.C., Mitchell, R., and Crawford, R.J. (1981) Hepatitis B virun markers in blood donors in the west of Scotland. *Medical Laboratory Sciences,* 38, 405–407.

Bath, G.E., Davies, A.G., Dominy, N.J., Peters, A., Raab, G., and Richardson, A.M. (1993) Imprisonment and HIV prevalence. *Lancet,* 342, 1368.

Bellis, M.A., Weild, A.R., Beeching, N.J., Mutton, K.J., and Syed Q. (1997) Prevalence of HIV and injecting drug use in men entering Liverpool prison. *British Medical Journal,* 315, 30–31.

Bennetto, J. (1996) Prisoners use heroin to thwart drug tests. *Independent, 6 February.*

Bird, A.G. and Gore, S.M. (1994) Inside methodology: HIV surveillance in prisons. *AIDS,* 8, 1345–1346.

Bird, A.G., Gore, S.M., Burns, S.M., and Duggie, J.G. (1993) Study of infection with HIV and related risk factors in young offenders' institution. *British Medical Journal,* 307, 228–231.

Bird, A.G., Gore, S.M., Cameron, S., Ross, A.J., and Goldberg, D.J. (1995) Anonymous HIV surveillance with risk factor elicitation at Barlinnie Prison. *AIDS,* 9, 801–808.

Bird, A.G., Gore, S.M., Hutchinson, S.J., Lewis, S.C., Cameron, S., and Burns, S. on behalf of European Commission Network on HIV infection and hepatitis in Prison (1997) Harm reduction measures and injecting inside prison versus mandatory drugs testing: results of a cross sectional anonymous questionnaire survey. *British Medical Journal,* 315, 21–24.

Bird, A.G., Gore, S.M., Jolliffe, D.W. and Burns, S.M. (1992) Anonymous HIV surveillance in Saughton Prison, Edinburgh. *AIDS,* 6, 725–733.

Burns, S.M., Brettle, R.P., Gore, S.M., Peutherer, J.F., and Robertson, J.R. (1996) The epidemiology of HIV infection in Edinburgh related to the injecting of drugs: an historical perspective and new insight regarding the past incidence of HIV infection derived from retrospective HIV antibody testing of stored samples of serum. *Journal of Infection,* 32, 53–62.

Carvell, A.L.M. and Hart, G.J. (1991) Risk Behaviours for HIV infection among drug users in prison. *British Medical Journal,* 300, 1383–1384.

Cassidy, J., Biswas, S., Hutchinson, S.J., Gore, S.M., Williams, O. (1999) Using self-completion questionnaires to assess prisoners' health and needs: a cross-sectional survey at two male prisons. *Prison Journal, in press.*

Connor, S. (1995a) Thousands of prisoners face HIV screening. *Independent, 29 January.*

Connor, S. (1995b) Drug tests 'threaten AIDS virus study'. *Independent, 3 February.*

Crofts, N., Stewart, T., Hearne, P., Ping, X.Y., Breshkin, A.M., and Locarnini S.A. (1994) Spread of bloodborne viruses among Australian prison entrants. *British Medical Journal,* 310, 285–288.

Dolan, K., Wodak, A., and Penny, R. (1995) AIDS behind bars: preventing HIV spread among incarcerated drug injectors. *AIDS,* 9, 825–832.

Dore, G.J., Kaldor, J.M., McCaughan, W. (1997) Systematic review of role of polymerase chain reactionin defining infectiousness among people infected with hepatitis C virus. *British Medical Journal,* 315, 333–337.

Dufour, A., Alary, M., Poulin, C., Allard, F., Noel, L., Trottier, G., Lepine, D., and Hankins, C. (1996) Prevalence and risk behaviours for HIV infection among inmates of a provincial prison in Quebec City. *AIDS,* 10, 1009–1015.

Farrell, M. and Strang, J. (1994) Drug users in prison. *British Medical Journal,* 309, 271–272.

Frischer, M., Leyland, A., Cormack, R., Goldberg, D., Bloor, M., Green, S. *et al.* (1993) Estimating the population prevalence of injecting drug use and infection with human immunodeficiency virus among injecting drug users in Glasgow, Scotland. *American Journal of Epidemiology,* 138, 170–181.

Gill, O.N., Noone, A., and Heptonstall, J. (1995) Imprisonment, injecting drug use, and bloodborne viruses. *British Medical Journal,* 310, 275–276.

Gore, S.M. (1999) Prisons need randomised controlled trials! *In preparation.*

Gore, S.M., Bird, A.G., and Strang, J.S. (1999) Random Mandatory Drugs Testing of prisoners: a biased means of gathering information. *Journal of Epidemiology and Biostatistics,* 4, 3–9.

Gore, S.M., Bird, A.G., Cameron, S.O., Hutchinson, S.J., Burns, S.M., Goldberg, D.J. (1999) Prevalence of hepatitis C carriage in Scotish prisons: Willing Anonymous Salivary Hepatitis C surveillance linked to self-reported risks. *Quarterly Journal of Medicine,* 92, 25–32.

Gore, S.M., Bird, A.G., Hutchinson, S.J., and Goldberg, D.J. on behalf of EC Network for HIV and Hepatitis Prevention in Prisons. (1999) Prisons need strict protocols for Hepatitis B and HIV outbreaks. *Manuscript in preparation.*

Gore, S.M., Brettle, R.P., Burns, S.M., and Lewis, C.S. (1998) Pilot study to to estimate survivors of 1983–84 prevalent hepatitis C infections in Lothian patients who tested positive or negative for hepatitis B surface antigen in 1983–84. *Journal of Infection,* 37, 159–165.

Gore, S.M., Brettle, R.P., Burns, S.M., and Lewis, C.S. (1998) Early mortality in undiagnosed but prevalent (in 1983–84) HIV infection in Lothian injectors who tested hepatitis B surface antigen positive (group A) or negative but were high risk for blood-borne virus trnasmission (group B) in 1983–84. *Journal of Infection,* 37, 166–172.

Gore, S.M., Bird, A.G., and Cassidy, J. (1999) New Prison Service Drug Strategy: in accord with prisoners' views about the drugs problem in prison. *Communicable Disease and Public Health, in press.*

Gore, S.M., Hutchinson, S.J., Cassidy, J., Bird, A.G., and Biswas, S. (1998) Needs formula for minimum number of drug rehabilitation places in a prison. *Communicable Disease and Public Health, in press.*

Gore, S.M. and Bird, A.G. (1998) Drugs in British prisons. Policies need outside scrutiny if they are to do more good than harm. *British Medical Journal,* 316, 1256–1257.

Gore, S.M. and Bird, A.G. (1998) Study size and documentation to detect injection-related hepatitis C in prison. *Quarterly Journal of Medicine:* accepted for publication

Gore, S.M., Bird, A.G., Burns, S., Ross, A.J., and Goldberg, D. (1997) Anonymous HIV surveillance with risk-factor elicitation: at Perth (for men) and Cornton Vale (for women) Prisons in Scotland. *International Journal of STD and AIDS,* 8, 166–175.

Gore S.M. (1996) Contribution to Discussion of League Tables and Their Limitations: Statistical Issues in Comparisons of Institutional Performance. *Journal of the Royal Statistical Society,* Series A, 159, 425–426.

Gore, S.M., Bird, A.G., and Burns, S.M. (1996) HIV epidemiology in prisons: Anonymous voluntary HIV surveillance with risk factor elicitation. In: *Deaths in Custody. Caring for People at Risk,* A. Liebling ed. London: Whiting and Birch Ltd. pp. 114–142.

Gore, S.M., Bird, A.G., Burns, S.M., Goldberg, D.J., Ross, A.J., and Macgregor, J. (1995) Drug injection and HIV prevalence in inmates of Glenochil prison. *British Medical Journal*, 310, 293–296.

Gore, S.M., Bird, A.G., Burns, S.M., Goldberg, D., Ross, A.J., and Macgregor, J. (1995) Anonymous HIV surveillance with risk-factor elicitation at Glenochil Young Offenders' Institution. *AIDS*, 9, 662–664.

Gore, S.M. and Bird, A.G. (1995) Cross-sectional Willing Anonymous Salivary HIV (WASH) surveillance studies and self-completion risk factor questionnaire in establishments of the Scottish Prison Service. *ANSWER*, 29 September, 1–4.

Gore, S.M. and Bird, A.G. (1995) Mandatory drugs tests in prisons. *British Medical Journal*, 310, 595.

Gore, S.M., Bird, A.G., and Ross, A.J. (1995) Prison rites: starting to inject inside. *British Medical Journal*, 311, 1135–1136.

Gore, S.M. and Bird, A.G. (1993) No escape: HIV transmission in jail. Prisons need protocols for HIV outbreaks. *British Medical Journal*, 307, 147–148.

Government Statistical Service (1997) *Statistics of offences against prison discipline and punishments, England and Wales 1996*. The Stationary Office Cm 3715, London.

Government Statistical Service (1997) *Prison statistics, England and Wales 1996*. The Stationary Office Cm 3732, London.

Gruer, L. and Macleod, J. (1997) Interruption of methadone treatment by imprisonment. *British Medical Journal*, 314, 1691.

Gruer, L., Wilson, P., Scott, R., Elliott, L., Macleod, J., Harden, K., Forrester, E., Hinshelwood, S., McNulty, H., and Silk, P. (1997) General practitioner centred scheme for treatment of opiate dependent drug injectors in Glasgow. *British Medical Journal*, 314, 1730–1735.

Haw, S.J., Higgins, K.M., Bell, D., Johnston, B.B., and Richardson, A.M. (1996) Evidence of continuing risk of HIV transmission among injecting drug users from Dundee. *Scottish Medical Journal*, 41, 3–4.

HIV and AIDS Surveillance in Scotland. (1995) *AIDS News Supplement to the Weekly Report, December 1995*.

Hutchinson, S.J., Goldberg, D.J., Gore, S.M., Cameron, S., McGregor, J., McMenamin, J., and McGavigan, J. (1998) Hepatitis B outbreak at Glenochil Prison during January to June 1993. *Epidemiology and Infection*, 121, 185–191.

Hutchinson, S.J., Gore, S.M., Frischer, M., Taylor, A., Goldberg, D., and Patterson, W. (1999) Economic implications of injecting in Glasgow: analysis of drug expenditure. *British Journal of Psychiatry, in press*.

Hutchinson, S.J., Gore, S.M., Goldberg, D.J., Yirrell, D.L., McGregor, J., Bird, A.G., Leigh-Brown, A.J. (1999) Completing the epidemiological account of HIV outbreak at Glenochil Prison. *Edipemiology and Infection, in press*.

Jurgens, R. (1996) *HIV/AIDS in Prisons: Final Report*. Canadian HIV/AIDS Legal Network and Canadian AIDS Society, Montreal.

Kennedy, D.H., Nair, G., Elliott, L., and Ditton, J. (1991) Drug misuse and sharing of needles in Scottish prisons. *British Medical Journal*, 302, 1507.

Lush, P. (1994) Drug users in prison. *British Medical Journal*, 309, 674.

Maden, A., Swinton, M. and Gunn, J. (1991) Drug dependence in prisoners. *British Medical Journal*, 301, 880.

Mason, D., Birmingham, L., and Grubin, D. Substance use in remand prisoners: a consecutive case study. *British Medical Journal*, 315, 18–21.

McBride, A.J., Ali, I.M., and Clee, W. (1994) Hepatitis C and injecting drug use in prisons. *British Medical Journal*, 309, 876.

McIntyre, P.G., Laszlo, J., Appleyard, K., and Ogden, G.R. (1996) Modified enzyme immunoassay to detect Hepatitis C virus antibodies in oral fluid. *European Journal of Clinical Microbiology and Infectious Diseases*, 15, 882–884.

McMenamin, J., Goldberg, D., Pithie, A., Green, S., Cameron, S., Williams, F., Middleton, D., Yirrell, D., Leigh-Brown, A., Glabraith, I., Henderson, N., and Farrell, A. (1997) HLA antigens

A1, B8, DR3 predict rapid progression in an IDU cohort infected with an identical strain of HIV in a Scottish prison. *Lancet* (submitted for publication).

McNeil, A.J., Yap, P.L., Gore, S.M., Brettle, R.P., McColl, M., Wyld, R., Davidson, S., Weightman, R., Richardsom, A.M. and Robertson, J.R. (1996) Association of HLA types A1-B8-DR3 and B27 with rapid and slow progression of HIV disease. *Quarterly Journal of Medicine, 89,* 177–185.

Power, K.G., Markova, I., Rowlands, A., McKee, K.J., Anslow, P.J., and Kilfedder, C. (1991) Sexual behaviour in Scottish prisons. *British Medical Journal,* 302, 1507–1508.

Poynard, T., Bedossa, P., Opolon, P. for the OBSVIRC, METAVIR, CLINVIR and DOSVIRC groups (1997) Natural history of liver fibrosis progression in patients with chronic Hepatitis C. *Lancet,* 349, 825–832.

Ramsbotham, D. (1996) *Patient or Prisoner?* London : Home Office.

Report of an independent review of drug treatment services in England (chairman: Reverend Dr. John Polkinghorne) (1996) *Task Force to review Services for Drug Misusers.* London: Department of Health.

Seaman, S.R., Brettle, R.P., and Gore, S.M. (1998) Mortality from overdose among injecting drug users recently released from prison: database linkage study. *British Medical Journal,* 316, 426–428.

Shewan, D., Gemmell, M., and Davies, J.B. (1994) Prison as a modifier of drug using behaviour. *Addiction Research*, 2, 2, 203–216.

Smith G. (1997) Prison HIV scare 'worse than feared'. Mother of former inmate supports doctors' claims that epidemic has spread outside jail. *Scotland on Sunday, 16 March.*

Steel, C.M., Ludlam, C.A., Beatson, D., Peutherer, J.F., Cuthbert, R.J.G., Simminds, P., Morrison, H. and Jones, M. (1988) HLA halpotype A1 B8 DR3 as a risk factor for HIV-related disease. *Lancet,* 1, 1185–1188.

Taylor, A., Goldberg, D., Emslie, J., Wrench, J., Gruer, L., Cameron, S,. Black, J., Davis, B., McGregor, J., Follett, E., Harvey, J., Basson, J., and McGavigan, J. (1995) Outbreak of HIV infection in a Scottish prison. *British Medical Journal,* 310, 289–292.

Unlinked Anonymous Surveys Steering Group. (1996) *Unlinked anonymous HIV seroprevalence monitoring programme in England and Wales: data to the end of 1995,* London : Department of Health,.

Ward, J., Mattick, R., and Hall, W. (1992) *Key issues in methadone maintenance treatment.* Sydney: University of New South Wales Press.

Wellings, K., Field, J., Johnson, A.M., and Wadsworth, J. (1994) Editors. *Sexual Behaviour in Britain. The National Survey of Sexual Attitudes and Lifestyles.* Penguin Books Ltd., London.

World Health Organization (1993) *Global Programme on AIDS: WHO guidelines on HIV infection and AIDS in prisons.* Geneva: WHO Global Programme on AIDS.

Yirrell, D.L., Robertson, P., Goldberg, D.J., McMenamin, J., Cameron, S., and Leigh Brown, A.J. (1997) Molecular investigation into outbreak of HIV in a Scottish prison. *British Medical Journal,* 314, 1446–1450.

Chapter 8

DEVELOPMENT OF HIV/AIDS POLICY IN THE DUTCH PRISON SYSTEM

Maarten van Doorninck and Wouter de Jong

The development of HIV/AIDS policy in the Dutch prison system covers a period of approximately ten years. It originated in 1985 in a single prison where guidelines were drawn up for the staff. These guidelines were the basis for the first circular, published in 1987, in which the Ministry of Justice formulated the HIV/AIDS policy for the Prison Service, and 1996 saw the publication of the second HIV/AIDS circular presenting the actualised HIV/AIDS policy for the Prison Service. The departmental working group AIDS and Detention, a co-operation between judicial and non-judicial organisations, had a crucial role in the development of the Prison Service HIV/AIDS policy and still has. This working group prepared the 1996 circular and took some important initiatives in order to improve HIV/AIDS prevention and care in prisons. Non-judicial organisations participated in the working group, influenced public opinion, parliament and the Ministry of Justice and stimulated the practical implementation of the HIV/AIDS policy. All this resulted in increased support among prison governors for the HIV/AIDS policy and a growing number of prisons that now work on the implementation of the policy guidelines.

This chapter describes the development of the HIV/AIDS policy in the Dutch prison system. It describes both the interaction between actors within and outside the prison system and the development and implementation of the policy. The chapter begins by describing the Dutch prison system and the policy regarding imprisoned drug users and continues with a description of the development of the HIV/AIDS policy in the past.

The closing comments will first search for an explanation for the gradual increase in the support the policy has received. For this purpose six Prison Service officials who hold a key position in the development of the HIV/AIDS policy in the prison system were interviewed. Also, the co-operation between judicial and non-judicial organisations is evaluated. Finally, suggestions are given for the future improvement of both the HIV/AIDS and drugs policies in the Dutch prison system.

THE DUTCH PRISON SYSTEM

For a long time Holland had less prisoners than other countries. Increasing numbers of offences and longer prison sentences, however, caused a growing shortage of cells. The number of delinquents who could not be detained due to this shortage caused an outcry in public opinion and in parliament and lead to plans for a considerable building programme to greatly increase the number of cells. Between 1991 and 1996, the number of prison cells for men and women over 18 years old increased from 7500 (4.99 per 10,000 inhabitants) to 12,000 (7.74 per 10,000 inhabitants) spread over 42 prisons and remand prisons, (Ministry of Justice 1995a, 1996a, 1996b; Tweede Kamer, 1994, CBS 1991, CBS 1996).

In 1996, 38,756 prisoners (25.0 persons per 10,000 inhabitants) entered the prison system, the majority (60 per cent) in remand prisons. Of all prisoners, 4.2 per cent were female and approximately 50 per cent were not born in the Netherlands (32 per cent had a foreign nationality).

The Dutch prison system is widely differentiated. There are separate prisons for men and women detainees, for short and long term sentences, for juvenile offenders and for prisoners who have been sen-

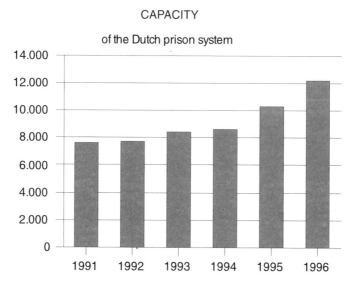

FIGURE 8.1 CAPACITY OF THE DUTCH PRISON SYSTEM, 1991–1996.

tenced to receive psychiatric treatment. Many prisons have separate units for psychotic detainees, for drug users, for prisoners who do not function well in groups, for high security prisoners. In total, the Ministry of Justice presently has 43 various categories, each with its own specific form of security and guidance.

All prisons and remand prisons for adults are controlled by the Prison Service of the Ministry of Justice. In addition 7 of the 17 juvenile prisons and 3 of the 7 psychiatric penitentiary institutions are part of the Prison Service. The rest are controlled by private organisations. The wide diversity in categories of prisons has enabled prison governors to gradually assert more influence on their particular prison's policy. The institutions are now governed more globally by the Prison Service. Annually, the report and the working plan for each prison is discussed with the prison governor which results in the settlement of the annual budget. The circulars are another governing instrument and these also have gradually acquired a more general character. The 1996 AIDS circular, per example, is less specific than that of 1987.

The task of the Prison Service is 'to execute imprisonment and detention measures in a safe, efficient and dignified manner'. Since the eighties there has been a more business-like approach to prison policy and in 1994 it was decided to further regulate prison life, such that prisoners should spend more time working, with less time for recreation and less time spent in the open air (Tweede Kamer, 1994). At present a new weekly schedule is being phased in. Between 8.30 a.m. and 9.00 p.m. prisoners spend 40 hours per week in their cells, 26 hours working, 9 hours at recreation, 10.5 hours on airing and 9 hours on other activities. Special programmes will be offered to a minority of the prisoners (estimated at 20 per cent) who are assumed to be motivated to improve their social situation. Examples of such programmes are professional skill training courses and addiction guidance units (AGUs, formerly called drug free units, DFUs) for drug users. Previously all kind of special programmes were available to all prisoners.

As a rule, prisoners each have their own cell. There are, however, some limited exceptions, partly due to the shortage of cells. A small number of short sentence prisoners (less than 2 months detention) can voluntarily be placed in a double cell and most foreigners awaiting deportation are detained in wards. Depending on the prison, the wards contain between 24 and 72 detainees, guarded by prison guards and officers. Prison guards work outside the cell blocks and are responsible for guarding and transport. Prison officers work in teams within the cell blocks with the accent on prisoner guidance. After having received the basic training for prison guards, officers take a supplementary 15-day course on social skills. In the daytime there are 2 prison officers on duty for every 24 prisoners.

MEDICAL CARE IN THE PRISON SYSTEM

Every prison has at least one prison doctor who is head of a medical service. A full-time doctor is employed for every 300 detainees; one nurse is available for every 50 males or 30 females. As soon as a prisoner is admitted, the doctor acquaints himself with the medical status and thereafter holds checks at regular intervals (Ministerie van Justitie 1993a and 1993b). Prisoners are allowed medical attention on the day of arrival or, at the latest, on the second day. Usually the prisoner is first seen by a nurse, since most prison doctors work part-time and run their own general practice as well. Some doctors are only actually present in a prison for a few hours per week. Prison doctors are also responsible for prison hygiene. Beside these tasks, which are in the interest of prisoners, they also judge prisoners' capability for work. Any prisoner who for medical reasons is unfit for work needs a note from the prison doctor (or nurse). In free society the latter medical task is normally executed by special doctors because of the conflicting interests. Prison doctors are autonomous in their treatment of patients, which has lead to conflicting situations, for example regarding the prescription of methadone.

If detainees require medical attention, they can request a visit to the medical service, which is usually granted the same or the next day. If the necessary medical attention cannot be supplied, the detainee will be referred to the penitentiary hospital or a general hospital.

One of the problematic aspects of medical service in prisons is the fact that detainees consider doctors and nurses to be part of the judicial system. The prison doctor's function as medical officer, judging prisoners' capability to work, further hinders a confidential doctor-patient relationship. Detainees formally have the right to consult another doctor, but they have to pay the fee themselves, which in practice limits this right. In 1997 a detained drug user claimed the right to receive (methadone) treatment from his drug service doctor. He won his case, but the appeal of the Prison Service is still pending.

Medical care in prisons has been widely discussed in the past few years. After complaints resulting from four deaths, the National

Ombudsman published a critical report highlighting the conflicting areas, such as the lack of communication and cooperation between the medical services and the prison officers. The Minister of Justice requested a committee to further investigate the problems which resulted in a report with several proposals for improvement (Ministerie van Justitie, 1995b). The most important recommendations were that doctors should be physically present and should be better skilled to deal with the detainees' particular problems such as drug addiction and mental illnesses. The committee also submitted proposals for better co-operation between medical services, prison psychologists, probation officers and other prison staff. One of the trouble spots regarding prisoner care was caused by rigid adherence to the formal division of tasks.

Next the committee stated a more consistent medical policy within the whole prison system was necessary. In the case of a transfer, a prisoner could be subjected to new medical standards due to the absence of general guidelines. The committee further advised to clarify the relation between the Medical Inspectorate of the Prison Service (MI) and the general Health Inspectorate of the Health Ministry. The Minister of Justice approved most recommendations in 1995 and requested the Prison Service to prepare their implementation.

One of the consequences of the committees report is that the Medical Inspectorate of the Prison Service (MI) will be transformed into a Bureau for Prison Health Care. Until 1997 the Prison Service had its own medical inspectorate (MI) which supervised medical care and advised on medical policy of the prison system. The MI could also give advice on individual medical cases. Requests for early release on medical grounds were always dealt with by the MI. The Prison Service MI was bound to report to the Health Inspectorate of the Health Ministry, but in practice both organisations had different opinions on what issues had to be reported.

In 1998 the formal position of the new Bureau for Prison Health Care and its relation with the general Health Inspectorate is not defined. The name however suggests that the bureau will have a less formal position than the former MI.

DRUG POLICY IN PRISONS

Approximately one third of the annual intake of detainees used hard drugs such as heroin and cocaine before being detained. That means that in 1995, about 10,000 hard drug users entered the prison system, including an error margin due to recidivism. Exact statistics are not available because the figures are based on prisoners voluntarily providing information and some prisoners withhold the fact that they used drugs before imprisonment. Drug using prisoners are not equally spread over the prisons. Most of them stay in remand prisons and in prisons for short sentences.

Drug use in prison is prohibited and abstinence is required for several reasons. Firstly, the use of illegal drugs is seen as conflicting with the function of the prison system. Secondly, it is judged to be an important cause of recidivism. Thirdly, as one of the interviewed Prison Service officials stated, abstinence is required in order to function in penitentiary life. At the moment there is not a uniform policy regarding the supply of medication. Until a few years ago all drug users were expected to have recovered from their dependency within 1 or 2 weeks. The choice of medication is left up to the doctors. Sometimes methadone is prescribed but other doctors only prescribed sedatives. Methadone prescription has gradually been accepted in more prisons, but still some prison doctors refuse to prescribe it. The Minister of Justice announced in 1996, following the advice of the previously mentioned investigative committee, that she aimed to enforce a uniform methadone policy. In the same year a prisoner nevertheless had to claim the right to continuation of methadone treatment in court after his transfer to an other prison. As with the previously mentioned case this prisoners' claim was accepted, but the appeal of the Prison Service is also still pending.

Prisoners can be given random urine tests for control of drug use, but the budget for this is limited. If positive results are obtained, disciplinary action will be taken. Despite the recent strengthening of the drug policy, drug use does take place in prisons. According to ex-prisoners, the staff are even willing to look the other way regarding the use of cannabis because of the sedative effect of the drug. Although the use of hard drugs is prohibited, it does not prevent them from being smuggled into prisons. Results of research in Amsterdam amongst 191 ex-detainee drug users showed that 36 per cent had used heroin, 20 per cent cocaine and 55 per cent cannabis during detention (Van Haastrecht, 1996). In this study only 5 injecting drug users (3 per cent) reported to have injected drugs during their last period of imprisonment, and none of them reported to have used syringes or needles that had been used by someone else before. In 1997 Van Haastrecht conducted a feasibility study on HIV prevalence and risk behaviour in one wing of a Dutch remand prison. The study was part of the research programme of the 'European Network for Prevention of HIV infection in Prisons'. Of the 98 prisoners participating in the study 9 reported ever having injected drugs, and 4 of them had injected in the month before imprisonment. None of the prisoners reported ever having injected in prison (Van Haastrecht, 1998).

The low rates of injecting in Dutch prisons and the seeming absence of sharing can until now not be explained on basis of thorough investigations. It is true that approximately 70 per cent of the drug users in the Netherlands actually smoke their heroin and cocaine, although life time prevalence of injecting among opiate users is about 70 per cent. Several personal reports of drug users show that drug users who normally inject change too smoking or sniffing when imprisoned. These ways of consuming drugs are easier to hide from prison officers and more safe, as sterile syringes are not available in prisons. Drug users' organisations however report that they regularly hear from drug users that drugs are injected and injecting equipment is shared. Members of prison staff unofficially report too that drugs sometimes are injected and that syringes are sometimes stolen from the medical service. These reports however do not show to what extend prisoners inject or share. The two studies of Van Haastrecht show low prevalence rates for injecting and no sharing. Prison governors state that it is very rare to find syringes and other paraphernalia during cell inspections.

ADDICTION GUIDANCE UNITS (AGUS)

In 1996 there were 446 cells available at AGUs (formerly called Drug Free Units) to drug users. Most drug users however stayed in ordinary prison units among other detainees. In AGUs drug users can prepare themselves for further treatment of their addiction after release. The units are staffed with prison officers who followed a 25 day course supplementary to the standard training for prison officers and probation officers from drug service organisations. AGU prisoners receive individual and group guidance. Control on drug use through urine tests is more intensive in these units. If positive results are obtained, the prisoner will be returned to a closed wing.

HIV IN PRISONS

Precise statistics on HIV/AIDS problems in prisons are not available because, as in the case of drug use, the figures are based on information supplied voluntarily by the detainees during their medical examination. Apart from those detainees who are unaware of their

	1990	1991	1992	1993	1994*
HIV positive reported at entry	133	172	182	136	147
HIV tests carried out in prison	259	383	417	517	414
HIV diagnosed after prison test	42	28	35	21	36
AIDS diagnosed reported at entry	19	18	34	30	12
AIDS diagnosed in prison	7	6	10	14	2

source: Medical Inspectorate Prison Service
* results of two remand prisons are missing
FIGURE 8.2   REGISTERED PRISONERS WITH HIV AND AIDS 1990–1994.

serostatus, an unknown number with seropositive status withhold this information for fear of experiencing negative consequences.

Prisoners can voluntarily undergo an HIV test. A protocol for this test was set up in 1995, which states that prisoners should be fully informed on advantages and disadvantages of the test and consent to it. The following figures show the medical service's registration of reports of illness and test results.

Neither the decline in reported HIV infections in 1993, nor the decline in reported AIDS diagnoses in 1994 can be explained from a decline in any of the groups with high HIV prevalence. The national figures for the same years only show a gradual decline (Inspectie voor de Gezondheidszorg, 1997).

After 1994 the Medical Inspectorate stopped gathering the data on HIV since it was to much work to gather the data and because of the restricted value of the collected data, as these were based on voluntary reports from prisoners.

On the basis of the estimated number of imprisoned drug users who have injected once or more (approximately 5000 people) and assuming HIV is present in 10–20 per cent of this population (30 per cent in Amsterdam, 12 per cent in Rotterdam, 10 per cent in the Maastricht region and 2–5 per cent in some other cities) it is estimated that in 1995 between 500 and 1000 prisoners infected with HIV entered the system. This estimation can be challenged as it is based on the assumption that most prisoners with HIV are injecting drug users. Van Haastrecht however found in his feasibility study in a remand prison that three of the 98 prisoners were infected with HIV, of whom only one had ever injected (Van Haastrecht, 1998). Furthermore, the estimation is based on the assumption that 50 per cent of drug users ever injected drugs, although reliable figures are not available. Of new clients of all Dutch drug services a minority (13.7 per cent) reported recent injecting (Ouwehand, 1997). In an HIV prevalence study among drug users in Rotterdam, 494 of the 701 drug users (70 per cent) reported ever having injected (Wiessing, 1995).

Officially, HIV infected prisoners are not treated any differently from the other detainees. The 1987 circular stated that 'stigmatisation, segregation or concentration of HIV infected prisoners is impermissible'. Despite this, there are several known cases of HIV infected prisoners undergoing negative experiences from both co-prisoners and staff (De Man, 1994). Another interviewed Prison Service official stated that prisoners with HIV/AIDS appear to have a low status among other prisoners, comparable to that of sex offenders. The limited opportunities to receive support from partners, friends and family increases the likelihood of psychosocial problems. In some cases the prison management decides on a transfer to a special cell block where extra support and guidance can be offered (Kools, 1996). Prisoners with HIV also reported being excluded from group activities, such as sport, because of expected trouble with other inmates (NCAB, 1994). The prisoners concerned could perceive these measures as segregation or discrimination on the grounds of their serostatus. The management, however, reasons that they have to protect these detainees and avoid trouble with other inmates.

Despite the fact that all staff have been informed about HIV/AIDS and other infectious diseases, they are not always able to prevent undesirable behaviour and attitudes among the prisoners. Sometimes the staff even encourage it, because, as educational programmes reveal, staff can be extremely afraid of infection and distrustful of available information on the likelihood of infection (Van Doorninck, 1996). In other cases the staff have gradually become used to HIV problems, especially in prisons which regularly hold prisoners with HIV.

In a small society like a prison, it is difficult to keep ones serostatus information confidential, either from staff or from prisoners. Medical files, for example, can be read by administrative staff. When a prisoner is transferred from another prison, a transport staff member accompanies a prisoner into a specialist's consulting room, or there is an awkward silence when a prison officer asks the nurse what is wrong with one of the prisoners. For prisoners it is hard not to speak about loaded personal information, such as having HIV. A confidential chat with a co-prisoner or a sympathetic officer can lead to the prisoner's serostatus becoming public knowledge. Therefore some medical staff advise against prisoners undergoing HIV tests in prison (Van Doorninck, 1996).

THE DEVELOPMENT OF THE DUTCH PRISON HIV/AIDS POLICY

As mentioned previously, in 1987 the first circular announcing the HIV/AIDS policy was published by the Prison Service. It stated that prisoners with HIV and AIDS should not be segregated or treated differently from other prisoners. It also named a number of preventive supplies which should be present in every prison and made recommendations regarding their use and supervision. Listed under the obligatory supplies were, for example, working gloves, disposable shaving gear, condoms and a first-aid protocol after needle stick or bite injuries. The circular also stated that regular informatory sessions should be available to both staff and prisoners. Many preventive measures were described to minimise the risk of infection for staff and detainees during their daily routines.

The circular further stated that it was almost impossible to specify general instructions regarding psycho social problems. It was the responsibility of the management to ensure adequate treatment and guidance for HIV infected prisoners. Together with the Ministry, suitable methods should be sought for the treatment of those prisoners with the physical symptoms of HIV, implying hereby the possibility of early release.

National Co-ordination

In 1989 the Health Ministry asked the Ministry of Justice to contribute to the national HIV/AIDS prevention programme by setting up an educative programme in prisons, especially for foreigners and drug users. Both ministries established the interdepartmental working group 'AIDS Education in Penitentiary Institutions'. Although denied by the Prison Service, the growing criticism on the HIV/AIDS policy in the prison system was probably a reason for the establishment of this working group. The task of the working group was to develop proposals to intensify HIV/AIDS and STD education in prisons. Prison governors, civil servants from both Ministries and experts from non-governmental organisations such as the former Netherlands Institute on Alcohol and Drugs (since 1996 Trimbos-instituut, further: NIAD/Ti), the National Commission on AIDS Control (NCAB) and the STD Foundation were invited to participate in the working group.

The working group first made an inventory of the existing situation in a selected number of prisons, and this revealed that most prisons had organised informatory sessions, but rarely on a regular basis and usually only for prison staff. These sessions were usually only made available to the staff when an incident had occurred.

The working group recommended that all prisons should assign a nurse who would be responsible for co-ordinating HIV/AIDS activities and, anticipating the final advice, it initiated a first series of HIV/AIDS training courses for these nurses in 1990. Nurses were chosen to fulfil a co-ordinating role in HIV/AIDS education in prisons because of their availability for individual and confidential contact with prisoners. The working group asked the STD Foundation to compile and distribute a presentation of folders and other informative material on HIV and STDs. Both the training course and the presentation were financed by the Health Ministry.

The working group's aim was to ensure that all prisoners receive comprehensive education on HIV/AIDS and STDs in order to prevent stigmatisation of drug users and homosexuals. In its final report of 1991, the working group proposed development of integrated activities in every prison. Group educational sessions should be combined with individual counselling whereby more attention could be paid to prisoners' individual circumstances. Besides these education and counselling activities, materials should be made available to enable the staff and detainees to prevent infection. However, since drug use in prison is prohibited, neither syringes nor disinfectants could be permitted. Instead the working group recommended to advise drug users to smoke their drugs or to disinfect syringes by boiling them in their cell kitchen.

The group also recognised that prison staff are an important target group as well, both for self-protection purposes and in order for them to support HIV/AIDS education for prisoners with whom the have daily contact. The working group further proposed to establish national co-ordination and support to the prisons through creating a consultant post. Finally, they suggested involving regional health and drug services with the development and implementation of HIV/AIDS prevention in prisons.

After the working group's recommendations were submitted in January 1991, nearly 18 months elapsed before the Ministry of Justice took action. Eventually a new working group was set up, this time established only by the Ministry of Justice, to develop more detailed activities and to promote the implementation of the first working group's recommendations. The new working group consisted of virtually the same people and organisations. Although not responsible for its work, the Health Ministry participated in the working group. In the next years the new working group instigated a number of measures which are described below. Since 1995 it has received an annual budget of approximately $125,000. A working plan is annually submitted to the Prison Service for approval. Gradually the scope of the working group is broadening from HIV/AIDS to other infectious diseases as a result of the recognition, through activities aimed at HIV/AIDS, that other infectious diseases also require more attention.

Training Courses for Prison Nurses

The first series of HIV/AIDS training courses for prison nurses was welcomed, although the two day course was too short for extensive training of educational and counselling skills. Therefore, in 1992 the working group proposed repeating the basic course and the development of an advanced course more specifically aimed at broadening the skills required for group and individual counselling. Both courses were offered by the Prison Service's Educational Institute, but now financed by the MI's training programme. In the years to follow the course was regularly repeated for new recruits. In 1995 the first advanced course was held. By the summer of 1998, approximately 180 nurses had followed the basic training course and 98 the advanced course.

The HIV/AIDS Consultancy

The first working group advised the appointment of special HIV/AIDS consultants to stimulate and promote the development of

HIV/AIDS education in prisons, with the emphasis on supporting the co-ordinating prison nurses. The first consultant was employed in 1993 for 10 hours a week. This was extended in 1994 to 20 hours a week, in 1996 to 40 hours, and in 1997 to 56 hours a week. The consultants' chief duties were advising prison management on HIV/AIDS policy and advising medical staff on the implementation of educational methods. In 1992 the working group had previously proposed the establishment of a network of co-ordinating prison nurses. In 1996, after the extension to 40 hours per week for consultants, the first regional meetings for prison nurses were organised. These meetings are now held twice a year. In 1997 the general director of the Prison Service recognised the broadened scope of the consultants' work and accepted changing their title and function to consultants on infectious diseases.

The HIV Test Protocol

It became apparent from the nurses' training courses that most prisons were not using a protocol for HIV testing, as was the norm in free society. The working group therefore adapted the existing protocol to the prison situation and this was sent by circular to all prison governors in 1994. The protocol stipulates that HIV tests may only be carried out when the detainee has been thoroughly informed of the consequences and then grants permission for the test to take place. It also contains guidelines for pre- and post-test counselling and confidentiality of medical information.

The New HIV/AIDS Circular

In 1994 the working group proposed that the Ministry review the 1987 circular. The old circular was seen as being out of date, due to there being a lack of balance in the attention paid to the different items covered by the circular. It contained 27 detailed guidelines for infection prevention, such as on the availability and use of working gloves for staff, the supply of razor blades for prisoners, and the temperature at which bedclothes should be washed. However, other areas were only briefly mentioned.

Due to the change in structure of the prison system, with the Prison Service allowing considerably more freedom to prison governors to develop their own prison policy, the main theme of the new circular was that prison governors are responsible for drawing up and applying HIV/AIDS policy in their prisons. The guidelines are formulated in more general terms and the 1997 circular therefore consists of a mere five pages.

The circular formulates the following principles for prison HIV/AIDS policy:

— Information on prisoners' serostatus should be dealt with carefully, both by medical and other staff, in order to prevent stigmatisation and to create a supportive climate for prisoners with HIV.
— Prisoners with HIV should be treated as non-infected prisoners. Labelling, segregation or concentration are inadmissible.
— Prisoners with HIV must receive the same medical treatment as non-imprisoned people with HIV.
— If adequate medical treatment cannot be offered, the MI can propose early release or treatment outside the prison system.

These principles are followed by the aims of Dutch prison HIV/AIDS policy:

— The prevention of HIV infection in prisons by supplying information and taking protective measures.
— Supplying adequate medical and psycho-social treatment for detainees with HIV or AIDS.
— Prevention of discriminatory treatment of prisoners with HIV or AIDS.

In order to achieve these aims, the circular states that HIV/AIDS information and education should be offered to all prisoners and staff, and that protective measures against HIV infection should be taken. Examples of suggested protective measures are wearing protective goggles and working gloves, making condoms available, and offering adequate assistance after needle stick or bite injuries. The circular however explicitly states that 'there are no possibilities to provide disinfectants for syringes'. With regard to the treatment of HIV infected prisoners, the circular refers to the HIV test protocol and suggests offering medical and psychosocial care to prisoners with HIV, this to be made available from both from prison staff and external organisations. Compared to the 1987 circular less attention is paid to specific instructions for prison staff. Instead, the targets for staff education are described, and it is recommended that education of staff should be aimed at both risk reduction and towards their contribution to the respectful treatment and guidance of prisoners with HIV.

HIV/AIDS Policy Recommendations and Pilot Prisons

As the guidelines in the circular were formulated in general terms, the working group decided to ease their implementation by producing a brochure with recommendations for drawing up prison HIV/AIDS policy. It mentions, for example, the different professional activities, like cleaning and cell inspection, which need specific safety instructions and it describes the conditions necessary for adequate medical and psychosocial treatment.

In addition to this brochure a number of prisons were to receive extra support in order to set up working examples of HIV/AIDS policy for all different types of prisons. The working group also proposed a national monitoring of progress within prisons. The circular, the instructions and some adapted methods for HIV/AIDS education were presented at a conference for prison governors organised by the working group in 1996. Almost all prisons were represented at this conference.

Booklet on Infectious Diseases

At the suggestion of the working group, NIAD/Ti produced a 12 page booklet on infectious diseases for all prisoners. The booklet described the infectious diseases that have impact on prison life (flu, tuberculosis, hepatitis B and C, HIV/AIDS and STDs) and gives advice on how to prevent infection and what a prisoner who is concerned about his health can do. The booklet also explains prison policy regarding infectious diseases, for example regarding tuberculosis screening and the fact that there is no need for segregation of prisoners with HIV. Since 1997 the booklet is handed out to all prisoners on entry. In order to emphasise the status of the information, it is offered on behalf of the prison management. Prison nurses report that they are more frequently consulted on infectious diseases, which suggests that the booklet improves the level of open communication on this issue. In 1998 the booklet was translated into four languages — English, French, Spanish and Turkish — in order to make the information accessible to foreign prisoners too.

Developments Outside the Working Group

Besides the improvements brought about by the departmental working groups, a number of other developments have influenced the HIV/AIDS policy in the Dutch prison system. Firstly, the various activities of non-judicial organisations will be described followed by a review of a number of pilot projects, and finally a review of research into HIV in prisons.

External Organisations

Despite the 1987 circular and other Prison Service activities, the prison system is regularly criticised by external organisations. One cause of criticism is that prison policy deviates from the policy applied within free society, for example regarding the restrictions on methadone treatment and the provision of facilities for safer drug use. The Prison System was also criticised on the fact that the 1987 circular was only partly executed. The majority of prisons had no structured education programme for prisoners, and only incidentally informed staff on HIV/AIDS.

In addition, the three external organisations represented in the departmental working groups undertook various outside activities, such as publishing articles, organising workshops and conferences and supporting pilot projects that were initiated by local health and drug services. Another active organisation is the Netherlands HIV Association, an interest group of people with HIV, which was regularly confronted with the problems of HIV infected prisoners. They aired their views through media publicity and through their connections with individual members of the working groups. In 1995 this association initiated a project in which the possibilities for confidential visits to prisoners with HIV by fellow sufferers outside prison were explored. Also the Amsterdam interest group for drug users (MDHG) and 'Act up!' regularly expressed their opinions.

Recommendations of the National Committee on AIDS Control (NCAB)

In May 1994 the NCAB submitted their advisory report 'AIDS and Detention' to the Ministers of Health and Justice. This paper contained 38 recommendations for reforming the policy on information, prevention, care, treatment, research, funding and policy structure. It received a divided response from the Ministries: The Health Ministry generally lent its approval to the recommendations, but the Ministry of Justice found the suggested measures too extreme, particularly those regarding the promotion of safer drug use in prisons through sterilisation of injecting equipment. Although the Ministers had announced that a joint response would be released, there was a long period of silence. Two years later, after questions had been raised in parliament, the government announced its views. The NCAB paper was found to be constructive and offered good opportunities for further policy development, including the actualisation of the 1987 AIDS circular. However, the recommendations regarding the supply of sterilising equipment were stated to be incompatible with recently strengthened drug policy.

In 1995 the NCAB again approached the Prison Service and this resulted in a proposal of NIAD/Ti for a national project to promote and support the development of HIV/AIDS prevention and care. The initial reaction was positive but during a second meeting a few weeks later the Prison Service announced that objections had been raised against placing this project with an external organisation like NIAD/Ti. Instead, the departmental working group was granted the previously mentioned annual budget.

PILOT PROJECTS

Various pilot projects have now been carried, mainly through the initiative of drug service organisations. Most of these innovative projects were subsidised by the Health Ministry and the national AIDS Fund with the aim of contributing towards adapting educational methods to the prison situation and passing these on to other prisons. The pilot projects cover the following subjects:

Utrecht: Wolvenplein Remand Prison

In 1991 the Utrecht drug service organisation started a group educational project for prisoners and staff. In 1994 a manual for group education was published and sent to all prisons. The project was funded by the drug department of the Health Ministry.

Amsterdam: Demersluis Remand Prison

In 1992 the Amsterdam drug service organisation started a project on individual counselling of imprisoned drug users by drug service probation officers. A manual for both individual and group counselling was published in 1996. The project was funded by the drug department of the Health Ministry.

Amsterdam: Havenstraat Remand Prison

In 1992 the prison staff and the Amsterdam health service organised information sessions for Surinam, Moroccan and Turkish prisoners presented by native speakers.

Doetinchem: De Kruisberg Semi Open Prison

In 1994 the regional drug service organisation started a project on group education sessions, specially aimed at sexual behaviour during leave and after release. Live theatre acts were used to illustrate moments in which decisions have to be made on safe sex. In 1995 a manual for educational sessions, a video with the dramatised theatre acts, and a folder designed as a driving licence (loving licence) was presented at a conference. The project was funded by the National AIDS Fund. NIAD/Ti supported the project by a funding donation for the video and reported on the development of the project (Van Doorninck, 1996).

Amsterdam: Havenstraat Remand Prison

In 1994 the staff of the educational department of the prison started a project in co-operation with the Amsterdam health service and the Amsterdam drug service, in which a CD-ROM for individual interactive HIV/AIDS education was developed. In 1996, this CD-ROM was presented at the previously mentioned conference for prison governors. The project was funded by the National AIDS Fund.

Following the positive response to this CD-ROM, the national working group initiated the production of a special CD-ROM for female prisoners. This CD-ROM was released in 1998. Based on experiences with HIV/AIDS projects for women outside prisons, the CD-ROM for women focuses on health issues such as pregnancy. This CD-ROM was produced by a project group which brought together the expertise of several organisations, and was funded by the Prison Service.

Dutch HIV Association (HVN)

In 1995 the HVN started a project to explore the possibilities for confidential contact between prisoners with HIV and fellow sufferers outside prison. The project showed that the issue of confidentiality presented the most difficult problems. For example, if a prisoner does not inform at least a limited number of prison staff of his or her serostatus, extra facilities for confidential visits cannot be arranged. In some cases a fellow sufferer can acquire permission to enter prison from an authorised, not HIV related, organisation. This project is funded by the National AIDS Fund.

The Hague: Scheveningen Penitentiary Complex

In 1996 The Hague buddy organisation started a project in which prisoners with HIV could receive confidential visits from their buddies. As with the HVN project, this project indicated that prisoners need a confidential relationship with members of the medical staff before extra facilities for confidential visits can be created. In 1997 the Trimbos-institute started a follow-up project to assess different ways to arrange visits by buddies. Both projects were funded by the National AIDS Fund.

Healthy from Inside to Outside

In 1997 the HIV/AIDS consultants of the Prison Service and Alletta, an organisation for women health care and promotion, started a pilot project in two prisons which resulted in the production of a manual to organise a series of group sessions for female prisoners. The project was funded by the Health Ministry and the manual was released in 1998.

OTHER LOCAL INITIATIVES

Besides these pilot projects, two initiatives have played an important role in the developments of the past few years. Firstly, the prison management of De Marwei prison in Leeuwarden installed a working group to develop a prison HIV/AIDS policy. A staff member of the regional HIV/AIDS council supported this working group. The prison HIV/AIDS policy that was adopted in 1994 was the first policy for a local prison and was used as an example for the AIDS circular of 1996 and the instructions for the development of prison AIDS policy by the departmental working group.

Secondly, in 1995 the Maashegge semi open prison included an HIV/AIDS education session in the introduction programme for all new prisoners. The first session is obligatory, participation in a follow up session is voluntary. Maashegge was thereby the first prison to implement HIV/AIDS education in the regular activity programme for prisoners.

RESEARCH

As previously explained, there are no reliable statistics on the extent of HIV/AIDS problems within the prison system. Over the years there have been various attempts, through research, to clarify the situation.

In 1990 the Catholic University of Nijmegen submitted a proposal for a feasibility study on the prevalence of HIV and the knowledge, attitudes and behaviour of detainees and staff in penitentiary institutions. The proposal was approved with the exception of the prevalence study which the Ministry of Justice deemed undesirable for fear of unrest amongst detainees if the extent of HIV infection among the prisoner population was publicly known. Also, this aspect of the research was not considered to be a priority for further development of HIV/AIDS prevention and care, a view supported by the NCAB .

In 1992, the study resulted in a report based on interviews with the management, staff and detainees of six prisons. The researchers' main conclusion was that, generally speaking, HIV/AIDS was not a cause of unrest, unless incidents such as fights occurred. In order to protect themselves in such situations, the staff often wanted to know which prisoners were HIV infected. Avoidance of contact with prisoners with HIV was noticeable, and this resulted in these prisoners becoming isolated. Another conclusion was that more attention should be paid to the prejudicial attitude of staff and inmates, particularly as information sessions about HIV/AIDS and infectious diseases reduced ungrounded fears of infection, and recommended that such sessions should therefore take place on a regular basis. The researchers also concluded that the availability of condoms, including condoms for anal sex, should be improved, for example by installing slot machines in toilets. This suggestions was of particular importance since there were future plans for double cells. Finally they concluded that the methodology employed was suitable for wide-scale research into the level of HIV/AIDS related knowledge among prisoners and staff, and their attitudes, risk perception and behaviour with respect to HIV/AIDS. However, the proposal for research on a national level was not approved for several reasons. Firstly, the Ministry of Justice, the Health Ministry and the NCAB rejected the proposed prevalence study. Secondly, the research methods received some criticism and finally, the research received no priority from the Prison Service.

The education and information project 'Criminality and Society' (K&S), the Amsterdam interest group for drug user (MDHG) and 'Act up!' asked the Institute of Criminology of the University of Utrecht to investigate medical care in prisons. Many shortcomings were identified in the official regulations and in their execution, and resulted in recommendations for improving facilities for supplying HIV/AIDS information, sterilising equipment and sterile syringes (Zijl, 1993). The results were submitted to the Medical Inspectorate and the Prison Service who acknowledged the value of this research and undertook consideration of a number of recommendations, but again criticised the research methods. The study had been carried out in one prison by a postgraduate student, and the conclusions of this single researcher in a single prison were found insufficient to provide a picture of the medical care in the whole prison system.

Two studies among drug users outside prison explored the relationship between risk behaviour, HIV prevalence, and imprisonment. In 1994, the National Institute for Public Health and Environment (RIVM) published the results of their research into drug users in Rotterdam which divulged that HIV infection was more probable among drug users who had been imprisoned two or more times (Wiessing, 1994). This could point to an increased risk by imprisonment but could also mean that drug users who are imprisoned more often lead a high risk lifestyle and thereby become HIV infected sooner.

The previously mentioned 1996 Van Haastrecht report published the results of a study among Amsterdam ex-detainee drug users. The respondents reported having used heroin (36 per cent), cocaine (20 per cent) and cannabis (55 per cent) during imprisonment. Five drug users (3 per cent) reported having injected drugs, of which four cases had done so once and one case three times, all without sharing syringes.

In 1996 NIAD/Ti proposed Dutch participation in international research of the European Network on HIV/AIDS Prevention in Prisons, co-ordinated by the Scientific Medical Institute of Germany (WIAD) and Regional Health Observatory (ORS) in Marseilles and funded by the European Commission. As in other countries, firstly a feasibility study on HIV/AIDS prevalence and risk behaviour of detainees was carried out in one Dutch remand prison in 1997. The results of this study were published together with the results of the studies in other countries in the final report of the network and in a Dutch scientific journal (Van Haastrecht, 1998). As cited previously the study found 3 HIV infected prisoners in a population of 98. Only one of these people reported having ever injected, and nobody reported ever having injected in prison.

Since the findings of Van Haastrecht do not confirm the assumptions of HIV-prevalence in prisons (low prevalence of injecting, sharing and HIV were expected, but the assumption was that most HIV infected prisoners are drug users), the Trimbos-institute proposed to participate in the follow-up study of the European Network and collecting data among 500 prisoners in 5 prisons. In 1998, the Prison Service had not yet decided on this proposal, but a discussion in the working group showed that most members thought such a study would not be useful for the further development of HIV/AIDS policy in the Dutch prison system.

CONCLUSION

The development of HIV/AIDS policy in the Dutch prison system covers a period of approximately ten years, marked by the Prison Service AIDS circulars of 1987 and 1996. The HIV/AIDS epidemic initially caused great concern among the personnel and detainees. In the following years less attention was paid to HIV/AIDS, as the problems within the prison system were considered to be controllable. During that period the Prison Service was regularly criticised by external organisations because the application of HIV/AIDS policy was not as intensive as that in free society. In recent years, however, there has been a gradual increase in supporting a more active HIV/AIDS policy. Two examples of this are the well attended conference for prison governors in 1996, and the growth in the number of institutions where Prison Service HIV/AIDS consultants are involved with the execution of HIV/AIDS prevention activities.

These closing comments on the development of the prison HIV/AIDS policy in The Netherlands search for factors that led to the increased attention on HIV/AIDS. For this purpose, interviews were held with six prison officials who were involved with this development.

If the number of detainees with HIV had grown in the past years it would explain the increased attention for HIV/AIDS. However this is not the case. Figures from the Health Inspectorate indicate that the HIV/AIDS epidemic has stabilised in Holland in the past few years (Inspectie voor de Gezondheidszorg, 1997). Figures on prevalence and incidence among drug-users are reasonably stable too (Van den Hoek, 1988; Van Haastrecht, 1991; Van Ameijden, 1992). The Prison Service MI figures also show no clear increase of reported HIV infections among prisoners. If there is a link between the increase of attention for HIV/AIDS and the number of detainees with HIV, then this has been an extremely slow reaction. It was already known in the eighties that HIV would constitute a serious threat to the health of drug users and that this would have consequences for everyone within the prison system. It is clear, however, that the number of detainees with HIV has not been the immediate cause of the considerable increase in interest in the HIV/AIDS issue over the last few years.

The characteristics of HIV/AIDS problems in the prison system have not undergone any radical changes in recent years. After the initial concern amongst the detainees and staff, the problems surrounding HIV/AIDS seem to have stabilised and are now classified as controllable. This is partly due to the policy that was formulated in 1987 and partly to a number of fundamental characteristics of the Dutch prison system.

The 1987 circular clearly stated the policy regarding treatment of detainees with HIV, such as labelling, segregation or concentration based on a prisoner's serostatus, is inadmissible. This was also repeated during the staff informatory sessions which were mainly organised after incidents had occurred. The result was that detainees with HIV were officially treated in the same way as other prisoners. However, not all staff were immediately convinced by the information they were given on transmission risks. Detainees with HIV were often ignored or avoided by those staff who were not acquainted with the problems surrounding HIV. Consequently, these staff members were unable to correct or prevent similar rejection by other prisoners. However, the policy was sufficiently specific to prevent or limit serious incidents.

This reduced the problems for HIV infected detainees to the level of individual problems which accordingly relieved the prison system from the acuteness of HIV/AIDS problems, and only incidental cases became publicly known. Reports from other sources showed that HIV positive prisoners experienced great difficulty during their detention. Some detainees reported their experiences during a workshop on HIV associated problems in prisons (NCAB, 1994 and 1995) and through interviews (Kools, 1996). The Prison Service Medical Inspector also published an article in which he stated that a lack of understanding is the main problem for prisoners with HIV (De Man, 1994). The detainees reported varying situations in prisons. In one prison they felt extremely isolated and even afraid of co-prisoners; in another prison they received more understanding from the staff. Recent reports by HIV/AIDS consultants confirm that many prison staff are used to dealing with these problems, but others are still of the opinion that they could protect themselves better by obligatory testing of detainees. These latter opinions have a negative influence on living conditions for detainees with HIV.

The two most outstanding fundamental characteristics of the Dutch prison system with regard to HIV/AIDS are cell accommodation and the guiding role of prison officers. A detainee in a Dutch prison generally has an individual cell, thereby reducing any threat constituted by sharing accommodation with an HIV infected prisoner. where incidents occurred, these mostly concerned communal activities such as the use of unit showers or sport. Such incidents were usually resolved when HIV infected prisoners adjusted to the situation, for example by showering last or not participating in sports. Some detainees were able to take a stand and acquire a full and worthy position within the prisoner group.

The Dutch prison system is outstanding in the area of special attention paid to the guidance of prisoners. Prison officers, having completed their prison guard training, follow an additional course on social skills. Their position in the cell block enables them to offer guidance to their group of detainees. In the most positive cases, in which they are used to dealing with HIV/AIDS associated problems, they can offer support to the detainees. In other cases they are at least able to observe and resolve tension in the cell block, which is of importance to HIV prisoners even if their problems are not fully respected.

The tendency towards individualisation of HIV/AIDS problems effects the amount of attention prison officers pay to these problems. The problems of HIV infected prisoners are not generally considered to be extremely serious when compared to psychiatric problems which seriously affect life in prisons. At the beginning of the nineties the issues of hostage taking and escapes demanded much more attention, and much of prison governors' time was taken up by the reorganisation of the Prison Service and expanding cell capacity. HIV/AIDS was considered to be controllable.

It can be concluded that the 1987 policy and a number of characteristics of the prison system influenced the nature of HIV/AIDS problems but there are no obvious changes which account for the increase of support to the HIV/AIDS policy in recent years.

One influencing factor may have been the release of the second AIDS circular in 1996. A comparison between the two circulars shows some distinctive differences. Firstly, the specific guidelines for preventive measures provided in the first circular were not mentioned in the second. One example of this is the temperature required for washing bedding. The absence of these details implies that the first circular was mainly aimed at providing clear, assuring instructions to management and staff. The second circular contained less specific details regarding safety measures and paid more attention to the various professional skills required from the staff. The working group's accompanying HIV/AIDS policy instructions states that prison guards should be able to carry out body-searches safely and that the medical staff should be able to carry out test counselling. All staff members are requested to support the HIV/AIDS policy in their daily work.

A second noticeable difference in the two circulars is that the second is adapted to the organisational changes that have taken place within the prison system. During the last ten years prison governors have been given more scope to adapt HIV/AIDS policy to the needs in their particular prisons. The Ministry now runs the prison system in more general terms. The 1996 circular explicitly states that the prison governors are responsible for HIV/AIDS policy. It continues to state the aims of prison HIV/AIDS policy and the subjects which should be dealt with. Whether prison governors actually do have a wider scope is questionable. The last circular also contains a number of requirements which are similar to those contained in the 1987 circular. The phrase 'an institution should continually offer AIDS education' from the 1996 circular can hardly be called more general or less obliging than the phrase 'good, regularly repeated AIDS education ..... is important' from the 1987 one.

But, nevertheless, the release of the 1996 circular and its better fit with the evolved organisational structure of the prison system will to a certain extent have contributed to the increase in support for HIV/AIDS policy. On the other hand, differences between both circulars are not that fundamental. The working group that edited the second circular even feared that just releasing it might not in itself be effective. It would mean that prison governors received the information but whether they really would take action was questionable. Many guidelines from the 1987 circular had been ignored. Although this circular contained the recommendation that provision should be made for HIV/AIDS information sessions for detainees, the actual organisation of this was very slow. It was seven years later, in 1994, before the first prison started these sessions. The working group therefore concluded that the release of the circular required some follow up in the form of support to prison managers and staff by the HIV/AIDS consultant and the monitoring of progress. The release of the new HIV/AIDS circular itself only partly explains why HIV/AIDS policy now receives more support from prison governors and staff.

Which brings us to another possible reason for the increased support for HIV/AIDS policy, namely the fact that the prison system has in recent years acquired its own expertise in the area of HIV/AIDS prevention and care. Previously, this expertise was only available in external organisations, such as the health and drug services who initially executed HIV/AIDS education programmes. The process of internalisation within prisons of expertise on HIV/AIDS prevention and care in the prison system took several years.

The first step was the training course for prison nurses. Initially this was carried out by the Prison Service Educational Institute but, due to the lack of in-house expertise, NIAD/Ti trainers were employed. This had the double advantage of supplying in-house expertise to the Prison Service and providing a platform for prison staff to discuss their practical experiences. Until then discussion of HIV/AIDS problems had been confined to prison governor level. The training course identified the problem areas for both prison staff and HIV infected prisoners, which gave the external organisations more insight and revealed the staff's willingness to improve the situation.

Pilot projects were the second step in the process of internalisation of expertise. Regional health and drug services had started educational programmes in prisons and funds were provided by the Health Ministry and the National AIDS Fund. Prison staff discovered that existing educational methods used in free society could be easily adapted for prison use. The fear that detainees would reject open discussion on HIV/AIDS or that it might even lead to unrest were proved to be unfounded. On the contrary, large numbers of detainees participated in the educational sessions and appreciated the fact that HIV/AIDS problems could be openly discussed.

The third step of internalisation was the appointment of HIV/AIDS consultants within the Prison Service, which was important as their tasks were exclusively involved with HIV/AIDS prevention and care. Initially the consultants required regular support from the external organisations but gradually they developed their own working methods and activities. In 1996 a national network of prison nurses was set up to further develop HIV/AIDS prevention in prisons. This network provided a structure for exchange of information between prison nurses all over the country and for further dissemination of innovative methods. The network meets twice a year. Besides these meetings, a newsletter produced by the HIV/AIDS consultants informs the members. Like the working group the HIV/AIDS consultant and the network have changed the scope of their activities and now pay attention to all infectious diseases.

The process of internalisation reveals the role of the external organisations. They strongly supported the prison system and initiated several new activities, both at national and regional level. Some of these organisations followed a strategy that can be characterised as dualistic. They both criticised the prison system for being slow in dealing with HIV/AIDS and offered support to the Prison Service to improve HIV/AIDS prevention and care.

The external organisations comprised many separate bodies with varying opinions and interests. Firstly there are the interest groups for drug users and HIV patients. Their role was mainly to express the views of their members. The former criticised the prison system for its repressive drugs policy and the associated risk drug users faced when injecting in prisons. The latter attacked the shortcomings in medical care and the lack of discretion regarding confidentiality of personal files. These two organisations also attempted to influence policy by publishing the results of an investigation into health care in the prison system (Zijl, 1993), although most suggestions were not accepted by the Prison Service.

The dualistic approach is more obvious in the work of the NCAB, the NIAD/Ti and the STD Foundation. These organisations participated in the departmental working group and exerted their influence outside the working group in order to improve the situation in the prison system. The NCAB produced a lengthy report in which the Ministers of Health and Justice were advised to conduct a more active policy. In co-operation with the NIAD/Ti and the STD Foundation, the NCAB organised conferences which delivered critical comments to the Prison Service. This caused some friction within the working group between representatives of the prison system and the external organisations. But because these organisations made an important contribution to the activities of the working group, this friction did not impair the working relationship.

It can be concluded that the role of the external organisations has been of great importance. They were an independent force responsible for keeping the HIV/AIDS on the agenda of the Prison Service, especially during the first years. They also provided support in the development of the policy and enabled the Prison Service to adapt the existing HIV/AIDS prevention and care methods for use in the prison system.

This has partially closed the discrepancy between the systems used in prison and in free society.

Although conditions appear to be favourable, it is still too early to determine whether the increased support for HIV/AIDS policy will actually lead to wider implementation. In any case, the setting up of a network of prison nurses and supplying all detainees with a folder on infectious diseases ensures that the issue remains under the constant attention of all institutions.

However, it cannot be concluded that all the recommendations supplied by the external organisations have been adopted by the prison system. Progress is mainly limited to the area of HIV/AIDS education. The more far reaching suggestions, for example to provide disinfectants for drug using detainees, have been rejected by the Prison Service. The advice for a harm reduction policy has also been discarded. Although the Minister has agreed to a uniform methadone medication policy, this has not yet shown any results. The new Prison Service methadone policy most likely will not match the policy and practice of drug services outside the Prison Service. There, methadone can be prescribed to all opiate addicted individuals. In 1996 and 1997 two detainees still had to take their cases for continuation of methadone medication to court and in both cases the Prison Service did not accept the court's decision and appealed against it.

The European Conference on Drug and HIV/AIDS Services in Prison, held in Amsterdam in February 1997, revealed that the drugs policy in the Dutch prison system is strongly based on abstinence in comparison with, for example, Switzerland and Germany (Trautmann, 1997). HIV/AIDS policy in Dutch prisons still focuses on education without providing the means to reduce risk, while outside the prison system it has for years been working policy to combine education with the distribution of syringes and other items which enable drug users to put the information into practice.

ACKNOWLEDGEMENTS

Interviewed Prison Service officials: Drs. M. Amoureus (staff member Prison Service, secretary departmental working group AIDS and prisons); Drs. J.G.A. van den Brand (prison governor Havenstraat remand prison, chair departmental working group AIDS and prisons); S. de Bruine RN (AIDS consultant Prison Service), Th. J. de Man, MD and A. van der Heijden, MD, (the former Medical Inspectorate Prison Service); Drs. Th. Molijn (Education Institute Prison Service).

References

Ameijden, E.J.C. van, Van den Hoek J.A.R., Van Haastrecht H.J.A., Coutinho R.A. (1992) The harm reduction approach and risk factors for HIV seroconversion in injecting drug users, Amsterdam. *American Journal of Epidemiology*, 136,(2), 236–243.

Centraal Bureau voor de Statistiek (CBS) (1992) *Statistisch Jaarboek 1991*. Heerlen, 1992.

Centraal Bureau voor de Statistiek (CBS) (1996). *Statistisch Jaarboek 1996*. Heerlen, 1997.

Doorninck M van. (1996) *Procesverslag van het AIDS-voorlichtingsproject in de penitentiaire inrichting De Kruisberg in Doetinchem*. Utrecht, NIAD.

Haastrecht, H.J.A. van, Hoek, J.A.R. van den, Bardoux, C., Leentvaar-Kuijpers, A., Coutinho, R.A. (1991) The course of the HIV epidemic among intravenous drug users in Amsterdam, The Netherlands. *American Journal of Public Health* 81, (59) p. 62.

Haastrecht, H.J.A. van, Hoek, J.A.R. van den, Coutinho, R.A. (1996) Low levels of HIV risk behaviour among injecting drug users during and following imprisonment in the Netherlands; *Vancouver; 11th International Conference on AIDS*, Abstract Tu.C.2549; 1996.

Haastrecht, H.J.A. van, Jong, W.J. de. (1998) HIV infecties en risicogedrag onder gedetineerden in een Nederlandse strafinrichting, in. *Tsg/Tijdschrift voor Gezondheidswetenschappen*, 76, 267–271.

van den Hoek, J.A.R., Coutinho, R.A., Van Haastrecht, H.J.A., Van Zadelhoff, A.W., Goudsmit, J. (1988) Prevalence and risk factors of HIV infections among drug users and drug using prostitutes in Amsterdam. *AIDS*, 2, (1), 55–60.

Inspectie voor de Gezondheidszorg (1996) AIDS in Nederland, kwartaaloverzicht per 1 oktober 1996; in: *AIDS-Bestrijding* Nr31; Amsterdam; Stichting Aids Fonds.

Interdepartementale werkgroep AIDS-voorlichting in justitiële inrichtingen (1991) Eindverslag van de interdepartementale werkgroep AIDS-voorlichting in justitiële inrichtingen. in: Doorninck M. van, *AIDS en Detentie, beleidsplan van het project AIDS en Druggebruik*, Utrecht: NIAD.

Ouwehand, A.W., Cruts, A.A.N., Vetten, L.J. de. Kerncijfers, Ladis (1996). Houten. IVV, 1997.

Kools J-P. (1996) Zitten met HIV. In *Mainline* (Amsterdam, Stichting Mainline).

de Man, Th. J. (1994) HIV in Dutch prisons, what is the main problem? In: *Iuris, Quaderns de Política Jurídica*; Núm. 2 -1994 (Barcalona: Generalitat de Catalunya, Departament de Justítia.)

Ministerie van Justitie (1993a) *Gevangenismaatregel van 23 mei 1953, laatstelijk gewijzigd 13 December 1993*. (Den Haag).

Ministerie van Justitie (1993b), *Huishoudelijk reglement voor het Huis van Bewaring*. (Den Haag).

Ministerie van Justitie (1995a) *Dienst Justitiële inrichtingen; Jaarverslag D&J 1994*; (Den Haag).

Ministerie van Justitie (1995b) *Zorg ingesloten, de organisatie van de medische zorg in de penitentiaire inrichtingen van het gevangeniswezen*, (Den Haag).

Ministerie van Justitie (1996a) *Dienst Justitiële inrichtingen; Jaarverslag 1995*; (Den Haag).

Ministerie van Justitie (1996b) *Dienst Justitiële inrichtingen; Jaarplan DJI '96*, (Den Haag).

Ministerie van Justitie (1996c) Opleidingsinstituut DJI; *Opleidingsgids 1996* (Den Haag).

NCAB (1994) AIDS en Detentie, AIDS-bestrijding in justitiële inrichtingen in Nederland (Amsterdam).

NCAB (1995). AIDS en detentie, verslag van het mini-symposium, 12–12–1994 Rotterdam. (Amsterdam: NCAB).

Trautmann, F., Doorninck, M. van. Verslag, van de 'European conference on drug and HIV/AIDS services in prison' in Amsterdam. in: *Bulletin* SPM 97/1. Utrecht, Trimbos-instituut.

Tweede Kamer (1994) *Werkzame detentie, beleidsnota voor het gevangeniswezen*; vergaderjaar 1993–1994, 22999, nrs. 10–11; Den Haag.

Wiessing, L.G., Toet, J., Houweling, H., Koedijk, P.M., van den Akker, R. en Sprenger, M.J.W. (1995) *Prevalentie en risicofactoren van HIV-infectie onder druggebruikers in Rotterdam.* Bilthoven, RIVM en Rotterdam, GGD Rotterdam en omstreken.

Willems, J., Schippers, G.M. en Breteler, M.H.M. (1992) *AIDS en Detentie, een exploratie van AIDS-gerelateerde problematiek bij hoger personeel, penitentiair inrichtingswerkers en gedetineerden in enkele penitentiaire inrichtingen in Nederland.* (Nijmegen : Vakgroep Klinische Psychologie en Persoonlijkheidsleer, Katholieke Universiteit Nijmegen).

Zijl M. (1993) *Gezondheidszorg in de bajes.* Utrecht, Wetenschapswinkel Rechten.

Chapter 9

DRUGS AND PRISONS: A HIGH RISK AND HIGH BURDEN ENVIRONMENT

Michael Farrell, Nicola Singleton and John Strang

Prisons remain one of the areas where there are considerable untapped opportunities for interventions with dependent drug users. It is also an environment that presents considerable risk for the transmission of blood-borne viruses, in particular the transmission of HIV and hepatitis C, with a number of studies identifying prisons as an independent risk factor for hepatitis C transmission (Gaughwin *et al.*, 1995; Stark *et al.*, 1995).

It is now well recognised that there are high concentrations of dependent drug users and injecting drug users in both male and female prisons in the UK, with there being higher rates of self-reported opiate dependence among the female prisoner population than in male prisoner populations (Advisory Council on the Misuse of Drugs, 1996).

Overall it is difficult to get a clear picture of how drug using characteristics of the prisoner population reflect the general populations from which they are drawn. In most general household surveys the rates of opiate use and dependence are very low, being well below 1 per cent in most surveys. Social deprivation is associated with higher rates of drug problems and dependence but this is unlikely to account for the high rates found among those in prisons. Higher rates were found in a pilot survey in a highly deprived locality, which reported levels of 3 per cent (Griffiths *et al.*, 1998), and a study of a homeless population reported high rates of alcohol and drug dependence (Farrell *et al.*, 1998).

Surveys of behaviour during imprisonment are necessary to provide an objective picture of the current situation in prisons. All these surveys are dependent on self reports of behaviour and require more detailed quantity frequency data to ascertain the exact nature of drug use in prisons. The following sections present data collected during recent surveys of prisoner populations carried out by the authors.

MENTAL HEALTH PROBLEMS WITHIN THE PRISONER POPULATION

There is now extensive data documenting the high levels of morbidity in the prison population. All of the national surveys which have been carried out in England and Wales indicate that within the prisoner population there is a significant number of people with alcohol and other drug related problems and dependence.

In a recent major survey of psychiatric morbidity in the prison population both the sentenced and remand, male and female population were surveyed (Singleton *et al.*, 1998). This involved structured interviews with a total of 3200 prisoners.

Of the overall sample, in the 12 months before entering prison about 20 per cent of the males and about 40 per cent of the females had received help for a mental or emotional problem. The female remand prisoners reported the highest rates of problems with over 22 per cent having ever been admitted to a mental hospital. The rates of psychotic disorder were estimated at 7 per cent for male sentenced prisoners, 10 per cent for male remand and 14 per cent for female prisoners. This is considerably higher than rates found in the general population where the estimated rate for psychotic disorder is 0.4 per cent. The most common personality disorder found in the prisoner population was Antisocial Personality Disorder, with approximately 60 per cent of the males and 30 per cent of the females displaying the characteristics of this condition. Assessment indicated that under 50 per cent of males and over 60 per cent of females were thought to have a neurotic disorder with a high prevalence of severe disorder. 2 per cent of the prison population had attempted suicide in the past week and approximately a quarter of males, and approaching half of females had a life time history of suicide attempts. Thus the prison population has a substantial excess of mental health problems when compared to the general population and this difference is likely to persist even if social inequalities are controlled for.

DRUG USE WITHIN THE PRISONER POPULATION

The Prison Psychiatric Morbidity Survey (Singleton *et al.*, 1998) also indicated high levels of substance abuse problems within the prisoner population, again considerably higher than those found in the general population. This study reported that over 60 per cent of male prisoners and approximately 37 per cent of female prisoners were rated as having a history of serious drinking problems.

Over 80 per cent of the sample reported smoking cigarettes, with a high proportion reporting heavy smoking. Smoking is an important activity for the prison population and tobacco is an important commodity for bartering with in prisons. In the Psychiatric Morbidity Survey, 85 per cent of male remand, 77 per cent of male sentenced, 83 per cent of female remand and 81 per cent of female sentenced

Table 9.1 Prevalence of smoking by prisoner type and sex.

	Male remand	Male sentenced	Female remand	Female sentenced
	%	%	%	%
Never regular	10	14	15	15
Ex-regular	4	8	3	3
Light (<10/day)	18	19	11	15
Moderate (10–19/day)	36	34	31	32
Heavy (20+/day)	31	24	41	34
Base	*1235*	*1109*	*185*	*581*

prisoners were current smokers (Farrell *et al.*, 1998). Details of smoking rates among this sample are shown in Table 9.1.

In the survey of psychiatric morbidity among adults living in private households, 32 per cent of the population reported current smoking. However, in the survey of psychiatric morbidity among homeless people and also in the survey of people in institutions catering for people with mental health problems (Farrell *et al.*, 1998) much higher rates of smoking (74 per cent and 70 per cent respectively) were reported.

High rates of heavy smoking (20+ per day) were found among all groups of prisoners, with 31 per cent of male remands, 24 per cent of male sentenced, 41 per cent of female remands, and 34 per cent of female sentenced reporting heavy smoking. In the household survey, only 11 per cent reported heavy smoking but these figures are similar to those of the homeless population in day centres, night shelters and hostels where 38 per cent of a survey sample report heavy smoking. The respondents in the Singleton *et al.* survey report very low rates of cessation with only 4 per cent of male remands, 8 per cent of male sentenced and 3 per cent of both female remand and sentenced reporting being an ex-regular smoker. This compares to 22 per cent of the general population as measured in the survey of psychiatric morbidity among adults living in private households.

The prisoner sample also reported high rates of hazardous drinking. Overall, women were more likely than men to have been non-drinkers in the year before coming to prison: 28 per cent of women on remand and 20 per cent of sentenced women said they had not drunk alcohol in the year prior to prison, compared with 16 per cent of male remand and 11 per cent of male sentenced prisoners. Among both men and women, remandees were more likely than sentenced prisoners to be non-drinkers. The AUDIT instrument was used to measure rates of

Table 9.2   Prevalence of harmful or hazardous drinking in year prior to entering prison.

	Male remand	Male sentenced	Female remand	Female sentenced
	Proportion of the population (%) (SE)			
AUDIT score				
Score: 0–7	42 (1)	37 (1)	64 (3)	61 (2)
Score: 8–15	27 (1)	33 (1)	16 (2)	20 (1)
Score: 16–23	13 (1)	16 (1)	6 (2)	8 (1)
Score: 24–31	10 (1)	10 (1)	6 (1)	7 (1)
Score: 32–40	7 (1)	4 (1)	8 (2)	4 (1)
Hazardous drinking (Score 8+)	**58 (0)**	**63 (0)**	**36 (1)**	**39 (0)**
Mean Audit Score	**12 (0)**	**12 (0)**	**9 (1)**	**9 (0)**
Base	*1243*	*1120*	*187*	*581*

hazardous drinking and indicates that men were roughly twice as likely to be hazardous drinkers as women. (Table 9.2)

The majority of prisoners had used illicit drugs and the overall reported rates of drug use were consistent with other prisoner surveys that indicate very high rates of ever and current use (ACMD, 1995). There were high estimated rates of dependence on heroin, methadone, amphetamine, cocaine and crack (Singleton *et al.*, 1998). Those with drug dependence were more likely to be assessed as being personality disordered, with the association being stronger for dependence on stimulants and opiates. Antisocial Personality Disorder accounted for the highest proportion of the correlation between drug dependence and personality disorder.

The Singleton *et al.* (1998) survey population was also characterised by high levels of drug injecting in the community. Of males on remand, 28 per cent reported ever injecting, 21 per cent reported regular injecting, and 17 per cent had injected in the month before prison. Of male sentenced prisoners the respective figures were comparable, with 23 per cent having ever injected, 16 per cent regularly, and 13 per cent in the month before imprisonment. Figures were higher for the females on remand, with 40 per cent reporting ever injecting, 34 per cent reporting regular injecting, and 28 per cent reporting that they had injected in the month before prison. For the sentenced female population 23 per cent reported ever injecting, 18 per cent regular injecting, with 14 per cent injecting in the month before prison.

Those dependent on opiates were most likely to report injecting drugs. In all sample groups, of those dependent on opiates with or without stimulant dependence in the year before coming to prison, about half reported injecting in the month before coming to prison. In contrast the proportion of those dependent on stimulants only who reported injecting in the month before coming to prison ranged from 14 per cent to 21 per cent and only 16 per cent of the stimulant dependent individuals reporting daily injecting.

The survey also looked at the risks factors associated with drug dependence in the year before prison. The study found that being born in the UK of white ethnic origin, leaving school before sixteen, being expelled from school, living off crime, being homeless, and having previous convictions were all significantly associated with being drug dependent. However, having been in an institution as a child and being taken into care as a child did not significantly discriminate between drug dependent prisoners and the rest of the prisoner population (Singleton *et al.*, 1998).

DRUG USE IN PRISON

Ongoing research involving the authors provides useful estimates of the level and nature of drug use during imprisonment. In this study, 19 per cent of sentenced males and 20 per cent of sentenced females reported using heroin during their current sentence, with 46 per cent of the sentenced males and 31 per cent of the sentenced females reporting using cannabis this time in prison. The rates in the remand population were slightly lower.

Injecting in Prison

Levels of injecting in prison reported by Singleton *et al.* were relatively low, with the vast majority (98 per cent) of the overall prisoner population reporting that they had never injected while in prison. Of those who had ever injected in prison, there was a trend for many to have injected intermittently rather than regularly. For the overall samples of male convicted and remand, 1 per cent reported injecting less than 10 times in prison. Within the female sentenced population, most of those who had injected in prison reported that they had done so less than 10 times. More frequent injecting was associated with the remand population, with 1 per cent of this group reporting injecting more than 10 times while in prison. Less than 1 per cent of the overall sample reported initiating injecting in prison.

Levels of injecting during current sentence were also low, with 2 per cent of adult remands reporting injecting in prison this time, 1 per cent of male sentenced prisoners, 2 per cent of female remand prisoners, and 2 per cent of female sentenced prisoners.

Surveys consistently report that 1–2 per cent of prisoners persist in injecting in prison (Bird *et al.*, 1997, Singleton *et al.*, 1998). Analysis of random mandatory drug testing (Farrell *et al. in preparation*) indicates that in the overall prisoner population, approximately 20 per cent test positive for cannabis and approximately 5 per cent test positive for opiates over time. Since the inception of the programme there has been a significant fall in the rate of cannabis positivity but no change in rates of opiate positivity.

The intermittent nature of use, and the short half-life of heroin could account for the differences between the self reported and the urine test data. The overall impression is that overall usage decreases on entry to prison but the risks associated with use substantially increase. The rates of opiate positivity do not change much with time and duration of sentence, indicating that there is a population of chronic heroin users who persist with use during long periods in prison. It is important to note that while there are substantial anecdotal reports of shifts in use from cannabis to heroin within prisons, the analysis of MDT data does not confirm this shift.

However there is a need for continued vigilance on this issue to determine if such a shift is occurring. Shewan *et al.* (1994) have reported on the shift in risk-taking behaviour among injectors entering prison, where those who continue to inject increase their risk-taking behaviour very substantially. One of the findings from Shewan *et al.* (1994) was that risk behaviour appeared to be more pronounced in those who had been treated with methadone before going to prison and then had that prescription stopped abruptly on entry to prison. To date, the majority of individuals who enter prison in the UK who have been prescribed methadone in the month prior to entry will have that prescription discontinued on entry to prison, with or without detoxification. Such discontinuation is likely to be associated with a substantial increase in risk-taking behaviour and is of particular concern for those who are on short term remand or short sentences where alteration in tolerance will also increase the risk of overdose on release from prison.

While rates of injecting within the prisoner population appear to be low, this does not leave room for complacency. Hepatitis C provides a particular cause for concern among injecting populations, with rates which are consistently reported to be between 50–70 per cent among injecting drug users, with lower seroprevalence among those with shorter histories of injecting (Crofts, *et al.*, 1997). It is estimated that

20 per cent of these hepatitis C positive individuals will progress to chronic liver disease and some to liver cancer. It is not clear what are the exact mechanisms of transmission but that hepatitis C is very efficiently transmitted by parental drug use. The high endemic rates of hepatitis C may also facilitate transmission. However international data also indicate that imprisonment is a specific and separate risk for the transmission of hepatitis C (Crofts, *et al.*, 1995; Stark *et al.*, 1995).

This provides a particular challenge for prison authorities in that the conventional view is that sterile injecting equipment should be used to prevent the transmission of hepatitis C. There is also a need to ensure that paraphernalia are not shared that may also contain the virus. The current advice on cleaning injecting equipment is that syringes should be flushed with cold, clean water twice and then flushed with undiluted bleach. Strategies to reduce hepatitis C transmission in prisons are likely to present a major public health challenge for the new millennium. Some countries such as Switzerland report the introduction of needle exchange in prisons with little associated problems, but there may be important differences in Swiss prisons where cells are all single compared to some of the multiple occupancy cells in British prisons.

Mandatory Drug testing results in added prison days for those who are found positive and is likely to have added to the time drug users are spending in prison. Gore and Bird (1996, 1998) have been critical of the spending on the random mandatory drug testing programmes and have argued that the money spent in this direction could have been more effectively spent on treatment and harm reduction interventions in settings that are hard pressed for resources.

The size of the problem and in particular the quantity and frequency of use within prisons remains unclear except that 5 per cent of the population are consistently positive for opiates. There is a high degree of consensus that drug users and dependent drug users constitute a major health burden within the prison system and there is a general agreement that there is a clear need to tackle this problem.

DRUG AND MENTAL HEALTH SERVICES IN PRISONS

The drug problem in prison has to be seen in the context of the broad range of social and mental health problems of this population and the need for a holistic integrated approach to the broader needs of this population. The function and role of prisons as part of the maintenance of law and order presents a challenge to society where demands for punishment and retribution are balanced with the desire to provide humane facilities that increase the likelihood that individuals can be rehabilitated to a constructive role in society.

Prisons are part of the broader criminal justice system that aims at correction of offending behaviour. Hough (1996) has written on the potentially strong support for drug treatment services in impacting on offending behaviour and there is a need to integrate these different services together. The recent Government Strategy (Lord President 1998) has committed major resources to the investment in new services for drug using offenders.

The issue of healthcare for prisoners is best seen in the context of the principle of equivalence, in that prisoners should ideally have the right of access to the same standard of health care as other individuals in society. The key challenge within the prison system is to address a major burden of mental health problems in a population who move at varying degrees of speed through prisons and back into the community. For this reason responding to the needs of drug users in prisons needs to be linked to the challenge of responding to drug users needs in the community.

In the context of community based drug treatment there is a clear consensus that a range of effective interventions are available and that it is cost effective to deliver such treatments. It is reasonable to assume that, potentially, effective rehabilitation opportunities exist within prisons. There appears to be a compelling argument for the cost benefits of investing in interventions that either divert people away from crime initially, or divert those in the criminal justice system away from custodial detention and for subsequent interventions within and after custodial detention that reduce recidivism. Despite the obvious nature of this argument, there has been a very slow take up of this approach. It is, however, reasonable to estimate that this will be a major area of growth in the treatment sector in the coming decade.

Treatment for drug users in the prison setting appears to be evolving at a rapid rate, with a range of pilot programmes based on different models of intervention. There appears to be substantial committment to the development of programmes provided in prison. There are, however, limited models of good practice to build on. It is important in this context that thorough evaluation of interventions in the prison setting is conducted, as the issues within prisons may make a substantial difference to both impact and outcome.

Prisons are faced with particular and complex challenges in maintaining control and providing care. They are faced with the challenge of reducing the supply of drugs entering prisons through visitors, staff and other routes. In a setting where there is a potentially high demand for drugs, particular problems of violence, intimidation and extortion can occur and can undermine the safety and integrity of the institution. Prison authorities need to maintain a steady vigilance to reduce the risks of trafficking, corruption and communal disorder and yet also have to provide humane conditions in which the prisoner population can live. The growth in the size of the prison population presents particular challenges and burdens to the effective running of establishments where additional resources are not always provided to back up the additional workload.

The establishment of drug treatment services in a prison setting requires good support from the prison administration. There are frequently problems of recruiting appropriately trained and skilled staff to work in the prison setting. There is a need for strong links between the programme and other aspects of the prison system to ensure and facilitate staff support and encouragement. Because of the complex nature of the problems associated with much of the prisoner population, successful programmes are most likely to be multidisciplinary teams combining a range of different skills. There is a need for links with community services and ideally new services provided in prisons should be structured to draw in and link with community services. However in many prisons the geographic area covered by the prison will be incompatible with ensuring good community links.

The needs of female prisoners are of particular concern in that they report very high rates of drug dependence, in particular of opiate dependence, and also report high rates of injecting drug use, high rates of self harming behaviour and high rates of general psychiatric morbidity. The women's prison population is small and tends to be concentrated in a small number of units at a major distance from the prisoners' families and communities. The health and social needs of women in prisons and the high rates of injecting drug use need specific consideration.

Standards of medical and psychiatric care in prison need substantial development and links with other NHS services if they are to respond to the demands being placed on them, and if they are to ensure that they are adequately resourced to fulfill their professional responsibilities. The prisons have developed a series of Health Care Standards including one for the provision of services for drug misusers. There is a need for a mechanism to ensure the implementation of standards to ensure that the best practice is delivered. The deaths of individuals in custody from both suicide and also some deaths from drug overdoses highlight the importance of rigorous clinical practice. The deaths of two prisoners who were started on methadone at a dosage of 50 mg. indicates the dangers of methadone when given to a person who is not tolerant of opiates, or when it is given in excess of recommended initiating doses. In general it is unwise to use more than 30 mg. of methadone as a starting dose. The prison system has limited capacity for careful observation of toxicity so that any issue of opiate toxicity should be referred to a general hospital where acute antagonisation with naloxone can be done.

CONCLUSIONS

In conclusion there has been a recent government commitment to addressing the needs of the prisoner population. However, the scale of the problem is such that a broad strategic integration between a whole range of services is needed if any meaningful impact is to be made on this large scale problem. Once society accepts its responsibility to put in place opportunities for rehabilitation the cost effectiveness of interventions to reduce recidivism are likely to be compelling. There is a real risk that unrealistic demands and expectations can be placed on the prisons to deal with problems that have not been effectively dealt with in other parts of society. The high concentration of problems in prisons means that modest and realistic targets need to be set if real progress is to be made in tackling this problem within the prison environment.

References

Advisory Council on the Misuse of Drugs (1996) Drug Misusers and the Prison System — an Integrated Approach. London: HMSO.

Crofts N., Stewart T., Hearne P., Ping X.Y., Breschkine A.M., and Locarnini, S.A. (1995) Spread of blood-borne viruses among Australian prison entrants. *British Medical Journal*, 310, 285–288.

Crofts N. and Aitken, C.K. (1997) Incidence of bloodborne virus infection and risk behaviours in a cohort of injecting drug users in Victoria, 1990–1995. *Medical Journal of Australia*, 167, 17–20.

Gore, S.M. and Bird, A.G. (1996) Cost implications of random mandatory drugs tests in prisons. *Lancet*, 348 (9035), 1124–7.

Gore, S.M. and Bird, A.G. (1998) Drugs in British Prisons. *British Medical Journal*, 316, 1256–1257.

Farrell, M., Howes, S., Taylor, C., Lewis, G., Jenkins, R., Bebbington, P., Jarvis, M., Brugha, T., Gill, B., and Meltzer H. (1998) Substance misuse and psychiatric comorbidity: an overview of the OPCS national psychiatric morbidity survey. *Addictive Behaviours*, Nov-Dec, 23(6), 909–18.

Farrell, M., McAuley, R., and Taylor, C. (*in preparation*) An analysis of MDT in English prisons.

Gaughwin, M.D. and Ali, R. (1995) HIV infection among injecting drug users in the South Australian methadone program. *Medical Journal of Australia*, 162, (5), 242–4.

Griffiths P., Farrell, M. and Howes, S. (1998) Local Prevalence Estimation. Can an Inner City Prevalence Survey Produce Useful Information? In 'Estimating the Prevalence of Problem Drug Use in Europe', EMCDDA Scientific Monograph Series 1. Luxembourg: Office for the Publication of the European Communities.

Hough, M. (1996) Drug Misuse and the Criminal Justice System: a Review of the Literature. Home Office Drugs Prevention Initiative, Paper 15. London: Home Office.

Lord President (1998) Tackling Drugs to Build a Better Britain: The Government's 10-Year Strategy for Drug Misuse. London: The Stationary Office.

Shewan, D., Gemmell, M., and Davies J.B. (1994) Prison as a modifier of drug using behaviour. *Addiction Research*, 2(2), 203–215.

Singleton, N., Meltzer, H., Gatward, R., Coid, J., and Deasy, D. (1998) Psychiatric Morbidity Among Prisoners in England and Wales. London: Office of National Statistics, The Stationary Office.

Stark, K., Muller, R., Wirth, D., Bienzle, U., Pauli, G., and Guggenmoos-Holzmann, L. (1995) Determinants of HIV infection and recent risk behaviour among injecting drug users in Berlin by site of recruitment. *Addiction*, 90(10), 1367–75.

Chapter 10

A REVIEW OF RISK BEHAVIOURS, TRANSMISSION AND PREVENTION OF BLOOD-BORNE VIRAL INFECTIONS IN AUSTRALIAN PRISONS

Kate Dolan and Nick Crofts

This chapter summarises research on drug use and blood-borne viral infections (BBVI) among prisoners in Australia.

HIV was first detected in Australian injecting drug users (IDUs) in the early 1980s (Blacker *et al.*, 1985). Despite early and extensive spread among the male homosexual community there has been little transmission among IDUs, among whom prevalence has remained below five per cent (MacDonald *et al.*, 1997). Of a total of 659 people newly diagnosed with HIV infection in 1997, only 23 (3.5 per cent) reported injecting drug use as a risk factor, while another 24 reported injecting drug use as well as homosexual contact (NCHECR, 1998). This is remarkable given that current estimates of the number of IDUs in Australia ranges from 100,000 to 150,000 (ANCARD, 1998). Control of hepatitis C virus infection (HCV) among IDUs has been less impressive. HCV has been detected in stored samples from IDUs from as early as 1971 (Thompson *et al.*, 1998) and prevalence has remained consistently high (approximately 65 per cent of IDUs are infected) over the last two decades (Crofts *et al.*, 1997).

HCV incidence among IDUs has been about 15 per cent, although there are signs that it decreased somewhat in the mid-1980s. This decrease coincided with the introduction of HIV prevention programmes and appears to be continuing, at least in some populations of IDUs (Crofts *et al.*, 1997). In other groups of IDUs, however, HCV incidence remains unacceptably high (Crofts *et al.*, 1995a). The low level of HIV and the high level of HCV in the community are reflected in Australian prisons. The prevalence of HIV infection is less than one per cent among prison entrants (Feachem, 1995) while about one third of prison entrants test positive for HCV (Crofts *et al.*, 1995b; Butler *et al.*, 1997).

Studying blood-borne viral infections (BBVI) and their prevention in the prison setting is a difficult but important task. The difficulties lie in gaining access to inmates, obtaining representative samples and reliable reports of risk behaviours, and collecting conclusive evidence of transmission in prison. The importance lies in the high level of inmate turnover, which means that BBVI transmission in prison threatens our ability to control transmission in the community when inmates are released. Research is required to evaluate the effectiveness of HIV prevention measures in prison settings, as little such evidence exists (Dolan, 1997a).

THE ORGANISATION OF PRISON SYSTEMS IN AUSTRALIA

Each of the six Australian states and two territories has its own prison system. There are no federal prisons and no national policy (nor mandate) for prisons in Australia. According to the 1996 National Prison Census, there were 18,193 prisoners, representing an imprisonment rate of 130 per 100,000 adult population. For indigenous Australians, however, this rate climbs to 3054 per 100,000. The overall prison population in Australia has increased by 58 per cent over the last decade (Australian Bureau of Statistics, 1997).

The prison systems and the prison health systems in all but two states come under the auspices of their local Department of Corrective Services. In New South Wales there is an independent health service, Corrections Health Service (CHS), which was in fact the first medical service in Australia, arriving with the first fleet in 1788. A renowned HIV immunologist, Professor Ronald Penny, chairs the CHS board and has facilitated research such as the Inmate Health Survey (see below). In private prisons in Victoria, private operators supply medical services to prisoners on contract.

Most prisons in Australia are publicly funded and operated. The state of Victoria is the major exception, where since 1997 two companies operate prisons that hold over 50 per cent of all prisoners. Private prisons also operate in NSW and Queensland, but house only a small minority of the states' prisoners. The one privatised prison in NSW, in a country town in the south, has been subject to an evaluation which found that it did not differ from other prisons in NSW with respect to the number of self harm episodes or assaults on staff or other inmates (Bowery, 1994). In Victoria the experience of privatisation has been both less examined and less comfortable, with nine deaths in custody in the largest private prison in 18 months, more than in the entire prison system in the three years leading up to privatisation. A major disadvantage of privatisation is the degree of loss of accountability, part of which is the increased difficulty in gaining access for research purposes.

THE HEALTH OF PRISONERS

From July 1996 to June 1997, there were 30 deaths in NSW prisons. All deaths are subject to an internal review by Corrections Health Service Administration and its Serious Incident Review Committee prior to the inquest by the State Coroner. Data on cause of death listed below are from CHS and may be modified on completion of the Coroner's reports. Of the 30 deaths, 2 resulted from murder, 10 from suicide, 4 from drug overdose and 14 from natural causes (Corrections Health Service, 1997).

A comprehensive health screen of a random sample of 800 NSW prison inmates, the NSW Inmate Health Survey, was conducted in 1996 (Butler, 1997). The Survey covered blood-borne viral infections as well as a comprehensive range of health indicators. Three quarters of female (73 per cent) and two thirds of male (64 per cent) respondents reported having used an illegal drug at some time in the past. After cannabis, heroin was the drug most commonly used, by 23 per cent of females and 18 per cent of males. In terms of drug use in prison, about one quarter of male and female respondents reported having used heroin. Reports of injecting in prison were a little higher at 32 per cent (female) and 21 per cent (male). Among the males injecting in prison, 69 per cent reported sharing needles, 55 per cent shared the drug, spoon or water and 70 per cent had cleaned the needle before using it. Eighteen males (3 per cent) and one female (1 per cent) reported that they started injecting in prison. Sixty four females and 146 males had become unconscious as a result of taking drugs at some time, but mostly in the community. Respondents were more likely to be under the influence of drugs (44 per cent of females and 32 per cent of males) than alcohol (17 per cent, 11 per cent) at the time of the offence.

RISK BEHAVIOURS FOR BBVI IN AUSTRALIAN PRISONS

A review of all prison research in Australia found that over 50 per cent of IDUs in each study reported injecting in prison (Crofts *et al.*, 1996). Questions about injecting in prison have ranged from time periods covering *ever injected*, to injected during *the last period of incarceration*, to injected during *periods of incarceration during the last year*. Eleven studies have examined the level of sharing by IDUs who reported injecting in prison. Very high levels of sharing — at least fifty per cent — have been recorded in all eleven studies with no reduction over time (cf. Crofts, *et al.*, 1996). There has been a general trend of increased bleach usage among prisoners, with three of the most recent studies finding over half of the IDUs using bleach to clean

Table 10.1   Techniques for cleaning injecting equipment.

Cleaning technique	In prison % (n = 31)
15 minute soak	10
Filled with Milton	13
Rinsed with bleach	7
N × N × N	30
2 × 2 × 2	32
Hot then cold water	10

syringes. However, the methods used for syringe cleaning vary greatly, as can be seen in Table 10.1.

Only the first two cleaning techniques in the above table could be considered to comply with the new syringe cleaning guidelines (ANCARD, 1993). The '2 × 2 × 2' method involves flushing the syringe twice with water, twice with bleach and twice with water, with the NxNxN method being a variation of this technique where the same procedure is adhered to more than two times. While there is consistent evidence of the level of risk behaviour occurring in prison, there is less evidence about the number of IDUs in prison.

In a Victorian study, 6 of the 36 people who reported injecting and sharing when last in prison also reported that was the first time they had ever shared syringes (Crofts *et al.*, 1995a). In a South Australian study, about 40 per cent of prisoners reported engaging in some risk behaviour in prison: 36 per cent reported having injected drugs, and another 12 per cent having engaged in anal sex (Gaughwin *et al.*, 1991).

The National Centre in HIV Epidemiology and Clinical Research conducts an annual one week study of approximately 20 needle and syringe exchange schemes in Australia (MacDonald, 1997). Clients are asked to complete a brief questionnaire and to provide a fingerprick blood sample. In the questionnaire, clients are asked if they were in prison in the preceding year, and if so whether they injected drugs while in prison. The results of these questions for five jurisdictions surveyed in 1996 appear in Table 10.2 below.

Fifty-eight needles and syringes confiscated or found in South Australian prisons were examined (Seamark & Gaughwin, 1994). Most (95 per cent) were one millilitre volume, had visible blood in 24 per cent, 59 per cent indicated repeated use and one third were wrapped in plastic. Twenty six per cent had a detachable needle, which allows more blood to be trapped in the dead space between the syringe barrel and the needle than with the fixed needle variety.

Table 10.2 Proportion of IDUs with histories of imprisonment, and proportion of those imprisoned who injected in prison, for males (M) and females (F), 1996.

Location	Imprisoned %	Injected % (of those in prison)
ACT M n = 59	22	46
ACT F n = 27	7	0
NT M n = 76	12	33
NT F n = 24	4	0
NSW M n = 335	25	35
NSW F n = 216	14	55
QLD M n = 356	7	64
QLD F n = 160	6	78
Vic M n = 307	18	30
Vic F n = 147	7	40

NATIONAL STUDY

The Australian Study of HIV and Injecting Drug Use (ASHIDU) was carried out in 1994 (Loxley *et al.*, 1995). The study sampled approximately 220 IDUs each in Sydney, Melbourne, Adelaide and Perth. The sample was stratified according to treatment status, residency, age and sexuality. A typical ASHIDU respondent was a single man, aged 28, who had not completed secondary schooling and was in receipt of government benefits. Overall, three per cent tested positive for HIV, 55 per cent for hepatitis C and 19 per cent for hepatitis B core antibody. The proportion of respondents in each city who had been in prison ranged from 23 per cent in Melbourne to 54 per cent in Sydney (See Table 10.3). Respondents in Sydney were more likely to report injecting in prison, but were less likely to report syringe sharing than respondents in other states.

PREVALENCE OF BBVI AMONG PRISON INMATES

Although several estimates of HIV prevalence have been conducted in correctional institutions, assessing the incidence of HIV transmission

Table 10.3 Prison characteristics of ASHIDU sample.

Variable	Sydney % (n = 219)	Perth % (n = 228)	Melbourne % (n = 216)	Adelaide % (n = 208)
Youth detention	37	19	15	19
Ever in prison	54	33	23	39
Injected last time	40 (n = 118)	38 (n = 75)	22 (n = 49)	29 (n = 82)
Shared syringes	56	81	73	71
Always bleached N&S	48	11	4	33
Any sex	9	9	12	4
Drug offence	53	51	46	56
On methadone	36	8	6	21

Table 10.4 Prisoners tested, new & previous HIV diagnoses, 1992.*

Location	No. of entrants	% tested	New diagnoses	Previous diagnoses	HIV prevalence %
NSW	8,632	99.9	8	39	0.5
Queensland	5,353	100	7	4	0.2
Victoria	3,999	99.9	3	15	0.5
Sth Australia	5,939	30.1	0	14	0.6
West Australia	5,530	33.4	1	2	0.2
Nth Territory	1,803	65	1	0	0.1
Tasmania	1,222	48	0	0	0
ACT	242	na	0	1	na
Total	32,720	68	20	75	0.4

* Source: NCHECR, 1998. na = not available

within a prison system poses considerably greater challenges (Dolan, 1997b). Most prisoners serve short and repetitive sentences which hampers the identification of the probable location of transmission of infections such as HIV. There are a number of ways to monitor the transmission of blood-borne viral infections in prison. Such methods include compulsory screening, mathematical modelling and outbreak investigations.

Since 1991, most jurisdictions in Australia have conducted large scale compulsory HIV testing of inmates. The coverage and results of testing Australian prison entrants for HIV appear in Table 10.4. In 1992, there were over 32,000 prison entrants of whom approximately two thirds (68 per cent) were tested for HIV infection. Only 95 cases (0.4 per cent) of HIV infection were detected. Of these cases, 75 had been previously diagnosed and 20 were new diagnoses. Virtually all prison entrants in the three most populous Australian states (NSW, Queensland and Victoria) were tested for HIV in 1992. These data show that HIV infection was rare in the population from which inmates were drawn (predominantly IDUs in the community).

Compulsory HIV testing of NSW inmates was discontinued in 1995. The reason cited was the enormous cost and the few detected cases. The cost of detecting each new case of HIV infection was estimated to be approximately $A50,000 (G. Vumbaca, personal communication, 1996).

THE PROPORTION OF IDUS AMONG PRISON INMATES

Estimations of the Number of IDUs among Prison Inmates

By using the prevalence of infection among inmates and among IDUs in the community, it is possible to estimate the proportion of prisoners

Table 10.5 Estimations of the number of IDUs among prison inmates.

BBVI	Prevalence in prison	Prevalence in IDUs in community	% prisoners who are IDU
HIV	1	2	50
HBV	31	50	62
HCV	38	64	59

who have a history of IDU. Using HIV, HBV and HCV prevalences, the proportion of prisoners with such a history ranges from 50 to 62 per cent. These data are shown in Table 10.5. With a census of 6411 inmates in 1997 (Corben, 1998), there would have been between 3205 and 3975 IDU inmates in NSW prisons.

TRANSMISSION OF BBVI IN PRISON

A study of hepatitis among prison entrants in Victoria found a very high incidence of hepatitis B (12 per cent) and hepatitis C (18 per cent) but not HIV (0 per cent) among prisoners with multiple entries within the study year (Crofts *et al.*, 1995b). However, it was not possible to determine whether the infections were acquired in or out of prison. Incidence among young male IDUs prison entrants was nearly 40 per cent and was associated with shorter stays in prison.

A MATHEMATICAL MODEL OF HIV TRANSMISSION IN PRISON

HIV incidence in NSW prisons has been estimated by mathematically modelling data from surveys of current and former prisoners (Dolan *et al.*, 1998c). In 1993, 185 injecting drug using (IDUs) ex-prisoners (Dolan *et al.*, 1999) and 181 current prisoners were surveyed (Dolan *et al.*, 1998a) to derive the following data: mean duration of imprisonment (54 weeks); mean number of inmates using each needle (30); mean number of shared injections per IDU per week (lower 0.13 and higher 0.41) and proportion of IDUs using bleach to clean syringes (mean 70 per cent). Other parameters included: cleaning with bleach destroyed HIV in used injection equipment on 10 per cent of occasions; HIV prevalence in IDUs on prison entry was five per cent; the probability of infection from sharing an infectious needle was 0.67 per cent; initial HIV prevalence in IDUs in prison was 0.8 per cent and the initial prevalence of HIV in needles was 10 per cent. HIV transmission was simulated under a modified 'Needles That Kill' model (Kaplan, 1989). That model was used to estimate the incidence of HIV by testing syringes returned to a needle exchange in New Haven.

When using the lower (and higher) values for frequency of shared injections of 0.13 (and 0.41) the prevalence of HIV in IDUs in prison was estimated to be between 0.8 per cent to 6.7 per cent (12.2 per cent) over 180 weeks. Between 38 and 152 IDUs were estimated to have become infected with HIV in NSW prisons in 1993. The minimum number of inmates infected with HIV while in prison in NSW in 1993 was estimated to be 38. This model was very sensitive to the values for frequency of shared injections. Additional measures are required to reduce the frequency of shared injections and thus decrease HIV transmission in NSW prisons.

HIV OUTBREAK

The first confirmed report of an Australian inmate becoming infected with HIV was reported in 1994 (Dolan et al., 1994a). Independent claims by injecting drug users of acquiring HIV in prison were investigated. IDUs and their prison contacts were interviewed about injecting, sexual and tattooing risk behaviour. Their prison and medical records were inspected. An expert panel assessed medical file entries for evidence of primary HIV infection. Epidemiological data indicated at least four IDUs acquired HIV in prison and most probably from shared injection equipment. HIV transmission is difficult to prove in prison populations. HIV transmission in prison has substantial public health implications as most drug using inmates soon return to the community.

This study illustrates some of the difficulties in the demonstration of HIV transmission in prison. The researchers became aware of a possible outbreak by chance. Obtaining ethical approval was an extremely protracted process, which required the assistance of a legal expert. Inmates were wary of admitting risk behaviour with potential serious legal consequences which were outlined in the consent form. These difficulties may partly explain why so few cases have been reported from prison to date.

PREVENTION OF INFECTION IN PRISON

Implementation of Recommended Legislative Changes in Prisons Relating to Infectious Diseases

A review of implementation of recommended prevention measures was conducted in 1998 (ANCARD, 1998). Condoms and bleach are now available to inmates in three of the eight jurisdictions. Methadone maintenance treatment remains available only in NSW, although there are plans to introduce methadone programmes in two other jurisdictions. Needle and syringe exchange programmes are not available in any Australian prison (ANCARD, 1998). Overall very few changes have occurred over the last five years.

AN EVALUATION OF A CONDOM PROGRAMME IN NSW PRISONS

A trial of condom provision in three NSW prisons in early 1996 was prompted by prisoners taking legal action against the Government. Prisoners argued that failure to provide condoms was a breach of the Government's duty of care. Although the court case was rejected on the grounds that there were too many claimants (52), the judge invited them to lodge a new case with fewer claimants. While a new case was being prepared, the Department of Corrective Services commenced a trial of condom distribution in three correctional centres.

During the 26 week trial, 13,527 condoms were dispensed from vending machines in the three correctional centres in NSW (Lowe, 1996). The average number of condoms per inmate during the 6 month trial was 12. A survey was distributed to all inmates in the three centres, but the response rate was very low, at $n = 69$ (7 per cent). Of those responding, 84 per cent supported the continued distribution of condoms, but only 26 per cent had obtained condoms from the vending machine. Of these, 50 per cent had used the condoms for sex, while the rest obtained condoms for the resealable plastic bag for storage (33 per cent) or wanted the lubricant for self masturbation (17 per cent). The resealable plastic bag was intended for the disposal of used condoms.

Seventy six per cent of respondents thought that sex occurred in their prison, with one quarter admitting having sex. The most common forms of sex were; oral (75 per cent), anal sex (69 per cent), mutual masturbation (60 per cent) and rubbing/massaging (56 per cent). Among those who reported engaging in anal sex, 64 per cent reported using condoms on all or most occasions while having anal sex. Just over half (55 per cent) reported using condoms when having oral sex. Half of the respondents reported flushing condoms down the toilet. Some respondents were unhappy about the location of the vending machines, especially the lack of privacy. One quarter of respondents reported being harassed by officers and inmates when obtaining condoms. However, there was general support from the inmates. There was no evidence of occupational health and safety problems. Nor any evidence of negative unintended consequences such as rape or condoms being used as weapons (Lowe, 1996). A follow up study of all correctional centres was conducted in 1998.

The Bleach Programme in NSW Prisons

Bleach has been provided in NSW prisons since 1990 and was available from medical staff, prison officers and inmates on request. Syringe cleaning instructions have been revised recently (ANCA, 1993). There have been two evaluations of the NSW bleach programme for prisoners (Dolan *et al.*, 1998; Dolan *et al.*, 1999).

The First Bleach Study

Correctional staff educators handed out self completion surveys to all inmates who volunteered for AIDS education courses in 12 prisons between May and December in 1993. The survey was conducted in 12 prisons which represented nearly half (41 per cent) of all adult correctional institutions in NSW (Dolan *et al.*, 1994b).

A total of 181 surveys were returned. The sample accounted for just under three per cent of the NSW prison population as recorded in the 1993 Census (*n* = 6386). The sample was similar to the prison population in the Census.

Over a third of respondents (38 per cent, n = 171) reported that they had easy access to bleach in the four weeks before the survey. Inmates reported using bleach to clean their cells (26 per cent, n = 150), injecting equipment (20 per cent), toilets (17 per cent) and tattooing equipment (5 per cent). Almost two thirds of respondents reported a history of injecting (64 per cent, n = 177) while most IDUs reported having injected in prison (68 per cent, n = 113) at some time. In order to provide a timeframe for questions, respondents were asked about the prison in which they were surveyed. One quarter of respondents (26 per cent) reported injecting while three quarters (76 per cent) reported sharing syringes in prison. Most respondents (96 per cent) who shared syringes, reported cleaning them with bleach. One sixth (16 per cent) of respondents reported sharing tattooing equipment, with two thirds (63 per cent) of these using bleach to clean the tattoo needle. Overall, forty per cent of respondents reported engaging in HIV risk behaviour in prison. Respondents (n = 35) who reported sharing syringes were asked how they cleaned the last syringe they had shared. The most common (51 per cent) cleaning method was the 2 × 2 × 2 procedure. The shared use of tattooing equipment in prison was reported by one sixth (16 per cent, n = 176) of respondents. Most (63 per cent n = 27) of these respondents reported cleaning the tattoo needle with bleach.

The Second Bleach Study

Between July and September 1994, all inmates who were to be released within a two month period from one of six prisons (which had been selected by the Department of Corrective Services as being representative) were visited and asked to telephone a toll-free number for an interview once released. Inmates were given unique identifiers, which were used to verify the authenticity of callers. Respondents were asked for an address (not necessarily theirs) to which a $50 postal note was sent as an incentive to call (Dolan *et al.*, 1996a, 1998a).

In 1994, 229 of 279 (82 per cent) inmates nearing release were visited and asked to telephone for an interview once released. Just under half (45 per cent) of the 229 inmates visited telephoned for an interview within the allotted time. There were no statistical differences between inmates who telephone and those who did not with respect to age, sex, number of prior imprisonments and length of the last prison sentence. Approximately half (54 per cent) the sample reported that they had been in prison for committing an offence to support their drug use. Three quarters (76 per cent) admitted having a drug or alcohol problem prior to prison entry. Approximately one third (29 per cent) reported being positive for hepatitis C infection.

A little over half of respondents (54 per cent, n = 102) reported an awareness of the Department's policy on bleach provision. Of the 50 inmates who had attempted to obtain disinfectants, 56 per cent reported having easy access to at least one type of disinfectant. The main factor which impeded access to disinfectants (40 per cent, n = 50) was that they were simply unavailable in prison. Some respondents (20 per cent, n = 50) reported that prison officers were reluctant to provide disinfectants when requested. Reports of negative consequences of the provision of disinfectants were rare (less than 4 per cent). However, many respondents reported being searched (24 per cent, n = 102) or having their names recorded (22 per cent, n = 102) when requesting disinfectants. Some (41 per cent, n = 102) respondents thought that other inmates had injected or shared syringes because disinfectants were available.

Sixty-four per cent of all respondents reported a history of drug injection and over half of these reported injecting during their last prison sentence. Among the 65 IDU respondents, reports of sharing syringes (83 per cent) and attempts to clean syringes were both high (96 per cent, n = 65). Among the 31 IDU respondents who reported sharing syringes, most (62 per cent) reported following the old guidelines for syringe cleaning. About one quarter of respondents who shared syringes reported using the revised syringe cleaning method (23 per cent, n = 31).

Over one third of respondents (38 per cent, n = 102) reported receiving a tattoo in prison. Injectors were significantly more likely to report engaging in tattooing in prison (48 per cent, n = 65) than non-injectors (22 per cent, n = 37). Only a few respondents with a history of injecting reported being sexually active in prison (4 per cent), yet most male respondents thought condoms should be available (79 per cent, n = 86). Among the 55 respondents who injected before prison, 11 per cent reported syringe sharing. Among the 26 respondents who reported injecting after prison, four per cent reported sharing syringes.

Feasibility of Syringe Exchange in NSW Prison

The introduction or trial of syringe exchange programmes in prison is very controversial in Australia. An inmate stabbed a prison officer with a syringe, and the officer subsequently seroconverted to HIV infection (Egger and Heilpern, 1991). The officer has since died, but not before suing the Department of Corrective Services over the size of compensation. A former Federal Minister for Health and a former President of the Australian Medical Association have urged serious consideration of Prison Syringe Exchange (PSE) programmes. Some stakeholders in the correctional system, such as prison officers, have vehemently opposed consideration of PSE and proposed industrial action if a PSE is implemented.

A study examined the feasibility of PSE by the use of focus groups with key stakeholders in the New South Wales (Dolan *et al.*, 1996b; Rutter *et al.*, 1996). The views of stakeholders will directly influence the operation of a PSE. Groups comprising prison officers, prison medical staff and ex-inmates provided information on likely safety issues associated with a PSE, emphasising the necessity for effective, broad-range treatment and harm minimisation programmes in prisons for injecting drug users. Groups questioned the implementation and effectiveness of existing HIV prevention programmes. The primary concern of all groups was the current policy of the Department of Corrective Services which opposes the introduction or exchange of syringes in any capacity. Prison officers were also unanimously opposed to PSE. This issue would need to be negotiated and co-operation of prison staff secured before implementation of any pilot PSE could be considered.

A frequently offered suggestion for reducing security risks of a PSE was the allocation of specialised sections of prisons to deal specifically with selected drug injectors. These specialised wings might provide a broad range of treatments and harm minimisation strategies, possibly including PSE. Custodial and medical staff for these sections would volunteer and be trained and clearly appraised of their own roles and the goals of the unit.

Several options for implementing and evaluating a PSE were suggested. The relative merit of each option was discussed in detail in a report (Rutter *et al.*, 1996). The introduction of a PSE in NSW is feasible only if strict guidelines are followed. The strenuous opposition to PSE under any circumstances by members of the prison officers group was noted. The strength of this opposition, if sustained, is likely to be a critical factor. Recommendations included education on hepatitis C for prisoners and prison workers, community education on prison public health issues, improved access to liquid bleach, methadone treatment, hepatitis B vaccinations and condoms. A number of conditions need considering before piloting PSE. These included establishing a specialised drug treatment wing where prisoners and workers can volunteer to be, custodial and health staff should receive training, syringe exchange would be strictly on a one-for-one basis. The mechanism for exchange could be via vending machines, nursing staff, an outside agency, or at an 'injecting room'. If the key stakeholders agreed on a pilot, this should be subject to certain conditions including no increase in risk of infections to staff, inmates, or visitors from assault, occupational injury, or accidental injury to visitors.

Details of monitoring the pilot PSE were outlined in the report. Basically it would involve monitoring a treatment wing and control wing for two years. This should start 6 to12 months before implementation of PSE. Inmates would be tested for hepatitis B, hepatitis C and HIV every 6 months. Training, availability of bleach in both wings and hepatitis B vaccination of all suitable participants should be maximised. Suitable inmates should be offered methadone maintenance treatment.

The New South Wales Prison Methadone Programme

The NSW prison methadone programmes is one of only a few such programmes in the world (Dolan and Wodak, 1996). The NSW prison methadone programme began in 1986 as a pre-release programme targeting IDUs with extensive drug careers and multiple periods of incarceration. Inmates with less extensive drug careers and fewer episodes of incarceration are now admitted to the methadone programme. The programme has been expanded and modified to reflect a maintenance treatment philosophy. The aims of the current programme are to reduce heroin injection and minimise the spread of blood-borne viral infections. There are approximately 800 clients on the programme at any time. Inmates can enter the programme while in prison.

A retrospective comparison of reports of drug use in prisons for persons who received standard drug treatment, time limited methadone treatment and methadone maintenance treatment was conducted (Dolan *et al.*, 1998b). Of 185 injecting drug users recruited, 105 (56 per cent) reported receiving standard care only (Group I), 32 reported receiving time limited methadone treatment (Group II) and 48 reported being maintained on methadone while in prison (Group III). The maximum mean dose of methadone was 52 mg (Range = 20–110) for Group II and 95 mg (Range = 65–210) for Group III. Group II received methadone for approximately three quarters of their prison sentence. Group III received methadone for the entire period of their incarceration.

The Groups were similar on basic demographic characteristics and drug use and prison histories. Members of Group I were younger than those in both other Groups. Group III contained significantly fewer males than the other Groups. Subjects in Group III were less likely to report injecting heroin, sharing syringes and scored lower on an HIV Risk-taking Behaviour Scale than Group I and Group II even though there was no significant difference between Groups on injecting any drug in prison. These results are summarised in Table 10.6.

This study provided the first evidence that methadone maintenance treatment can reduce injecting risk behaviour among inmates, but only when a moderately high dose of methadone was provided and for the entire period of imprisonment. This finding has important implications because IDU prisoners have remained at very high risk of contracting blood-borne viral infections while IDUs in community settings have decreased their risk of contracting HIV over the last decade. Even though there was no difference in the level of injecting between Groups, there were significant differences in the level of syringe sharing. A randomised controlled trial of the NSW prison methadone programme is currently underway and expected to be completed by mid 1999. Two other Australian states are planning to commence prison methadone programmes in 1999.

CONCLUSION

Although there has been a large amount of research in Australian (mostly NSW) prisons, it has to date had little impact on policy. The

Table 10.6 Self reported risk behaviour in prison for subjects receiving standard care (I), time limited methadone treatment (II) and methadone maintenance (III).

Variable	Group I (n = 105)	Group II (n = 32)	Group III (n = 48)	Group I vs Group II	Group I vs Group III	Group II vs Group III
Injected in prison %	46	56	31	ns	ns	ns
Injected heroin %	38	50	15	ns	$X^2 = 2.6^{**}$	$X^2 = 3.4^{***}$
Shared syringes %	39	47	21	ns	$X^2 = 0.8^*$	$X^2 = 0.7^*$
HRBS[A]	6	8	3	ns	$Z = -2.3^*$	$Z = -2.87^{**}$

ns = not significant
$^{***} = 0.001$; $^{**}p < 0.01$; $^*p < 0.05$ A = HIV Risk-taking Behavioural Scale (Darke et al. 1991).

evaluation of a condom trial was followed by statewide distribution of condoms in NSW prisons, but this was more likely related to Prison Department being sued by prisoners. Even though the case never came to fruition, there were strong indications that the court would have ruled against the Prison Department. Presumably the Department thought it better to plan the introduction of condoms rather than be forced to provide them without sufficient time for planning.

Bleach programmes have been safely implemented in Australian prisons without adverse consequences for prison staff or inmates. However, in the NSW study, many prisoners reported difficulties in obtaining disinfectants. This is cause for concern as the programme had been in operation for three years before this research. Given that prisoners have a low level of literacy and are rule breakers by definition, the level of uptake was good. However, widespread promotion of the revised syringe cleaning method is still required in Australian prisons. Most respondents who reported sharing syringes also reported cleaning syringes with a disinfectant while in prison. This was a substantial improvement since 1989, when only 30 per cent of NSW prisoners who reported sharing syringes also reported boiling syringes in water or cleaning syringes with a disinfectant (Potter and Conolly, 1990).

The emergence of hepatitis C as a public health threat, and the repeated demonstration of high incidences among injecting drug users even in the context of widespread and seemingly highly successful harm reduction approaches, has brought the issue of control of blood-borne viruses in Australian prisons into starker relief. Because of the success of these programmes in reducing the spread of HIV among Australian IDUs, leading to very low prevalences of HIV among prison entrants, the threat of HIV transmission in Australian prisons could be treated by prison authorities as a 'potential' or even 'theoretical' threat. The demonstration of hepatitis C transmission in prisons, coupled with the extremely high prevalences in inmates, has changed the scenario to one of actuality. The Australian prison system has so far, by and large, failed to cope with either of these threats, and shows marked reluctance to do so. It is perhaps sadly the case that it will be legal considerations, rather than public or personal health imperatives, which eventually do bring about change. The continued privatisation of Australia's prisons, however, could be a force for prevention of change or even worsening of the situation with regard to blood-borne virus transmission.

References

ANCARD (1998) Legal Working Party. Canberra: AGPS.

Australian Bureau of Statistics (1997) Prisoners in Australia, 1996. Melbourne: Commonwealth of Australia.

Australian National Council on AIDS (1993) New syringe cleaning guidelines for HIV. National AIDS Bulletin, July, 4.

Blacker, P Tindall, B Wodak A and Cooper D. (1985) Exposure of Intravenous Drug users to AIDS retro virus, Sydney 1985. Aust NZ J Med, 686–690.

Bowery, M. (1994) Junee: one year on. Sydney: NSW Department of Corrective Services, Research Publication no. 29.

Butler T. (1997) Preliminary Findings from the Inmate Health Survey of the inmate population in the New South Wales Correctional System. Sydney: NSW Department of Corrective Services.

Butler T., Dolan K., Ferson M., McGuiness L., Brown P., and Robertson P. (1997) Hepatitis B and C in New South Wales prisons. Prevalence and risk factors. Med J Aust, 166, 127–130.

Corben, S. (1998) NSW Inmate Census 1997. Summary of Characteristics. Sydney: NSW Department of Corrective Services.

Corrections Health Service (1997). Annual Report 1996/97. Sydney: Corrections Health Service.

Crofts N., Thompson S., Wale E., and Hernberger F. (1995a) Risk behaviours for blood-borne viruses in a Victorian prison. Aust NZ J Criminol , 29, 20–27.

Crofts N., Stewart T., Hearne P., Ping X.Y., Breschkin A.M., Locarnini S.A. (1995b) Spread of blood-borne viruses among Australian prison entrants. Br Med J, 310, 285–288.

Crofts N., Webb-Pullman J., and Dolan K. (1996) An analysis of trends over time in social and behavioural factors related to the transmission of HIV among IDUs and prison inmates. Canberra: AGPS.

Crofts N., Jolley D., Kaldor J., van Beek I., Wodak A. (1997) Epidemiology of hepatitis C virus infection among injecting drug users in Australia. J Epidemiol Community Health, 6, 692–697.

Darke S., Hall, W., Heather, N., Ward, J., and Wodak, A. (1991) The reliability and validity of a scale to measure HIV risk-taking behaviour among intravenous drug users. AIDS, 5, 181–185.

Dolan K., Wodak, A., and Hall W. (1999) HIV prevention and risk behaviour in prison: a bleach programme for inmates in NSW. Drug Alcohol Review, 18(2), in press.

Dolan K., Wodak A., and Hall W. (1998a) A bleach programme for inmates in NSW: an HIV prevention strategy. Aust N Z J Public Health, 22, 838–840.

Dolan, K., Wodak, A., and Hall, W. (1998b) Methadone maintenance treatment reduces heroin injection in NSW prisons. Drug and Alcohol Review, 17(2), 153–158.

Dolan, K., Wodak, A., Hall, W., and Kaplan, E. (1998c) A mathematical model of HIV transmission in NSW prisons. Drug and Alcohol Dependence, 50, 197–202.

Dolan K. (1997a) HIV in Australian Prisons: Transmission, risk behaviour and prevention. PhD thesis. Sydney: UNSW.

Dolan, K. (1997b) AIDS, Drugs and Risk Behaviour in Prison: State of the Art. International Journal of Drug Policy, 8(1), 5–17.

Dolan K., Shearer J., Hall W., and Wodak A. (1996a) Bleach is easier to obtain but inmates are still at risk infection in New South Wales Prisons. Technical Report No 34. Sydney: National Drug and Alcohol Research Centre.

Dolan K., Rutter S., Wodak A., Hall W., Maher L., and Dixon D. (1996b) Is syringe exchange feasible in a prison setting? Med J Aust, 164, 508.

Dolan K. and Wodak A. (1996c) An international review of methadone provision in prisons. Addiction Research, 4(1), 85–97.

Dolan, K., Hall, W., Wodak, A., and Gaughwin, M. (1994a) Evidence of HIV transmission in an Australian prison (Letter). Med J Aust, 160, 734.

Dolan K., Hall W., and Wodak A. (1994b) Bleach Availability and Risk Behaviours in Prison in New South Wales. Technical Report No 22. Sydney: National Drug and Alcohol Research Centre.

Egger, S. and Heilpern, H. (1991) HIV/AIDS in Australian Prisons. In 'HIV/AIDS and Prisons Conference Proceedings', J. Norberry, S.A. Gerull and M.D. Gaughwin (eds). pp. 65–83. Canberra: Australian Institute of Criminology.

Feachem, R. (1999) Valuing the past.... investing in the future. Evaluation of the National HIV/AIDS Strategy, 1993–94 to 1995–96. Canberra: Australian Government Publishing Service.

Gaughwin, M.D., Douglas, R.M., and Wodak, A.D. (1991) Behind bars — risk behaviours for HIV transmission in prisons, a review. In 'HIV/AIDS and Prisons Conference Proceedings', J. Norberry, S.A. Gerull and M.D. Gaughwin, (eds). pp 89–107. Canberra: Australian Institute of Criminology.

Kaplan, E. (1989) Needles that kill: Reviews of Infectious Diseases, 11, 289–298.

Lowe D. (1999) Consulting evaluation of the condom trial in three correctional centres in New South Wales. Final report to the Department of Corrective Services. Sydney: NSW Department of Corrective Services.

Loxley, W., Carruthers, S., and Bevan, J. (1995) In the same vein. First report of the Australian study of HIV and injecting drug use. Perth: ASHIDU, NCRPDA, Curtin University of Technology.

MacDonald, M., Crofts, N., and Kaldor, J. (1997) HIV prevalence and risk behaviour in needle exchange attenders: a national study, Med J Aust, 166, 237–240.

National Centre in HIV Epidemiology and Clinical Research (1998) Australian HIV surveillance report, 14(2), April.

Potter F. and Connolly L. (1990) AIDS: the sexual and IV drug use behaviour of prisoners. Sydney: Research and Statistics Division, NSW Department of Corrective Services.

Rutter, S., Dolan, K., Wodak, A., Hall, W., Maher, L., and Dixon, D. (1996) Is syringe exchange feasible in a prison setting? An exploratory study of the issues. Technical Report No. 25 National Drug and Alcohol Research Centre, Sydney.

Seamark, R. and Gaughwin M. (1994) Jabs in the dark: injecting equipment found in prisons and the risk of viral transmission. Aus Journal of Public Health, 18(1), 113–116.

Thomson J.A., Rodger A.J., Thompson S.C., Jolley D., Byrne A., Best S.J., and Crofts N. (1998) The prevalence of hepatitis C in patients admitted with acute hepatitis to Fairfield Infectious Diseases Hospital, 1971–1975. Med J Aust, 169, 360–364.

Chapter 11

THE MACRO AND MICRO LOGIC OF DRUGS AND PRISONS

John B. Davies and David Shewan

THE MACRO-LOGIC

Drugs, Dangers and Definitions

For reasons which have very little to do with their pharmacology, potency or 'dangerousness', and a great deal to do with accidents of history, geography and politics, we find ourselves in a situation where legal sanctions are applied differentially to psychoactive substances. The first group of such substances may be legally used, legally sold, distributed and under certain conditions advertised, and Governments receive revenue from their sale. A second set of psychoactive substances, however, are illegal, manufactured under variable and frequently uncontrolled conditions, distributed and used clandestinely, and no government revenue is obtained.

The distinction between the two sets is regularly portrayed in the popular media as fundamental. In some way the pharmacological and physiological hazards of using the first or 'legal' group of drugs are legally defined as acceptable or if not acceptable, at least not as a cause for judging their use and distribution to be illegal. On the other hand, the second set are defined as in principle more dangerous by an order of magnitude such that their illegal status is justified, and their media descriptions frequently contain adjectives attesting to their lethality. Furthermore, whilst the popular media are happy to talk about the 'use' and 'misuse' of those drugs in the first group (especially alcohol and prescription drugs), the second group are normally accompanied by terms such as 'abusive' or 'addictive', with simple 'use' not being an acknowledged possibility. The reasons, however, for categorising drugs in this way stem primarily from the historical dominance of Western societies, certain mores and climates of the times, and accidents of climate and geography which have little to do with the actual chemical and pharmacological properties of the drugs concerned. These facts have been well described elsewhere (e.g. Berridge and Edwards, 1981) and although the arguments surrounding this case have been well put, one final point is worth reiterating by way of introduction. The drugs available to a community in the absence of international travel depend very much on factors related to geography and climate. Thus, for example, in Mexico mescaline obtained from the peyote cactus might be described as a 'generic drug'. On the other hand, the coca plant, from which cocaine is manufactured thrives in South American countries. Opium poppies flourish in the fields of Afghanistan so that heroin is the locally available psychoactive substance. In a similar way the climate of Scotland is suited to the growing of certain grains, giving rise to the excellent malt whiskies of that region. Hop fields in the south of England provide the basis for beer. The point being made is that the drugs available to a community tend to be the ones that are available locally due to particular conditions of climate and agriculture. In recent times this picture has been supplemented by synthetic manufactured drugs. It seems possible that what has happened over the past several decades is that due to unequal power relationships between countries, we have come in some sense to trust the drugs which we grow, manufacture and consume ourselves whilst preserving a deep mistrust and fear of substances used for similar purposes in other parts of the world by strange and 'foreign' people who lack our 'understanding' of these things. In other words, the drug laws as they have developed are basically ethnocentric. It is worth remembering, for example, that in certain Middle Eastern countries alcohol is the illegal drug, the one which is viewed with the same abhorrence, perhaps, as heroin is viewed in the west.

For reasons that do not bear close scrutiny, the 'drug wars' thus represent a battle to uphold a set of rules and regulations that have limited scientific or logical basis. The distinction between safe and unsafe drugs which may carelessly be supposed to underlie the difference between the legal and illegal drugs simply does not exist, as even a casual glance at health and mortality statistics will testify. There are similar misrepresentations of the facts with regard to the 'addictive' nature of drugs. Strong but seldom mentioned evidence exists that addiction, or addictive use, is not an inevitable consequence of illicit drug use, and that set and setting play a crucial role in shaping the nature of a drug habit (Cohen, 1995). As with alcohol controlled or non-addicted use is common or with some drugs even the norm. Even controlled heroin users and controlled cocaine users can be found (e.g. Shewan, Dalgarno *et al.,* 1998; Harrison and Mugford, 1994) though these facts receive little media attention. On the other hand, the panics cultivated with respect to ecstasy are, arguably, not justified by the facts. Despite media coverage of this 'lethal drug', ecstasy-related deaths in Scotland for the year 1996 number just 7, whilst deaths involving benzodiazepines (minor tranquillisers) number 109 (I.S.D., 1998). Furthermore recent research (Sherlock, 1997) shows that a majority of young ecstasy users suffer no consequences to their health or social functioning (assuming they manage to escape the arm of the law) and find a weekend dance accompanied by the use of ecstasy just as rewarding and no more problematic than the use of alcohol on a Saturday night to accompany a game of darts or dominoes. For reasons which are difficult to understand, these plain and obvious facts about drugs however receive little publicity, and are seldom featured in newspapers or television programmes about drugs, which instead focus on the problems of addiction as though they were prototypical. It is as though we were to describe the whole of alcohol consumption by reference to that smaller group of people we call alcoholics. Such a description would not do justice to the range of consumption and use patterns, nor the benefits as well as the costs of alcohol use. Open debate, however, is not publicly permitted within the area of illicit drugs.

Rights and 'the Common Good'

Given the above situation in which an arbitrary and unsustainable distinction is made between illegal and legal substances, on the basis of claims about their properties which are exaggerated or simply untrue, the issue arises as to what right a government has to exercise particular powers with respect to those drugs which are judged illegal. The issues here concern individual freedoms and civil liberties, but they also involve a uniquely philosophical problem concerning the western notion of 'rights'. The traditional starting point for discussions of rights and civil liberties is the essay by J.S. Mill, 'On Liberty' (Mill, 1859; cited in Friedman and Szasz, 1992) which has been much quoted in this context. When defending illicit drug use on the basis of individual rights it is customary to abstract from Mill that sentence which basically says people have a right to do to themselves whatever they wish provided it does not interfere with the rights of others to do the same ('the only purpose for which power can be rightfully exercised over any member of a civilised community against his will is to prevent harm to others'). On the other hand, Mill also extended this argument to concede that a breach of duty to others could constitute harm as envisaged in the above quotation. Thus (for example) if by using drugs one was in breach of one's duty to one's family Mill's definition could by extension be used to curtail that individual's right to use those drugs. This qualification by Mill is the link to the public health argument which says that an individual's right to do what they wish may be controlled or curtailed not because it involves harm to the individual but because costs are imposed on his/her immediate family; and it is a short step from family 'others' to society at large.

It is therefore only a short step from what Mill actually said in total (as opposed to what he said in one widely quoted sentence) to public health arguments of the type offered by Beauchamp. Thus with respect to alcohol, Beauchamp (1987) writes 'public health paternalism in regulating alcohol commerce seeks to protect the common good, not the good of any particular person' (p. 75). Consequently whilst according to Mill the individual is 'the person most interested in his own well-being': 'and the interest which any person ... can have in it is trifling,' this sentiment can be subordinated to a higher (or at least a different) principle involving duty to others. In discussing public health paternalism Beauchamp advocated as a general group principle 'The lives we save together might include my own'. He goes on to argue that public health paternalism encourages concern for the wider good, for co-operation and group solidarity in solving problems, concluding with the note that these are community virtues (p. 76). On such a basis, therefore, it could be argued that it is reasonable to curtail illicit drug use on the basis that this is for the common good because the behaviour in question imposes a cost on the community as a whole. Unfortunately Mill's qualifier about duty to others provides the means by which the alleged rights of the individual to do unto himself what he wishes may be set aside in favour of a larger common good. From this point of view it then becomes a final very short step indeed to argue that since the costs of illicit drug use to the community as a whole are (it is claimed) massive the most extreme measures are justified in the interest of the common good. This, therefore, includes severe legal penalties, including imprisonment.

It has been argued elsewhere that drug use/misuse would be better treated as a health problem, rather than as a legal issue (Davies, 1997). Whilst there may be advantages to such a separation of legal and health issues, the two are difficult to separate; they are currently intertwined in a socially destructive fashion. Exaggerated concerns and mythical beliefs about the powers of drugs to undermine health actually form the very basis for the war on drugs, and the associated legal sanctions. Let us be clear about this. Politically motivated health policies on drugs, based on frequently grotesque exaggerations of the true picture (see Harding, 1998) form the very life-blood for prison and other punitive sentences. The two draw sustenance from each other; and severity of sentencing is justified directly by the nature of the health arguments. It is because drugs are so dangerous to health and social functioning (so it is argued) that it is necessary to imprison those who deal in them; and the more exaggerated the picture, the more imprisonment becomes necessary.

The health argument is thus the underpinning and justification for custodial sentences for drug offences; the health consequences of taking illegal drugs are judged to be sufficiently devastating to the community to justify gaol sentences for who those who deal in them; and most street users are also dealers at some level (Hammersley, Morrison *et al.*, 1990). In some countries the death penalty is imposed. The reader may note the irony of using gaol sentences, or the death penalty, to impose certain standards of public health.

THE PROBLEM OF REFLEXIVITY

The problem with any public policy which claims to operate at the level of what is good for society is that the system of intervention proposed (whatever its nature) is also, or becomes, part of that society. It is not imposed disinterestedly, as if from afar, by some entity divorced from that society, but by people and systems which are very much an integral part of it. It is not, and cannot be, a controlled experiment. Furthermore, society does not react passively to the intervention, but modifies its actions (the people who comprise it modify their individual actions) to take into account the nature of the intervention. In other words, the intervention affects it's subject matter. It is quite possible to look at some problem, plan an intervention, implement it, and then find that as a consequence, over time, the problem has changed its nature by adapting to the intervention; perhaps to the extent that the policy is no longer advantageous, or is even possibly harmful, because the problem is no longer the same as it was to start with.

The simplest examples of this type of thing might concern immunisation schemes. Once the false-positives exceed the base rate in the population, the intervention actually does more harm than good. A more contentious example might be harm-reduction education for primary school children. Such education is intended to target users, but if an audience is largely composed of non-users, more interest may be stimulated than harm is reduced (Davies, 1986). Finally, and most difficult to demonstrate, is the way in which social problems come to be described and conceptualised in ways that are shaped by the policies devised to address them. In other words, policy and response comprise a dialectical dance, with both sides prompting and yet simultaneously responding to the other.

Blame Cultures, Verbal Reports and Attributional Style

At the present time, the system of legal sanctions surrounding drug use indicates that drug use takes place within a 'blame culture'. There is good evidence from other sectors on the consequence of blame cultures, especially where the costs and benefits are high. In high consequence industries (e.g. airlines, nuclear industry, rail transport) problems which come to light are usually investigated through official channels. However, in firms and organisations where a 'blame culture' exists, such investigations usually result in (or are perceived as usually resulting in) disciplinary action against individuals (Wright and Davies, 1997). There may even be a preference to find out and punish those responsible, rather than to find out why a given system allows, or stimulates, certain things to happen; and usually, it is cheaper to invest the blame in individuals than to change the system.

Drug use is prevalent in all sections of society, but harmful dependent use is social class related (Leitner, Shapland and Wiles, 1993). Similarly, a number of the risk factors associated with harmful use are also class related (Davies and Farquhar, 1995). It is cheaper however, to punish individuals than to address the risk factors; and since the dominant Western societies have basically adopted the philosophical and social bases of a badly-run corner shop (see for example, the much vaunted slogan, 'United Kingdom PLC') we may expect the cheaper and easier options to be taken. Thus where harmful drug use and socially damaging drug trading is predicted by, for example, unemployment and social incoherence, it is cheaper to put those manifesting the dependent variable in prison than to address the independent variables.

But social policies also have an impact on the way problems are conceptualised. Within a blame culture, explanations become more and more functional as the costs of transgression increase. The function is to ensure that responsibility is deflected from the individual. Thus in some industries where a blame culture exists, incident reports consist of little other than external uncontrollable attributions. Things fail or malfunction; computers make 'errors'; or other people are responsible for creating the adverse conditions in which the event took place. Individual responsibility is often totally missing from such reports. Industrial reporting systems such as CIRAS (a confidential human factors reporting system used by railway companies) and CHIRP (a similar system used by airlines) are a direct response to such patterns of reporting. Under these 'blame free' conditions, where the possibility of disciplinary consequences or punishments is removed, it becomes possible to produce accounts which give primacy to 'human factors', and in which people do things (rightly or wrongly) for reasons, displaying volitional behaviours and decision-based acts. Not only can organisations learn more from these accounts, but the behaviours described are often capable of individual modification, control and change.

Where a *social policy* is based on blame and punishment, the same thing happens as occurs within any 'blame culture'. For example, when homosexual behaviour was illegal, the behaviour was conceptualised as a condition beyond the choices of the individual; and 'treatment' (often based on aversion therapy) was the appropriate 'cure'. With the change in the legal status of homosexual behaviour, people were free to openly voice their sexual choices as acts of preference (Crisp, 1985), sometimes even describing these as deliberate acts of political protest (see Carol, 1994). Change in legislation changed homosexuality from an illness or 'condition' to an act of volition or preference (Davies, 1997).

If we now address the problem of drug use within a society where social policy places such behaviour firmly within a blame culture, we can foresee the consequence. Where the behaviour is legally and/or socially sanctioned, forms of explanation will be encouraged that are external in nature. These will include peer-pressure, inability to cope, stress, genetic predisposition, and helpless states of addiction created by the drugs themselves. We can also predict that where drug use is not so sanctioned, drug use would more frequently be seen as being based on decisions, volitional acts and as fun which is deliberately sought.

The conclusion is therefore that sanctioning drug use by means of legal penalties, including imprisonment, creates a societal reaction whereby value is added to explanations for use which are external. It only remains to add that research evidence (Eiser *et al.*, 1977a, 1977b,

1985; DiClemente, Prochaska *et al.*, 1991) shows that belief that one is addicted is a factor which actually predicts uncontrolled use and inability to stop. The circularity is thus clear. Prison and other sentences for drug offences lead to the conceptualisation and description of drug use in non-volitional terms (i.e. in terms of 'helpless addiction'). This conception is a frightening one, and thus justifies an increase in the sanctions necessary; this produces an even higher premium on external forms of explanation; and so forth in an increasing spiral. That is where we stand at the moment with respect to drug problems; and by actually making the problem worse, we create the need for new and more costly (in economic and human terms) interventions.

Interventions That Incapacitate

The suggestions made above are not new, (Davies, 1992; 1997) nor are they specific to drug problems. In other areas of public health, interventions of various kinds have led others to speculate about similar themes. Most recently May, Johnstone and Rose (1997) have described the 'expert patient' whose modes of self-description and attributional style increase rather than decrease dependence on service provision; and in private correspondence has made reference to people who 'become addicted to incapacity'. The difference between the general area of public health and the specific issue of drug policy, however, is that the 'incapacity' argument is reinforced by gaol sentences where drugs are concerned.

From the point of view of medical ethics or 'rights', the arguments described above by Beauchamp (*op cit.*) seem to be coherent, whether one agrees with health paternalism or not; and anarchy is hardly the answer. Nonetheless, it is quite possible for interventions based on strong moral or ethical principles to have effects which are indefensible. The public health arguments which ultimately underpin drug policy are clearly of this nature. Deliberate volitional behaviour with respect to drugs is punishable, whereas helplessness receives the blessing-in-disguise of the health services. Within a blame culture such as surrounds drug use, a premium is placed on patterns of thinking and of use which elevate 'helplessness' to the level of a key concept. This process is given the equivalent of a rocket-assisted-take-off by incorporating into the system the ultimate sanctions of gaol and in some places death sentences. The way to escape the sanctions is to believe in, and to act out (in effect, to become) the helpless addict. This creates greater demand for service provision, and thus escalates the problem to a scale far greater than it would have been without the suffocating hand of health paternalism. Not only are the prisons full, but there is an escalating demand for services for helpless addicts, and the criterion for agency success has insouciantly become the fact that client numbers continually escalate rather than go down. Thus, well-intentioned (arguably) health philosophies underpinned by a woefully inappropriate set of legal sanctions, combine to make the problem worse, and shape cognitive and behavioural frameworks within which the 'helpless addict' becomes the standard drug-use role, rather than the occasional bit-part extra.

To put this another way, prison sentences are one of the ways in which health paternalism manifests itself in the attempt to 'protect society' from the dangers presented by illicit drugs. This is justified by the types or argument put forward by Beauchamp, and these can be traced back to the writings of Mill. However, such arguments only justify *the act of intervening*. They do not justify any particular policy adopted *as an intervention*. Such policies still have to be justified pragmatically, on the basis of synthetic propositions (Ayer, 1936) about whether they actually make things better or worse, and may not be taken as subsumed under the metaphysical (or 'nonsensical') debate about 'rights' or 'duties' which justify the act of intervention. It is the suggestion here that underpinning drug-related health interventions with prison and other penalties actually makes the problem worse than it was before. Whether thus suggestion is true or not, it is clearly now the moral obligation of health paternalists to demonstrate that their interventions *in toto* have in fact achieved what was envisaged; namely, that drug policy within a blame culture has produced results which are to 'the common good'. It is interesting to speculate about the nature of the evidence that would be adduced to support this cause, and as to how convincing it would look, given the solid evidence for increasing prevalence of drug-related harm over the last two decades.

THE MICRO-LOGIC

In the above paragraphs we have discussed the broad frameworks within which legislative action is justified with respect to illegal drugs and their use; and the philosophical bases for intervention in the interest of the 'public good'. We have also raised a number of issues concerning the use of punitive sentences as a means of dealing with the problems of illicit drug use, and suggested that in a number of respects the 'public good' is not in fact being served and that the approach may even be counterproductive. Certainly, all our best preventative efforts through the law, customs and education result in nothing other than an accelerating increase in prevalence (so *use* is certainly not being prevented) and there are side effects from the 'blame culture' within which we place illicit drug use which may actually exacerbate the problem at an individual level.

Nonetheless, we still have to live in the real world; a world in which drug problems continue to escalate, in which convictions for drug offences continue to rise, and in which large and increasing numbers of people find themselves imprisoned for drug offences. Furthermore, because of the nature of prisons and the selective nature of the clientele, the prison environment is one within which a majority of inmates will already have some involvement, frequently a major involvement, with drugs regardless of what they were actually sentenced for. This situation creates problems for prison systems and for inmates, and has to be dealt with. It is worth noting that one of the best ways to find a high representation of drug users in a single delimited space is to go to a prison.

The process by which this group of people arrive in custody is an interesting one, containing as it does a number of contradictions. In many countries the response to drug *users* is to send them to prison, whereas in others the intention to *supply* is the key feature, with simple possession being dealt with more leniently. The United States stands out as a particularly good example of the former; that is, a policy under which people are imprisoned for drug possession. In other countries, such as Britain, relatively few people are sent to prison for simple drug possession, but instead a high proportion of the prisoner population (approximately a third of the Scottish prison population (Power *et al.*, 1992) are drug users who have been incarcerated for petty crimes of dishonesty (Shewan *et al.*, 1994) rather than a drug offence *per se*. Where prevailing models of addiction propose that the addict's drug use and drug-related behaviour are defined as being *out of control* to a greater or lesser degree there would appear to be a contradiction between this perspective and the response of the criminal justice system.

From the perspective of the medical model, a more humane response to the criminal-addict would be treatment rather than punishment. However, as discussed earlier in this chapter, while medicalisation of drug problems may be more humane than the criminal justice system, it still begs the question in theoretical terms of whether the drug addict can be judged as not culpable for behaviour which is antisocial. For example, the relationship between drugs and crime is one of the more notoriously unresolved areas of drugs research, with considerable debate centring around the proposition that the association between drug use and crime is such that drugs are the *cause* of criminal behaviour (the *addict* has to steal because he/she is in the grip of a *compulsive habit,* which *has* to be fed). Increasingly this view is being challenged (Clayton and Tuchfeld, 1982; Hammersley *et al.,* 1989), particularly within more mainstream forensic psychology and criminology (Blackburn, 1994; Osgood *et al.,* 1988). Blackburn (1994) states:

> Mythologies about alcohol and drug use have fostered the belief that they are prominent causes of criminal acts, particularly violence. However, research indicates that delinquency and substance use are part of a deviant lifestyle originating in a variety of factors, and any association may be incidental. (Blackburn, 1994, p. 228).

Such a position challenges models of addiction which give prominence to pharmacological and psychopathological factors. This does not however mean that the response to people who use drugs and commit crimes would be necessarily entirely punitive. If one's aim is to both reduce crime *and* the prisoner population then it is not inconsistent to look for alternatives to custody which involve rehabilitative interventions which include drug treatment interventions. This does not perpetuate 'mythologies about alcohol and drug use', but rather views and responds to alcohol and drug use as one aspect of a deviant and problematic lifestyle, and views drug problems in the context of broader psychological and social factors (cf. Alexander, 1994; Cohen, 1990; Davies, 1992; Orford, 1985; Robins *et al.,* 1980; Shewan *et al.,* 1998; Zinberg, 1984). This approach also has the advantage of being supported by empirical research rather than popular belief.

There is still considerable debate within criminology, and between psychology and criminology, as to the theoretical basis of crime and the implications for responding to crime (Blackburn, 1994; Lilly, *et al.,* 1989; Young and Matthews, 1992). Much of the debate in this area centres round the concept of deviance as rational or irrational, and the question of whether the criminal or society should be described as 'pathological'. In some ways, the medicalisation of drug use and drug addiction falls squarely within this debate. By seeking to promote treatment rather than punishment as an option for the criminal drug addict, the medical model, it can be argued 'pathologises' the individual, thereby diminishing his responsibility, but at the same time reducing the opportunity for recognising and debating the impact of societal factors on drug-related behaviour. In practical terms, this may keep more drug users out of jail, but the question of whether this involves swapping one repressive system for another remains open to question (Cohen, 1990).

Therefore, the extent to which it can be argued that drug use is a mitigating factor in crime, and a justification for not sending someone to prison, relies more on pragmatic considerations concerning the appropriateness and effectiveness of imprisonment for particular types of offender and offence than it does on the disease model of addiction. To adopt a more liberal position with regard to imprisoning people who use drugs it is not necessary to accept the disease model. It is, however, necessary to adopt a more liberal approach to societal definitions of, and responses to crime.

According to a disease model of addiction, it might be predicted that the drug users who make up a sizeable proportion of the prisoner population in many countries would be characterised by destructive, chaotic use, and this behaviour would worsen in the bleak and oppressive setting of prison. The potential for the prison setting to act as a conduit for HIV transmission within the prisoner population and thence into the community has been a major concern of public health researchers and policymakers (Advisory Council on the Misuse of Drugs, 1988; Farrell and Strang, 1991; Harding, 1987, 1990; Power et al., 1992; World Health Organisation, 1990) who wisely faced up to the worst case scenario where drug users in prison were unable, or unwilling, to reduce their risk taking behaviour while incarcerated. Research in Scottish prisons has paid particular attention to patterns of injecting and sharing of injecting equipment in gaol (Shewan et al., 1994, 1995; Gore and Bird, 1995; Power et al., 1992). These studies indicate that while drug use, and risky drug use, is a worrying feature of prison life in Scotland, drug use in prisons is generally characterised by a reduction in levels of use, and for the majority of prisoners, a reduction in HIV-risk behaviour, when the in-gaol habit is compared to the patterns of use prior to imprisonment. These were welcome findings in the light of concern over the potential of prison to act as the setting for high levels of HIV transmission. This should not lead to any feelings of complacency, however. High risk behaviour does occur in Scottish prisons with serious repercussions, as evidenced by the outbreak of HIV transmission in HMP Glenochil (Taylor et al., 1995). However, as the potential of the prison environment to act as a modifier of drug using behaviour has been recognised, behavioural change in the prison environment should not simply be seen as representing an increase in high risk behaviour — prisons have the potential to decrease, as well as maintain, increase or reintroduce, high risk drug using behaviour. Positive outcomes have been reported in terms of behavioural change among clients of in-prison drug services in Scotland (Shewan et al., 1996).

At the present time, there are in the region of 6,000 people in prison in Scotland. Of this population, the most reliable prevalence studies carried out in Scottish prisons has suggested that between 25–30 per cent have a history of drug injecting (Gore and Bird, 1995; Power et al., 1992); that is, something in the region around 1600 people. It has been estimated that 5 per cent of this injecting group are HIV positive, around 80 people (Gore and Bird, 1995). In terms of numbers alone, drug use and prison represents a considerable challenge to prison authorities, creating extra demand on prison medical services (Scottish Prison Service, 1993a), and bringing with it the potential for disruption to prison regimes (Tomasevski, 1992).

Over the past decade, the problems created by drug use in prisons in has become increasingly recognised, researched and better understood. Scotland has been progressive in responding to drugs and prisons, and one feature of this response has been the prominent role given to research in informing policy and practice (Scottish Prison Service, 1994). At the same time, those involved in research have also sought to add to the knowledge base concerning drugs and prisons.

Injecting drug users are well represented in the Scottish prison population. The first prevalence study carried out in Scottish prisons found that 27.5 per cent of prisoners were injecting prior to imprisonment (Power et al., 1992). Results from the innovative Willing Anonymous HIV Salivary (WASH) Surveillance studies provide the most comprehensive and up-to-date estimates of drug injectors in Scottish prisons, and are reported in full elsewhere in this book. The authors of these studies reported that 27 per cent of the prisoner populations in the eight penal establishments had a history of injecting drugs (range 17 per cent–66 per cent). All of these rates are higher than that estimated in a recent study in England, which reported that 11 per cent of prisoners in a representative sample of English prisons had been inject-ing drugs before imprisonment (Maden *et al.*, 1992).

Given the significant numbers of drug injectors housed in Scottish prisons, HIV/AIDS is therefore an issue of considerable importance. It has been estimated that an average of 4.6 per cent of drug injectors in Scottish prisons are HIV positive (Gore and Bird, 1995). The potential for prisons to act as an epidemiological bridge for HIV transmission (Harding, 1987) has begun to be addressed by the Scottish Prison Service (Scottish Prison Service, 1994). Current injecting among the Scottish prison population is likely to be a problem for a small but significant minority of prisoners. Power *et al.* reported that 7.7 per cent of their total random sample had injected at least once while in prison, and that 28 per cent of drug injectors had injected while in prison. Gore and Bird (1995) reported that 51 per cent of injectors had injected in prison at some point.

Power *et al.* (1992) reported that of those who had injected in prison, 74 per cent had shared injecting equipment at some time. Shewan *et al.* (1994), found that 75 per cent of those who had ever injected in prison had shared at some point while incarcerated. This figure had dropped to 25 per cent of those who had been injecting in the community prior to current sentence but remained constant at 75 per cent for those who had injected during their current sentence. In Scottish prisons, therefore, while injecting is confined to a minority of prisoners, the rates of sharing of injecting equipment among this group are high.

Current prison sharers present a particular challenge to policy on drug use and HIV in prison, and to public health policy generally. In the studies by Power *et al.* (1992) and Shewan *et al.* (1994, 1995) there was evidence to suggest that most injectors were aware of the risks of sharing injecting equipment in prison and consequently made some effort to clean equipment with whatever was available, with use of bleach being common. As such, Scottish Prison Service Policy (SPS evidence to SAC) on supporting the discreet availability of materials for cleaning equipment and providing instructions in how best to do so is to be welcomed.

The reduction prescribing of methadone within Scottish prisons has been shown to be effective (Shewan *et al.*, 1996), but the provision of this service remains patchy in Scottish jails. In the Shewan *et al.* 1994 study, being prescribed methadone prior to imprisonment was associ-ated with a move towards either stopping or cutting down injecting and sharing. On entry to prison, however, where all methadone prescriptions were abruptly discontinued, there was a strong trend for prior methadone prescribing to become closely identified with sharing of injecting equipment.

It may be that those being prescribed methadone who are subsequently imprisoned represent an atypical group. Alternatively, these results could be seen in the context of the abrupt cessation of methadone scripts generally, with prison serving as an additional penalty. Applying either analysis it is significant that current sharing in prison generally (not just of the methadone group) represents a reinstatement of previous drug using behaviour in prison. Those who were currently sharing injecting equipment in prison were characterised by having injected a wider range of drugs within prison, both during current and previous sentences, suggesting a willingness to take chances within the prison system, allied to a knowledge of how to find a way around security. This could also apply to these individuals obtaining and using injecting equipment in prison.

The association between methadone prescribing and sharing of injecting equipment in prison can be further analysed according to the principles of drug, set, and setting (Cohen, 1995; Zinberg, 1984). Insufficient data is available from this study, particularly with regard to set, to provide a conclusive analysis, but the following interpretation is worth considering. In terms of the main drug involved, methadone has the reputation of being 'difficult' to withdraw abruptly from (George, 1990; Gossop et al., 1987). The set of the individuals concerned is likely to have been negative, not only with regard to entry to prison (although this does not differentiate this group from other participants), but also with the cessation of their methadone script. In addition the previous drug using behaviour in prison of this group is likely to have been a contributor to set, in that it provided a forerunner for behaviour which was entirely contrary to their drug using behaviour before entry to prison. It should also be borne in mind that a high proportion of this group were HIV positive, again likely to have a highly negative influence on set. It is still a source of frustration to the authors that this trend in the data only became apparent after the conclusion of the data collection part of this study, and that fuller information could not be gained about this group, and that this analysis rests uncomfortably close to being on the wrong side of speculation. Nonetheless, it does seem likely that a particular combination of drug and set lead, for this group, to prison being a setting for high risk behaviour.

Clearly, prisons are going to continue to admit a number of people who are being prescribed methadone while in the community. The strong association between discontinuation of these prescriptions and subsequent sharing of injecting equipment meant that a rethink was necessary on the response within prisons to prisoners who are on prescriptions in the community. It has been argued that a detoxification programme with reduction based oral prescribing should be routinely offered to all prisoners on admission who present with a drug problem (Farrell and Strang, 1991; Shewan *et al.*, 1996).

Drug use is a part of prison life in Scotland, but it would be unwise and unhelpful to sensationalise its incidence and impact on prison life. Clearly, some difficult decisions have to be made regarding prison policy on drug use. However, the interests of both those who live and work in prisons, and the community in general, will be best served by a harm reduction policy which is realistic within the context of the functions of the prison system. It is widely acknowledged within the prison system that drug free prisons are not a realistic goal; to suggest otherwise, and to develop future strategy on such a basis, would be misleading and detrimental to ensuring stability within the prison population.

Future policy on drug use and prisons has to be based on an awareness and understanding of the complex relationship between drug using behaviour, criminal justice policy, the function of prisons, and the characteristics of prison regimes. Since the mid-1980s, the Scottish Prison Service have affirmed their commitment to the tasks and responsibilities of prisons being those of custody, order and opportunity (Coyle, 1991; Scottish Prison Service, 1990, 1992, 1993a, 1993b, 1994). The primary objective of prison is punishment, that punishment being the deprivation of liberty for the time laid down by the court (Foucault, 1977). However, people are sent to prison *as* punishment, not *for* punishment, and there is, therefore, no contradiction between the primary objective of prison and the secondary objectives of offering all prisoners, including drug users, the opportunity for rehabilitation.

CONCLUSIONS

In conclusion, it can be seen that the problems created by drug use in prison populations can, in principle, be tackled at two more or less distinct levels. The broader policy issues concern the appropriateness of the 'War on Drugs' as a framework for tackling drug problems, and the assumption that such a war can be won. Sending people to gaol for drug offences is one aspect of that war. However, it seems unlikely that government policy will change from the basically entrenched stance adopted by parties of all persuasions despite the almost total lack of any evidence that a drug prevention approach is working.

On the other hand, there are pressing problems arising from the numbers of incarcerated people in prison and the prevalence of drug use within that population. Independent of whether gaol is the best place for people convicted of drug-related offences or not, and the difficult logics that surround this issue, it is apparent that positive steps can and should be taken once they are there, in the interests of individual health and harm reduction. It has been argued in the above paragraphs that such an approach is desirable and pragmatic. It also coincides with previous arguments concerning 'the public good'.

On the other hand, the problem is not without its own dangers. Drug rehabilitation should not be seen as a *primary* objective of prisons, and for drug users to be sent to prison on that basis would be an extremely retrograde step for drug policy and criminal justice policy generally. As Cohen (1990) has pointed out, medical control of drug use can be as, or even more oppressive than legal control. How much more oppressive a combination of the two would be. But, where it is considered fit to send drug users to prison on the basis of the crime they have committed, there is no contradiction in trying to provide them, or any other prisoner, with the maximum opportunity for constructive change. In this way, rather than fighting a war of attrition against drugs and drug users, prison authorities will be in a better position to stabilise the impact of drugs on prison life, and also to move towards a more participatory and positive role within the broad-based response required in relation to drug use and HIV.

References

Advisory Council on the Misuse of Drugs (1988) *AIDS and Drug Misuse, Part 1*. London: HMSO.

Alexander, B. (1994) Do heroin and cocaine cause addiction? In Brisson, P. (ed.) *L'usage des Drogues et la Toxicamanie (Vol. II)*. Montreal: Gaetin Mouin.

Ayer, A.J. (1936) *Language, Truth and Logic*. London: Gollancz

Berridge, V. and Edwards, G. (1987) *Opium and the People*. London: Yale University Press.

Beauchamp, D. (1987) Life-style, public health and paternalism. *In* Doxiadis, S (*ed.*). *Ethical Dilemmas in Health Promotion*. Chichester: Wiley and Sons.

Blackburn, R. (1993) *The Psychology of Criminal Conduct*. Chichester: Wiley.

Carol, A. (1994) *Nudes, Prudes and Attitudes: Pornography and Censorship*. Cheltenham: New Clarion Press.

Clayton, R.R. and Tuchfeld, B.S. (1982) The drug-crime debate: obstacles to understanding the relationship. *Journal of Drug Issues*, Spring, 153–166.

Cohen, P. (1995) Drug effects: we need more theory. *Addiction Research*, 3,1, i–iii

Cohen, P. (1990) *Drugs as a Social Construct*. Amsterdam: Universiteit van Amsterdam.

Coyle, A. (1991) *Inside: Rethinking Scotland's Prisons*. Edinburgh: Scottish Child.

Crisp, Q. (1985) *The Naked Civil Servant*. London: Harper Collins Ltd.

Davies J.B. (1986) Unsolved problems with mass-media drug education campaigns: three cautionary tales. *Addiction Research*. 1, 1, 69–74.

Davies J.B. and Farquhar, D. (1995) *Risk and Protective Factors Associated with Adolescent Drug Use*. Report submitted to Home Office Drugs Prevention Initiative: London

Davies, J.B. (1992) *The Myth of Addiction* (1st ed.) Reading: Harwood Academic Publishers.

Davies, J.B. (1997) *The Myth of Addiction*. (2nd ed.) Reading: Harwood Academic Publishers.

Davies, J.B. (1997) *Drugspeak: the Analysis of Drug Discourse*. Reading: Harwood Academic Publishers.

DiClemente, C., Prochaska, J.O., Fairhurst, S.K., Velicer, W.F., Velasquez, M.M., and Rossi, J.S. (1991). The process of smoking cessation: an analysis of precontemplation, contemplation, and preparation stages of change. *Journal of Consulting and Clinical Psychology*, 59, 2, 295–304.

Eiser, J.R., Sutton, S.R., and Wober, M. Smokers, non-smokers and the attribution of addiction. (1977a) *British Journal of Social and Clinical Psychology*, 16, 329–336.

Eiser, J.R. and Sutton, S.R. (1977b) Smoking as a subjectively rational choice. *Addictive Behaviours*, 2, 129–134.

Eiser, J.R., van der Pligt, J., and Raw, M. (1985) Trying to stop smoking: effects of perceived addiction, attributions for failure, and expectancy of success. *Journal of Behavioural Medicine*, 8, 4, 321–341.

Farrell, M., and Strang, J. (1991) Drugs, HIV, and prisons. *British Medical Journal*, 302, 1477–1479.

Foucault, M. (1977) *Discipline and Punish: The Birth of the Prison*. London: Allen Lane.

George, M. (1990) Methadone screws you up. *International Journal on Drug Policy*, 5, 1, 24–25.

Gore, S.M. and Bird, A.G. (1995) Cross-sectional willing anonymous HIV salivary (WASH) surveillance studies and self-completion risk factor questionnaire in establishments of the Scottish Prison Service. *Answer*, 29th September, 1–4.

Gossop, M., Bradley, B., Philips, G.T. (1987) An investigation of withdrawal symptoms shown by opiate addicts during and subsequent to a 21-day in-patient methadone detoxification procedure. *Addictive Behaviours*, 12, 1–6.

Hammersley, R., Forsyth, A., Morrison, V., and Davies, J.B. (1989) The relationship between crime and opioid use. *British Journal of Addiction*, 82, 899–906.

Hammersley, R., Morrison, V., Davies, J.B., and Forsyth, A. (1990). *Heroin Use and Crime: a Comparison of Heroin Users in and out of Prison*. Edinburgh: Scottish Office.

Harding, G. (1998) Pathologising the Soul: the construction of a 19th century analysis of opiate addiction. In Coomber, R (ed.), 'The Control of Drugs and Drug Users.' London: Harwood Academic Publishers.

Harding, T. (1987) *AIDS in Prison*. Geneva: University Institute of Legal Medicine.

Harding, T. (1990) HIV infection and AIDS in the prison environment: a test case for the respect of human rights. In Strang, J., and Stimson, G.V. (eds.), 'AIDS and Drug Misuse'. London: Routledge.

Harrison, L. and Mugford, S. (1994). Cocaine in the community. *Addiction Research* (special issue), 2, 1, 1–134.

Leitner, M., Shapland, J., and Wiles, P. (1993) *Drug Usage and Drugs Prevention: the Views and Habits of the General Public*. London: Home Office Drugs Prevention Initiative.

Lilly, J.R., Cullen, F.T., and Ball, R.A. (1995) *Criminological Theory: Context and Consequences*. London: Sage.

Maden, A., Swinton, M., and Gunn J. (1992) A survey of pre-arrest drug use in sentenced prisoners. *British Journal of Addiction*, 87, 27–33.

May, C., Johnstone, F., and Rose, M. (1998) *Back pain and the expert patient.* University of Manchester. Department of General Practice. (under review).

Mill, J.S. (1859) 'On Liberty'. Cited from Friedman, M., and Szasz, T. (1992). *On Liberty and Drugs*.Washington: Drug Policy Foundation.

Orford, J. (1984) *Excessive Appetites.* London: Wiley.

Osgood, D.W., Johnson, L.D., O'Malley, P.M., and Bachman, J.G. (1988) The generality of deviance in in late adolesence and early adulthood. *American Sociological Review*, 53, 81–93.

Power, K.G., Markova, A., Rowlands, A., McKee, K.J., Anslow, P. J., and Kilfedder, C. (1992) Intravenous drug use and HIV transmission amongst inmates in Scottish prisons. *British Journal of Addiction*, 87, 35–45.

Robins, L.N., Helzer, J.E., Hesselbrock, M., and Wish, E. (1980) Vietnam veterans three years after Vietnam: How our study changed our view of heroin. In Brill, L. and Winick, C. (eds.) 'The Yearbook of Substance Use and Abuse', pp.213–230. New York: Human Sciences Press.

Scottish Prison Service (1990) *Opportunity and Responsibility.* Edinburgh: Scottish Prison Service.

Scottish Prison Service (1992) *Sentence Planning.* Edinburgh: Scottish Prison Service.

Scottish Prison Service (1993) *Medical and Nursing Services in Scottish Prisons: Recommendations from a Review.* Edinburgh: Scottish Prison Service.

Scottish Prison Service (1993b) *Guidance on the Management of HIV/AIDS Prisoners.* Edinburgh: Scottish Prison Service.

Scottish Prison Service (1994) *Guidance on the Management of Prisoners who Abuse Drugs.* Edinburgh: Scottish Prison Service.

Sherlock, K. (1997) *Psychosocial Determinants of Ecstasy Use.* Ph.D. thesis. University of Leeds, Department of Psychology.

Shewan, D., Dalgarno, P., Marshall, A., Lowe, E., Campbell, M., Nicholson, S., Reith, G., McLafferty, V., and Thomson, K. (1998) Patterns of heroin use among a non-treatment sample in Glasgow (Scotland). *Addiction Research*, 6, 3, 215–234.

Shewan, D., Gemmell, M., and Davies, J.B. (1994) Prison as a modifier of drug using behaviour. *Addiction Research*, 2, **2**, 203–216.

Shewan, D., Macpherson, A., Reid, M.M., and Davies, J.B. (1995) The impact of the Edinburgh prison (Scotland) Drug Reduction Programme. *Legal and Criminological Psychology*, 1, **1**, 83–94.

Shewan, D., Macpherson, A., Reid, M.M., and Davies, J.B. (1995) Patterns of injecting and sharing in a Scottish prison. *Drug and Alcohol Dependence*, 39, 237–243.

Taylor, A., Goldberg, D., Emslie, J., Wrench, J., Gruer, L., Cameron, S., *et al.* (1995) Outbreak of HIV infection in a Scottish prison. *British Medical Journal*, 310, 293–296.

Tomasevski, K. (1992) *Prison Health: International Standards and National Practices in Europe.* Helsinki: Helsinki Institute for Crime Prevention and Control, affiliated with the United Nations. Publication Series No. 21.

World Health Organisation (1992) *Drug Abusers in Prisons: Managing Their Health Problems.* Copenhagen: WHO Regional Publications, European Series, No. 27.

Wright, L. and Davies, J.B. (1997) Setting up a third-party reporting system and human factors database with ScotRail. In 'International Disaster and Emergency Response' United Nations: IDNDR Conference Proceedings, The Hague, 242–248. Winchester: Andrich International.

Young, J. and Matthews, R. (1992) *Rethinking Criminology.* London: Sage.

Zinberg, N. (1984) *Drug, Set and Setting: The Basis for Controlled Intoxicant Use.* Yale: Yale University Press.

APPENDIX

Anonymous HIV surveillance in HM Prison Glenochil

Thank you for your help in this study which will enable us to plan better HIV care in prisons. We do not need to know your name nor any other form of identification when you complete this questionnaire. It goes to the Medical Research Council for analysis. No results will be reported which relate to fewer than 50 prisoners.

Please tick (√) the box beside the answer that applies to you

1   How old are you?

    under 26 years ☐
    26-30 years ☐
    31-35 years ☐
    36-40 years ☐
    over 40 ☐

2   Where did you live before coming into Glenochil Prison?

    Glasgow : Springburn, Maryhill, Possilpark, ☐   Edinburgh ☐
    Ruchill

    Glasgow : Easterhouse ☐   Dundee ☐

    Glasgow : Castlemilk ☐   Fife ☐

    Glasgow : Gorbals, Govan, Nitshill, Pollock ☐   elsewhere ☐

    rest of Glasgow ☐

3   How long is your present sentence?

    less than 1 year ☐
    between 1 and 3 years ☐
    more than 3 years ☐

4   When did your present sentence begin?

    in 1994 ☐
    in 1993 ☐
    in 1991 or 1992 ☐
    in 1990 or 1989 or 1988 or 1987 ☐
    in 1996 or 1985 or 1984 or 1983 ☐
    before 1983 ☐

5   Were you in Glenochil Prison at any time during   yes ☐
    January to June last year (1993)?   no ☐

6   How many times have you been inside before this   never ☐
    sentence?   once ☐
    2 or 3 or 4 times ☐
    5 or more times ☐

7   Have you been in a borstal or young offenders' institution?   yes ☐
    no ☐

8   Have you ever been charged with a drugs-related offence?   yes ☐
    no ☐

9   How much time have you done inside   less than 6 months ☐
    since January 1983?   between 7 and 12 months ☐
    between 1 and 3 years ☐
    more than 3 years ☐

Salivette   Sealed label-pair

Please fix sealed label here.

┌─────────────────────────┐
│   MRC   │
│ Medical Research Council │
│   Biostatistics Unit   │
│   Cambridge   │
└─────────────────────────┘

10	In which year did you first inject drugs (excluding insulin)?	NEVER INJECTED 1982 or earlier 1983-1985 1986-1988 1989-1991 1992 or later	

11	In which year did you last inject?	NEVER INJECTED 1982 or earlier 1983-1985 1986-1988 1989-1991 1992 or later	

12	Have you ever injected while inside?	yes no	

13	Did you start injecting while inside?	yes no	

14	Did you inject in Glenochil Prison during January to June last year (1993)?	yes no	

15	Have you ever taken the blood test for HIV?	yes no	

16	Did you have an HIV blood test in Glenochil Prison during January to June last year (1993)?	yes no	

17	Have you had an acute attack of hepatitis or yellow jaundice?	yes no	

18	In the last year before this sentence, how many women did you have sex with?	none 1 2 - 5 6 - 10 11 or more	

19	In the last year before this sentence, how many men did you have sex with?	none 1 2 - 5 6 - 10 11 or more	

20	Have you ever accepted money (or goods) for sex?	yes no	

21	Have you ever been paid for sex?	yes no	

22	Have you ever been treated for a sexually transmitted disease?	yes no	

23	Have you ever had anal sex with another man in prison?	yes no	

Thank you for answering this confidential questionnaire.

INDEX

Abstinence – 77, 178, 200
Addicts, prevalence in prison – 28, 57–59, 177–178, 215, 220–221
Aids, cases in prison – 61–62, 130–131

Blame culture – 238

Cannabis:
    use in prison – 33, 67, 126–129, 136, 178
    testing in prison – 65, 67, 71
Crime and drug use – 90–91, 243
Condoms, provision in prison – 6, 7, 16, 29, 31, 133–135, 182, 192, 222–225
Controlled drug use – 234
Counselling – 72–73, 183–184, 189

Drug-free prisons – 66
Drug-free areas – 69, 77, 175, 179
Drug testing – 14, 65, 67–68, 160–161, 178–179
Drug use:
    prevalence in prison – 33–34, 58–59, 126–129, 178–179, 217
    in prison compared to use in community – 33–34, 126–129, 179, 217
Drug wars – 1, 14, 93, 234, 249

Ecstasy – 236
Education: drugs and HIV/AIDS – 31, 77–79, 187–190, 227

Harm reduction: 28, 41, 68, 70, 75, 78, 85, 183
Heroin prescribing in prison – 13–14, 28–30, 38–41, 75, 83–84

Hepatitis:
    prevalence in prison – 37, 59, 64–65, 215, 219
    prisoners' knowledge of – 36–38, 40
    risk behaviour – 35, 58, 64, 217–220
HIV/AIDS:
    links with imprisonment – 62–64, 193–194, 221–222
    prevalence in prison – 30, 37, 59–64, 129–134, 178–182, 191–194, 215, 219
    prisoners' knowledge of – 36–38, 40, 192
    risk behaviour – 28, 35, 58, 129–134, 181–182, 217–220
    testing – 60–61, 133, 180, 182, 185, 220
Human rights – 119–122, 135, 235

Incarceration rates – 27, 57, 119–122, 174, 216
Injecting in prison – 58, 62, 178–179, 193, 218–221, 224–226

Mental health problems – 27, 58, 124–126
Methadone, prescribing in prison – 11, 12, 29, 41, 70, 73, 78, 81–83, 92, 178, 222, 227–228, 247–248

Outside agencies – 70–74, 188, 199–200

Prevention – 66–68, 72
Prisons:
    health services – 122–124, 176–177, 217